MISERICORDS
IN GREAT BRITAIN

A CATALOGUE OF
MISERICORDS
IN GREAT BRITAIN

BY

G. L. REMNANT, F.S.A.

WITH AN ESSAY
ON THEIR ICONOGRAPHY

BY

M. D. ANDERSON, F.S.A.

OXFORD
AT THE CLARENDON PRESS
1969

Oxford University Press, Ely House, London W. 1

GLASGOW NEW YORK TORONTO MELBOURNE WELLINGTON
CAPE TOWN SALISBURY IBADAN NAIROBI LUSAKA ADDIS ABABA
BOMBAY CALCUTTA MADRAS KARACHI LAHORE DACCA
KUALA LUMPUR SINGAPORE HONG KONG TOKYO

PRINTED IN GREAT BRITAIN
AT THE UNIVERSITY PRESS, OXFORD
BY VIVIAN RIDLER
PRINTER TO THE UNIVERSITY

PREFACE

THE inspiration of this work came from the acceptance by the late Bertram Plummer of the challenge implied in a sentence of Francis Bond's *Misericords* (O.U.P., 1910). In Chapter XXX, p. 224, it is stated: 'A vast number of misericords remains, especially in collegiate and monastic churches . . . But it is impossible to catalogue all the misericords in the parish churches. . . .' Plummer determined to attempt this huge task, and had made much progress, by both postal and library research and by personal visits to churches, when I met him at Etchingham, Sussex, through the introduction of the vicar. Thenceforward I gladly collaborated in the work by supplying Plummer with data and photographs collected in visits to churches in the southern counties. After his death in 1961 I set myself to finish the task.

It would be rash to state categorically that we have recorded every misericord in England, Scotland, and Wales. Every effort has been made to do so, and every avenue of research explored, but even after I had thought my work complete more unrecorded examples came to light, sometimes on a chance visit to a remote church. If there are misericords not mentioned in this volume I shall be glad to have details of them.

It would be quite impossible to acknowledge individually here all the help given by the many librarians, curators, parish clergy, historical and archaeological societies, and other helpers who responded so willingly and enthusiastically to our requests for information, and I ask them all to accept this expression of my gratitude. I have had also the ready co-operation of members of various photographic societies, who have sent me prints for identification of subjects in churches I have been unable to visit in person.

I wish to express sincere thanks to the Revd. J. C. Dickinson, M.A., F.S.A. and Miss Hilary L. Turner both of whom read the manuscript and made many valuable suggestions, and to Miss M. D. Anderson for her co-operation and for her constant help and encouragement.

G. L. REMNANT

CONTENTS

LIST OF PLATES

Photographs are by the author except where stated.

INTRODUCTION: MISERICORDS

HISTORICAL PURPOSE

I N the medieval Church the divine offices (Matins, Lauds, Prime, Terce, Sext, None, Vespers, Compline) were each said daily, and at the end of each office four psalms and canticles and hymns were recited. In addition, every priest other than the celebrant had himself to say a private mass daily.

The offices were said standing. Prayers, for instance, were said standing with uplifted hands. At a later date it was permitted to kneel at prayers. Sitting, however, was not customary, and was, in fact, severely discouraged.[1] The first concession to monks and canons who were weak or old and needed to relax was the provision of crutches.[2]

As a further and later *misericordia* (act of mercy), the seats were so constructed that they could be turned up like the seats in a modern theatre, and their undersides were provided with small projecting shelves which, when the seats were in this position, afforded some support to persons who sat on or leant against them.[3] These shelves, or misericords, were often carved with great skill.

This catalogue comprises all those misericords which were constructed for the original purpose of supporting the occupant of the stall, and also includes a number of seventeenth-century examples, such as a noteworthy group in County Durham, for the installation of which Bishop Cosin (1660–72) was responsible, and certain other examples of the period, believed in some instances to have come from the private chapels of Catholic families who returned to England at the Restoration. There are many good carvings of later date, including the present century, which were installed largely for decorative purposes, to fill gaps caused by decay in older sets, or to provide additional choir seating. They do not come within the scope of this book and are described

[1] F. Bond, *Misericords* (O.U.P., Oxford, 1910), p. 208.
[2] A. Wolfgang, 'Misericords in Lancashire and Cheshire Churches', *Trans. Lancs. and Cheshire Hist. Soc.* lxiii (1911), p. 7 9 f.
[3] Willis Clarke, *Observances i n use at the Augustine Priory of Saint Giles and Saint Andrew at Barnwell, Cambridges hire* (Macmillan & Bowes, Cambridge, 1897), pp. 81, 87.

b

in the catalogue as modern. One noteworthy group of these is in Henry VII's Chapel, Westminster Abbey, and was added to the existing stalls by George I in 1725 to provide additional seating for the Knights of the Order of the Bath, when he founded the Order in that year.

LOCATION

The oldest remaining set of misericords is at Exeter; it dates from the middle thirteenth century. The earliest known individual examples are at Christchurch (2), Henry VII's Chapel, Westminster (1), Hemingborough, Yorks. (1) (Pl. 43b), and Kidlington, Oxon. (5).

A vast number remains, especially in collegiate or monastic churches, and in parish churches, of which many have not been catalogued previously. Many old stalls in parish churches have been brought from monasteries which passed into secular hands at the Dissolution.[1] The stalls from Fotheringay, for example, appear to have been distributed among various churches in Northamptonshire, including Benefield, Hemington, and Tansor.

Many stalls have been lost by sheer neglect, or at the hands of iconoclasts, or in Victorian and even later 'restorations'.[2] Elsewhere, the eight returned stalls in Durham Cathedral were removed when Bishop Cosin's screen was taken down in 1846, and the Wimborne Minster stalls were cut up and mutilated in 1855. At Christchurch, where there are fifty-eight stalls, only thirty-nine misericords remain. Of the county of Dorset the infamous William Dowsing, smasher of images, glass, and pictures, reported in his journal: 'Destruction very complete.' In a restoration at St. Nicholas, King's Lynn, the stallwork was removed and the carpenter doing the work was told to burn it. Fortunately, he shrank from doing so, and when he told another of his patrons of the instruction, the stalls were rescued and presented to the Architectural Museum at Westminster, whence they were acquired with others by the Victoria and Albert Museum. At Chester five misericords were destroyed by Dean Howson on the grounds that 'they were very improper'. At Sherburn Hospital Chapel, Durham; Holy Rood, Southampton; and York Minster, amongst others, the stallwork perished by fire. In Ireland only one set remains, that of St. Mary's Cathedral, Limerick.

---

[1] See Appendix.
[2] H. Munro Cautley, *Norfolk Churches* (Adlard, Ipswich, 1949), p. 2.

The largest surviving collections are:

105 Salisbury Cathedral
96 St. George's Chapel, Windsor
92 Lincoln Minster
68 Beverley Minster
    King's College Chapel, Cambridge
66 Winchester Cathedral
65 Ely Cathedral
64 Chester Cathedral
    Wells Cathedral
62 St. Botolph's, Boston
    Norwich Cathedral
    New College Chapel, Oxford
53 Henry VII's Chapel, Westminster
50 Exeter Cathedral
46 Carlisle Cathedral
    Gloucester Cathedral
44 St. John's College Chapel, Cambridge
42 All Souls College Chapel, Oxford
    Worcester Cathedral
40 Hereford Cathedral
39 Christchurch Priory
38 Chichester Cathedral
    Hexham Abbey Church
37 Durham Cathedral
34 Lincoln College Chapel, Oxford

33 Ripon Minster
30 Pembroke College Chapel, Cambridge
    Manchester Cathedral
29 Magdalen College Chapel, Oxford
28 St. Andrew, Bishop Auckland
    Bristol Cathedral
    St. Lawrence, Ludlow
    St. David's Cathedral
26 St. Mary Magdalen, Newark
    St. Peter and St. Paul, Salle
    Holy Trinity, Stratford-on-Avon
25 Cartmel Priory
    All Saints, Leighton Buzzard
23 Beverley, St. Mary
22 Great Malvern Priory Church
20 St. Catherine, Beaumaris
    Holy Trinity, Coventry
    St. Mary the Virgin, Godmanchester
    St. Andrew, Greystoke
    St. Mary, Higham Ferrers
    All Saints, Maidstone
    St. Mary, Nantwich
    St. Mary the Virgin, Ottery St. Mary
    St. Asaph Cathedral

DATING

The accurate dating of misericords is very difficult. Documentary evidence from manuscripts or church archives is very rare. In the absence of such evidence a tentative assessment of date can be made from a study of stylistic variations in the shapes of the seat-ledges[1] or the subject-matter of the carvings. We may consider:

[1] G. C. Druce, 'Misericords; Their Form and Decoration', *Jour. Brit. Arch. Assoc.*, N.S. xxxvi (1931), p. 252.

1. *Shape*

Misericords of the thirteenth century use a simple semi-oval seat plan and small depth of moulding.[1]

Those of the first half of the fourteenth century use a seat plan which is rather more varied, usually concave at the sides, and, in front, either convex, straight with rounded ends, or slightly concave. Sometimes the top surface dips gently in the centre.[2] In the late fourteenth century there is a variant of this concave front type which has a central point in front.[3]

In the late fourteenth century also, seat plans became more complicated, having four or six sides either straight or concave, culminating in a point in front. This design provided more scope for the carver. The front moulding was at first deep, and cut in ribs or grooves, but later (this group lasted up to the Dissolution in the early sixteenth century) the moulding became less elaborate.[4] There is a variant of this group which has a straight front without a point. In some sets it appears with the type just mentioned.[5]

Most of the post-Reformation misericords revert to the simple plan of a seat with a straight front, usually for reasons of economy.[6]

The edge of the seat is, of course, always rounded for the comfort of the occupant, and in some earlier misericords this is all that is done in the way of moulding, e.g. those at Exeter and Hemingborough. In the latest examples the number of moulded ledges is increased, but moulding should not be taken as a criterion of date.

A misericord normally has a central carving with side supporters, i.e. subsidiary carvings to right and left of the main subject. In Winchester the supporters are larger than the centres. In an example at Lavenham no room has been left for supporters. In a few churches the supporters are omitted.[7] In some cases only the tip of the bracket is carved or the bracket form is more or less retained. In a few cases the misericords are all alike.[8] In this connection it may be noted that supporters seem to be peculiar to Britain. The author knows of no examples among European misericords.

[1] e.g. Exeter and Hemingborough (Pl. 43*b*).
[2] e.g. Chichester (Pl. 38), Ely, Gloucester, and Hereford Cathedrals
[3] e.g. Bodmin and others (Pl. 19).
[4] e.g. Beverley Minster, Carlisle, Chester, and Lincoln (Pl. 7*a*).
[5] e.g. Gayton, Higham Ferrers, Tong, and Wellingborough (Pl. 13*d*), *inter al.*
[6] e.g. Christchurch (Pl. 23), Wimborne, and Durham.
[7] e.g. Wakefield, Soham (Cambs.), King's College, Cambridge.
[8] e.g. Wingfield, Milton Abbey, and Lincoln College, Oxford.

In the majority of the carvings there is no relation between the subjects of the bracket and the supporters.

2. Date given

In a few cases the date is carved on the stalls or seats, e.g. at Ripon and Beverley Minster.

3. Donor

The name of the donor of the stall may be carved.

4. Heraldry

This may enable the name of the donor to be identified, but the disappearance of tinctures renders it uncertain.

5. Documentary evidence

Such evidence of foundation of a college or monastery will explain the presence of stalls in a church, but is not always reliable for their date: e.g. in cases where there has been rebuilding or refurnishing at a later date.

6. Foliage carving

The character is significant. It was conventional foliage early in the thirteenth century, trefoil (Pl. 3b), or cinquefoil. By the middle of the century the design was more refined, and in its last years conventional was replaced by naturalistic foliage.

In the first half of the fourteenth century this was replaced by bulbous foliage, abounding in the compound ogee curve, as at Ely and Hereford. The effect of the bulbous design resembled that produced by beaten metal, and the carvers may have been copying this type of ornament.

In the fifteenth century naturalistic foliated ornament very largely went out of fashion. In most parts of England the foliated capital tended to be supplanted by the moulded capital. Foliage was conventionalized once more and standardized, the favourite form being the lozenge-shaped or square flower, with or without stalks (Pl. 11b).

In the first half of the sixteenth century much of the foliage was conventional and uninteresting, but it returned occasionally to naturalistic forms of complicated and novel types.

A particular ornament may provide an approximate date, e.g. ball-flower was most common in stone carving between 1307 and 1327;[1] but it must be remembered that the carvers often copied from earlier patterns, and from ornament they saw around them.

7. Style of armour depicted

This also may provide an approximate date. For example, the helmet evolved from the early flat-topped variety (pl. 4a) to the visored helmet with pointed top (Pl. 44d), and still later changed to become close-fitting and skull-shaped. There was a parallel evolution in body armour and also in horse armour.[2] Similarly, the style of costume on a misericord can also be a useful guide to its date.[3]

Such are the various criteria for assessing the probable dates of misericords. However, it must immediately be emphasized that it is virtually impossible to date misericords really accurately, either on purely stylistic grounds or by assuming that the representation of armour or costume must be contemporary with the date of the carving. The carver may have copied his designs from older pictures, and it is known that some examples have been taken from the marginal illustrations in older books and manuscripts.[4]

There is ample evidence of great variation in the work of different carvers of the same period. Worcester and Lincoln Cathedrals are examples of this variation. Even carvers working side by side were apt to differ in their styles if they were of different generations. Unskilled work by village craftsmen is cruder (Pl. 17a), and tends to look much older than it really is. Some later carvings were copied from earlier groups that the carver had seen.

In the catalogue which follows, therefore, I have given the recorded evidence so far as I have been able to trace it, but otherwise the dating is approximate and tentative, and based on stylistic evidence.

[1] F. Bond, *Misericords* (O.U.P., Oxford, 1910), p. 219.

[2] C. Blair, *European Armour* (Batsford, London, 1958).

[3] C. Willett & P. Cunnington, *Handbook of English Medieval Costume* (Faber, London, 1952; *Handbook of English Costume in the Sixteenth Century* (Faber, London, 1954); D. C. Calthrop, *English Costume* (A. & C. Black, London, 1907).

[4] M. D. Anderson, 'Twelfth-Century Design Sources of Worcester Cathedral Misericords', *Archaeologia*, xcvii (1959), 165; J. S. Purvis, 'The Use of Continental Woodcuts and Prints by the Ripon School of Woodcarvers', *Archaeologia*, lxxxv (1936), 107.

THE ICONOGRAPHY OF
BRITISH MISERICORDS

by M. D. ANDERSON, F.S.A.

MISERICORDS are a very humble form of medieval art and it is unlikely that the most distinguished carvers of any period were employed
in making them, except, perhaps, during their apprentice years. Sometimes the King's Master Carpenters may have been concerned with the
planning of new stalls for such great cathedrals as Ely, Lincoln, or
Chester, but probably only in an advisory capacity. The names of the
men who actually carved particular misericords are never recorded.
The nearest we can come to such an attribution is to surmise that the
misericord of the Sovereign's stall in St. George's Chapel, Windsor,
would probably have been made by William Berkeley, since he was
then the chief carver on the pay roll. This misericord is unique in
showing a scene of contemporary history: the meeting of Edward IV
and Louis XI on the bridge at Picquigny (Pl. 1a). Yet, in spite of this
anonymity and the narrow limits imposed upon the carvers by the
function of the device, British misericords offer a wide range of
interest to those who study them carefully. Some of these half-hidden
carvings are so finely worked that they make us painfully aware of
what was lost with the almost total destruction of major works of wood
sculpture by the iconoclasts. The men who carved the 'Flight of Alexander' at Wells (Pl. 1b) with such dignified elegance, or portrayed with
such imaginative power the face of the Green Man at Coventry (Pl. 6a),
could probably have produced a Rood group, or a great reredos, as
majestic as anything still to be seen in northern Europe. Such master
craftsmen are, however, always rare; the majority of misericords show
only a primitive vitality of design, and are sometimes crudely worked.
Yet, at all levels of quality, these carvings reflect the minds of the men
who made them, and, if we study misericords as we might turn the
pages of painters' sketchbooks, they may teach us much about English
medieval craftsmen which is not recorded in any other form.

Paradoxically, it is the very unimportance of misericords as an art
form which has made them interesting historically. Even in the greatest

churches it does not seem to have been thought necessary for the misericords to conform to any coherent scheme of iconography, although
roof-bosses, which were equally inconspicuous, were often designed to
do so. Many of the carvers were clearly capable of executing any form
of didactic imagery that their clerical patrons desired, and these patrons
cannot have considered misericords too lowly a location for religious
themes, since they did not veto their inclusion in a general hotchpotch
of subjects. The grander the stalls the wider the variety of subjects
carved on them, but only in the village church of Ripple (see p. 168)
do we find a set of misericords with a consistent scheme of iconography.
This lack of over-all planning meant that the carvers probably enjoyed
a considerable measure of freedom in their choice and treatment of
designs, although subject to the final verdict of their employers. The
extent to which these clerical patrons played an active part in suggesting
certain subjects or banning others probably varied in each case with the
individuals involved, much as it would today, and their influence
tended to decrease in the later Middle Ages as the lay craftsmen achieved
a more independent economic status. Because of this freedom the
carver's work is often amusing in a naïve way, and sometimes includes
subjects which are mysterious, because he has divorced one incident
from the identifying context of the full story or has worked from his
inaccurate memory of a picture he had seen but not fully understood.

Since the iconography of misericords was thus determined by chance
rather than by scholarly planning, it seems more appropriate to consider its subjects within the context of the various ways by which
designs may have been presented to the carvers than to try to fit them
into an artificially logical pattern. But first we must briefly survey the
range of subjects likely to be found on an important set of stalls.

Biblical themes are always in the minority, and, even where they
do appear, seem to have been chosen at random. Thus in Gloucester
Cathedral we have the Shepherds on their way to Bethlehem, looking
up at the Star, but no misericord there shows their arrival. At Tong
(Salop) the misericord of the Master's stall bears an Annunciation with
a small figure of the Crucified Christ set on the stem of the Lily (Pl. 1c).
The erudite symbolism of the Lily Crucifix is unlikely to have been
understood by the carver, so his imagination was probably fired by
some design executed in another medium, which he reproduced in a
set of misericords that includes no other biblical subject.

Scenes from the lives of saints are also rare. St. George fighting the dragon is most often seen, but contests between men and monsters, or between aggressively confronted beasts, were so popular with the carvers, because ideally suited to the decoration of corbels, that one can rarely be sure whether the champion is a saint or a hero of romance. Even St. Margaret of Antioch, who appears constantly in other forms of church imagery because, having miraculously burst from the belly of a dragon which had swallowed her, she was considered as the special protectress of women in childbirth, is only shown on one misericord, at Sherborne (Pl. 1d). Had the carvers been influenced by considerations of cult her representations would have far outnumbered those of St. Giles, whose protective welcome of the hunted hind is only portrayed on one misericord—at Ely (Pl. 2a). A few misericords represent saints of local fame. At Chester St. Werburgh is shown resuscitating the cooked goose which had been killed in breach of her promise of protection given to the flock. St. Govan, journeying miserably in a ship to fetch the true form of the Mass from Rome, is shown at St. David's (Pl. 2b), and the martyrdom of King Edmund of East Anglia by Danish archers at Norton (Suffolk) (Pl. 2c). Whether these subjects were chosen because of the carver's special devotion to the saint, or because suitable designs were available for his copying, we cannot tell, but the carving of St. Govan being sea-sick looks more like one scene taken from a long sequence of pictures than an isolated portrayal. The ship-building misericord in the same cathedral (Pl. 2d) might have been copied from an earlier picture in the same sequence, showing the preparations for the saint's journey. The Evangelists appear occasionally, identified by their emblems: two winged oxen ramp heraldically beside St. Luke on a misericord at Cockington (Devon). More often the winged lion of St. Mark (Pl. 3a), or the eagle of St. John, appears as a single subject, with a scroll added to make clear its significance. The decorative value of an angel's wings was recognized by the carvers of all architectural details in medieval churches, and angels are very often shown on misericords, either holding musical instruments, or supporting shields on which are carved the arms of benefactors of the church.

The moral allegories which figured largely in other forms of church imagery seem to have had curiously little appeal to the carvers of misericords. The destruction of the stalls of Coventry Cathedral in the 1939–45 War has left one misericord, in St. George's Chapel, Windsor, as the only illustration of the Dance of Death, although full cycles are known to have been painted in the cloisters of St. Paul's Cathedral and elsewhere. The allegory of the Three Living and the Three Dead, so often painted on the walls of parish churches, was apparently never carved beneath their stalls. The influence of the allegorical analyses of sin is much more difficult to estimate, and will be discussed in a later context (see p. xxxix). Some subjects may have been meant to be realistic portrayals although symbolic interpretations seem probable. For instance, the fortified town shown on a misericord in Norwich Cathedral could either represent the actual city, or illustrate one of the literary allegories of the soul of man. The closed gateway that appears at Coventry and at New College, Oxford might be the ancient type of the Virginity of Mary or merely a decorative design. The soldiers' heads on the supporters of the New College example suggest that this may be an adaption of the basic 'Sir Yvain' design (see p. xxxiii), omitting the trapped knight.

The Bestiary was a source from which the carvers of misericords took many designs. They probably understood the symbolical meanings of the commonest subjects, such as the Capture of the Unicorn (see p. xxxvii), which symbolized the Incarnation and Passion of Christ, or the Pelican in her piety, bringing back to life the fledglings she had killed in a moment of exasperation, with blood from her self-wounded breast, symbol of Man's Redemption through the Blood of Christ. In the case of the rarer Bestiary subjects (see p. xxxv) the carvers may have worked from Bestiary pictures, or from their memory of sermon stories, without understanding the moralized interpretations given by the *Physiologus*.

Many misericords look as if their designs had been inspired by secular literature. These range from the few definitely identifiable subjects from the romances of chivalry, through a larger number of designs apparently taken from similar sources but not yet certainly identified, to the scores of carvings which illustrate popular fables, animal satires, proverbs, and so on. There are also large numbers of misericords which were purely decorative: foliage (rarely showing any close observation of nature), human figures contorted to fit the corbel, and heads that often show an individuality suggesting portraiture but can never be certainly identified. Between the clearly identifiable subjects and those as clearly not intended to convey any particular meaning lies a mass of work presenting a wide variety of iconographical puzzles. Medieval teachers, such as Hugh of Saint Victor and Honorius of Autun, regarded almost every object in the visible world as reflecting some spiritual counterpart, and this use of metaphors drawn from daily life was popularized by the preaching friars. If we were to compare all the figure subjects listed in Mr. Remnant's Catalogue with a complete analysis of medieval sermon *exempla*, with their racy vignettes of social life and their wide range of stories, the result would probably show that almost every carving might possibly have been inspired by some preacher's figurative language. On the other hand it might also have been based on the carver's own observation. It is misleading to assume that every detail in church imagery was meant to convey a religious message: but equally we cannot ignore the strangely broad spectrum of subject-matter with which medieval preachers coloured their instruction, and this does explain why themes that now seem incongruous in church imagery were accepted by medieval clerics. Both cosmic majesty and grotesque humour have their place in the great structure of medieval thought and art.

What evidence can we deduce from the surviving misericords as to how the carvers achieved their designs? The romantic nineteenth-century conception of medieval carvers delighting in their own creative powers, as wholly original designs took shape beneath their chisels, has been discarded, but we still have little certain knowledge of how they did get their designs. Did each carver make his own patterns on plastered boards, or did he rely on the master carpenter to do so? Did painters or illuminators provide drawings? We do not even know whether all carvers worked from drawings. The study of misericords cannot answer such questions fully, but it can throw light on what happened in certain cases, and these were probably typical of many others. The general impression given is that, while some carvers certainly repeated designs, with very free variations, and may have originated them, others as certainly copied any ready-made design which came their way. Wall-paintings, manuscript illuminations, and the woodcut pictures and marginal ornaments of early printed books, have all been identified as the originals of certain misericords. When both original and copy have survived, the indication they give of the extent to which a craftsman felt free to alter the design he was following provides a useful criterion of how much difference we may accept when trying to establish a connection between designs in different media.

Misericords also enable us to plot out the movements of some individual carvers, and to judge how far the designs they used were their personal property, or were used by other members of a team, like a sketchbook of basic patterns which each was free to vary at will. Exact repetitions are rare, though there are a few instances where lack of initiative, or of skill, has made the carver produce a whole set from one pattern. Further research is needed, though the possibilities are limited by the fact that relatively few carvers of misericords had such an individual style that we can distinguish their work from the general output of the same workshop. To illustrate the problems and potentialities of such study, let us look at three sets of cathedral stalls, those at Exeter, Worcester, and Lincoln.

The late thirteenth-century misericords of Exeter Cathedral are the earliest complete set in England, and here we see the carvers feeling their way towards mastery of a new task. The misericords with foliate designs are the most successful in making their ornament harmonize with the function of the central corbel (Pl. 3b), and these designs are so much akin to those of some contemporary foliate capitals that they may have been inspired by the work of more experienced stone carvers. In this connection it is relevant to note that the late thirteenth-century stall canopies of Winchester Cathedral follow the example of stone masons, even in methods of construction.[1] This subservience to more expert workers in other media is also apparent in the figure subjects at Exeter. It is easy to visualize these designs in what was most probably their original form, as drawings in a manuscript, because they have been copied with so little adaptation to their new purpose. There is no suggestion that the figures support the corbel, they are merely carved on its under-side, like toys beneath a shelf, and the supporters are often awkwardly cramped. The carvers evidently needed help in designing their work, and comparison of some of the misericords with contemporary manuscript illuminations shows where they sought it. The mermaid (Pl. 3c) whose human torso rises at right angles to her fish tail, and who probably once held a fish in each outstretched hand (one is now broken) to symbolize the souls of men in the grasp of the Tempter, is like a drawing in a thirteenth-century Bestiary manuscript in the British Museum (Sloane MS. 3544). Several thirteenth-century English Apocalypse manuscripts show the Locusts described in Chapter 9 of the Book of Revelation as 'horses prepared unto battle', with the heads

[1] F. H. Crossley, *English Church Woodwork* (1927), p. 15.

of crowned men and tails with scorpion stings, in a form very close to that of the strange figure on an Exeter misericord (Pl. 3*d*), which has a snake's head at the end of its tail. One manuscript in the Bodleian Library (Can. Bibl. Lat. MS. 62, fol. 13^v) even agrees in the shape and texture of the saddlecloth. The fact that the carver has given this creature human hands implies that he did not know its source, and no other detail of Apocalyptic imagery appears on the Exeter misericords. Why was this single subject chosen, and how did the carver get the design? Illuminated manuscripts were too precious to be used as models in a carpenter's workshop, so the most probable explanation is that a rough sketch, or an accidentally spoilt page, was given him by some illuminator. The same explanation probably applies to the misericord representing the Knight of the Swan (Pl. 4*a*), the mythical champion from whom Godfrey de Bouillon claimed descent. This subject appears at Exeter unaccompanied by any other romance subject, and thus illustrates one of the chief difficulties of identifying unusual figure subjects on misericords. They are shown isolated from their context and may well have been copied from some picture of a minor incident in a long series of illustrations. A misericord at Lincoln (Pl. 4*b*) represents what is clearly a scene from some romance, but the closest literary parallel I have yet found to it is a very unimportant episode in the adventures of Sir Perceval de Galles.

Another Exeter misericord of unusual interest shows an elephant so naturalistically correct, with the exception of its feet, that experts can say with certainty that it is African (Pl. 4*c*). As no howdah is shown on its back it is unlikely that the carver copied a miniature in a Bestiary, for the *Physiologus*, besides explaining the complex symbolism by which the elephant sometimes represents Christ, describes how eastern warriors fight from wooden towers on the backs of elephants, and this fortified tower is always illustrated. It is often our only means of identifying a medieval carver's very odd conception of an elephant. In 1255 an elephant was given to Henry III, and the drawing made of it by Matthew Paris[1] is so like the Exeter carving that we may safely assume this to have been based upon a similar sketch of the royal beast—an interesting example of the way in which iconographical features can sometimes help us to date carvings.

The uneven quality of the Exeter misericords, which has led to their being assigned to widely separated dates, and the fact that none of the

---

[1] *Chronica Majora*, Corpus Christi College, Cambridge.

distinctive designs found on them occurs in other churches, suggests that they were made by men permanently employed in the cathedral workshops. At Worcester there is stronger proof of this, since certain designs appearing on the misericords had been in use in the priory workshops for two hundred years.

The Worcester misericords were carved in 1379 and they include more biblical subjects than does any other set. There are no less than ten subjects from the Old Testament and some of these represent incidents so rarely illustrated that they can only have been derived from a very full series of typological designs in which the main events of the Gospel story were associated with the Old Testament episodes that supposedly foreshadowed them. Such a series is known to have existed in the twelfth-century wall-paintings of the Chapter House at Worcester, and a copy of some early verses records their subjects. Titles based upon these verses appear on some pages of thirteenth-century decorative designs in a manuscript at Eton College, and also identify the subjects of the enamel roundels on the twelfth-century Warwick ciborium now in the Victoria and Albert Museum. As such designs and verses were sometimes copied from one church to another, the fact that the same designs appear on misericords at Worcester made two hundred years later, but while the wall-paintings were still visible, is important evidence of their provenance. A full discussion of the relation between the Old Testament subjects on the Worcester misericords and those of the Eton manuscript and the Warwick ciborium has been published,[1] and one example only need be discussed here. The carving representing the Circumcision of Isaac (Pl. 4d) has two unusual and significant features. The first is that the child turns its head at a very awkward angle to take its mother's breast. This is not normally shown in scenes of circumcision, but it occurs in the Eton manuscript and on the Warwick ciborium. There is no suggestion in the Bible that Sara suckled Isaac at this moment, so the action may have been introduced as an allusion to a theme known to have figured in twelfth-century wall paintings at Bury St. Edmunds: Abraham's joy at the suckling of Isaac.[2] The second peculiarity of this misericord is that the officiating priest

[1] 'The Twelfth-Century Sources of the Worcester Cathedral Misericords', *Archaeologia*, xcvii (1959), pp. 165–78.

[2] The subjects of the Bury paintings are recorded in a manuscript in the College of Arms (Arundel, xxx). See M. R. James, *The Abbey of St. Edmund at Bury*, Cambridge Antiq. Soc. Octavo Publications No. 28 (1895).

has horns on his head, the identifying attribute of Moses. This does not occur in the corresponding miniature in the Eton manuscript, but a note written in the margin near it, in a later hand, refers to Exodus 4, the passage describing how Zipporah circumcised her child before Moses. It seems probable that this note was meant to direct some later copyist to substitute the incident from Exodus 4 as an alternative type for the Circumcision of Christ, and that the carver worked from some drawing in which this substitution had been made.

Another group of misericords at Worcester has clearly been copied from the calendar illustrations of some fine Book of Hours, although the original, if still extant, has not yet been identified. A dignified figure seated at a desk, with a large bird beside her, and the head of either a snake or a small dog emerging from the sleeve of her loose robe, was probably based on a drawing of *Dialectica*, for all these attributes can be paralleled in medieval manuscripts illustrating the Liberal Arts. Other unusual subjects occurring at Worcester, notably the 'Clever Daughter' (see p. xxxix) and the satirical representation of a joust (Pl. 5a), seem likely to have been copied from the marginal ornaments of illuminated manuscripts. All these subjects suggest that the carvers worked largely, if not entirely, from designs provided by the monks. Some of the Worcester misericords have been copied by modern carvers at Gloucester, but as their characteristic designs appear on no other medieval misericords the probability is that they were carved by men permanently employed by the cathedral priory.

A completely different system of organization is reflected in the stalls of Lincoln, made at some uncertain date during the time when John of Welburn was Treasurer, 1350–80. Unfortunately, the Fabric Rolls for this period have been lost, so that we cannot tell the names of the men employed, nor even whether the stalls were made in Lincoln, or brought there in ready-worked pieces for assemblage in the cathedral, as was done in the case of some alabaster retables and tombs. Since wood was generally available locally it seems more probable that a band of skilled carvers and carpenters moved from place to place as their services were required. From Lincoln they went on to make the stalls at Chester, c. 1390, and their work can also be seen in Holy Trinity, Coventry, and on some stalls from Roche Abbey, now in Loversal church, Yorks. W. R. None of the Lincoln misericords shows any evidence of having been worked from a design originating there, but the monks of Chester probably produced the design for the misericord illustrating the legend of their patron saint, St. Werburgh. The unique misericord illustrating the hunter throwing down glass balls to deceive a tigress while he rides off with her cub (Pl. 5b), is clearly based on some Bestiary manuscript, perhaps then in the Chester library.

Mr. John Harvey has suggested that the stalls of Lincoln and Chester show the influence of the royal carpenters, William and Hugh Herland, with the possible collaboration of William Newhall, the King's chief carpenter at Chester from 1377 to 1412.[1] Certainly some of the carvings show the handling of a master. The famous Falling Knight at Lincoln (Pl. 7d) is brilliantly designed. The twist of the horse's neck and the curve of the rider's body both convey the impetus of their imminent fall, and yet the whole group maintains a well-balanced unity with the corbel. It is carved with such care that a finger probing the underside of the knight's head feels detail that no eye can see, and it has been accepted as a true, and unique, record of how this particular form of armour fastened at the back, all other representations showing only the front. The identity of the Knight is mysterious. Although his lance pierces the neck of a dragon on the supporter, he cannot be St. George, for he is not victorious. He might symbolize the overthrow of Pride, like the falling knight in Hell, carved on the Romanesque portal at Conques, if an arrow sticking in his back did not provide the reason for his fall. Either the carver added this detail because he did not understand his model, or this is another unidentified subject from some romance.

The lack of records identifying the Lincoln carvers is particularly regrettable because one of them was an artist whose work is recognizably individual. At Holy Trinity, Coventry (Pl. 6a), he applied his sensitive modelling of the planes of a human face to give a sinister and romantic beauty to a subject common in all forms of architectural sculpture, the foliate mask, or Green Man. When the same sinister quality appears in a similar mask at Lincoln (Pl. 6b), between supporters showing the same boldly curving pair of leaves, we can feel reasonably sure that the two misericords were carved by the same pair of hands, and the difference in character between the two faces precludes any suggestion of their being two copies of a stock design. The Coventry Green Man might be the pagan nature god whose rites persisted into the Middle Ages in the spring festival of the May King, or Jack-in-the-Green, while at Lincoln he is more like one of the squalid bandits who haunted the medieval

[1] *Gothic England* (1947), p. 56.

forests. At Loversal we get yet another variant of the mask (Pl. 43*c*), still with the same supporters in which the carver clearly took too little interest to vary them. He was more concerned with perspective than most carvers of his time, and, when he carved almost identical griffins on the stalls of both Coventry and Lincoln, he was not content to show their raised wings in the normal heraldic convention, but tried to convey their lateral expansion by a curiously foreshortened curve.

Comparisons between other designs occurring on these various stalls suggest that certain patterns were the common property of the working team. Thus the subject of a wodehouse bestriding a lion and controlling it by means of a chain round its neck, which rarely occurs elsewhere, is repeated several times at both Coventry and Lincoln. At Coventry the carver produced a vigorous design, but with crude detail and chunky figures, while the version at Lincoln is free and elegant in line, but has little relation to the function of the corbel. Similarly with two carvings of Tristan and Iseult meeting under the tree in which King Mark has hidden in order to spy upon the lovers: the Chester version (Pl. 6*d*) is more sophisticated and correct than that at Lincoln, the difference being greater than can reasonably be explained as being a more successful second attempt by the same man. The reason why this scene of illicit love was acceptable in church imagery may be found in a French compilation of moralized stories called *Cy nous dit*. As the lovers, made aware of the presence of King Mark by seeing his reflection in a pool of water, kept their conversation innocent, so we, knowing that God sees all we do, should avoid sin. *Cy nous dit* uses the story of how Alexander enticed hungry griffins to carry him up into the sky, by holding lumps of meat, impaled on spears, above their heads, to illustrate how man should hunger for the beauty of Heaven; but in a Middle English *Alphabet of Tales*[1] 'Alexander's Flight', which is shown on several misericords (Pl. 1*b*), is made an example of ambition and pride. Some such moralization may also have been applied to the scene from the romance of Sir Yvain shown on misericords in five different churches, by several different carvers, for all reproduce exactly the same incident. The knight is seen from the back, riding through a castle gateway, the portcullis of which falls upon his horse's hindquarters. The supporters all show the men-at-arms who came to seize him when he was thus trapped. In the finest example, at Enville, Staffs. (Pl. 7*c*), these soldiers are shown as full-length figures standing in minor gateways; at New

[1] Early English Text Soc., o.s. 126–7.

College and Boston their heads appear over the battlements of towers; and at Lincoln and Chester only the heads are shown. Unless some moralization made the inclusion of these soldiers obligatory, surely at least one of the carvers would have substituted the damsel or the lion, both of whom play much more important parts in the romance. Some medieval scrolls bearing roughly written and illustrated verses on the Emblems of the Passion have survived,[1] and it is possible that similarly rough texts of moralized stories were once current, and that their illustrations served the carvers as basic designs. This might also explain why the mysterious subject of a lion being suckled by a mermaid appears on misericords in Hereford and Norwich Cathedrals and also at Edlesborough, Bucks. (Pl. 8b).

That medieval carvers were ready to copy designs from books is made clear at Ripon, where two scenes from the story of Jonah (Pls. 8d and 9a), Samson carrying away the gates of Gaza (Pl. 9c) and the spies bearing the grapes back from Canaan, are all certainly copied from the block-book Biblia Pauperum, printed in the Netherlands in the late fifteenth century. Dr. J. S. Purvis has identified many other instances of foreign engravings copied on misericords.[2] Amongst these is one in Westminster Abbey (north side, upper row 3), which is very close to the central figures in a print by Dürer, c. 1496 (Bartsch 93).

The early sixteenth-century misericords of Bristol Cathedral include several apparently based on the illustrations of some early printed edition of Reynard the Fox. The highly individual treatment of the head of King Noble, the lion, with his deep-socketed eyes and long mane (Pl. 9d), is very close to that in some surviving woodcuts from Wynkyn de Worde's Reynard the Fox, but none of these corresponds exactly to a misericord. Three other misericords at Bristol (Pl. 21b) are certainly based on grotesque subjects used as marginal ornaments in the books produced by such Parisian printers as Thielman Kerver and Simon de Vostre in the late fifteenth and early sixteenth centuries (Pl. 5d). Two of these grotesques were copied by different carvers in misericords at Throwley, Kent (Pl. 5c), and they also occur in stone carving on the de la Warr chantry at Boxgrove.

Whether the numerous misericords which represent foxes and apes performing human actions, such as studying urine flasks in parody of

---

[1] See R. Morris, Legends of the Holy Rood, E.E.T.S., o.s. 46 (1871).
[2] 'The Use of Continental Woodcuts and Prints by the Ripon School of Woodcarvers in the Early Sixteenth Century', Archaeologia, lxxxv.

doctors (Pl. 9*b*), were based upon drawings accompanying rough texts of animal fables corresponding rather vaguely to some branches of the Continental *Roman du Renard*, or merely record the carvers' verbal memories of such tales, it is impossible to tell. Yet it is permissible to guess that they record a rich field of popular fiction of which no text has survived. The favourite subject of this type shows a fox preaching to a congregation of geese in order to lure them within reach of his teeth (Pl. 35*c*). The fox wears a friar's robe that sometimes has a dead bird lodged in its cowl. This seems a strangely inappropriate subject for church imagery, but the beneficed clergy, who were often denounced by the Mendicant Friars as slothful and corrupt, probably welcomed this satire on the greed and hypocrisy of the Friars as a counter-attack; they even tolerated its expression in much cruder forms.

This proven tendency among the carvers to copy pictures from books may explain in part why the animal subjects which form one of the main iconographical categories of misericords show such a marked preponderance of the mythical and symbolical creatures described in the Bestiaries, as opposed to real ones. Dogs, cats, and chickens do appear, but mostly only as subsidiary elements in scenes of domestic life, while basilisks, dragons, and griffins abound. The supporter of a misericord in Ely Cathedral, which shows a stag eating a snake, must have been copied from a drawing akin to that in *Queen Mary's Psalter*, and illustrates the teaching of the Bestiary that the hart (symbolizing Christ) wages war on serpents, for anyone living in medieval England would have known that deer do not favour such a diet.

The following list includes the animals most often seen on misericords, with their symbolical meanings. Sometimes their symbolism is confusing. Thus the lion represents the Resurrection when it breathes upon its cubs, born dead, to bring them to life; it is a symbol of goodness when it fights the dragon, a very common subject (Pl. 10*b*); but it represents the Evil One when its jaws are rent by Samson. The Bestiaries say that when the lion is sick it eats a dead monkey, and this is shown on a misericord in St. George's Chapel, Windsor.

Amphisbaena. A winged serpent with a second head at the end of its tail. A symbol of deceit.

Antelope. Said by the Bestiary to have serrated horns with which it can cut down trees but to fall a prey to the hunter when these horns become entangled in bushes. It symbolized the man who, though armed with the two

Testaments, falls into the Devil's power when indulging in foolish pursuits. The heraldic antelope has the body of a tiger, short horns, and projecting tusks.

Ape. Symbol of fraud and deceit.

Asp. A form of serpent, generally shown winged. It was said to resist the wiles of the snake-charmer by laying one ear to the ground and blocking the other with its tail. Only certainly identifiable in this position, which does not appear in English churches, but small dragons with branching tails curled back towards their heads are sometimes tentatively described as asps.

Aspido Chelone. Confused with the whale. Little fishes attracted by its sweet breath were swallowed, but larger fish avoided it. Fish swallowing others are generally shown as dolphins.

Basilisk. Has a cock's body with a serpent's tail. Its glance can kill, but the weasel can attack it safely, provided it eats rue beforehand (Worcester, Pl. 10c).

Bat. Shown as a single subject on seven misericords, but never given the correct wing structure.

Bear. Only represented in scenes of bear-baiting, etc.

Blemya. A human monstrosity with no head but with a face in its stomach.

Camel. When it kneels to take up its load (Boston, Pl. 10d) it symbolizes Christ's humility in taking on the sins of the world.

Cat. Generally shown holding a mouse, in both Bestiaries and carvings.

Centaur. Half man, half horse. The man typifies Christ, the horse His vengeance on those who betrayed Him. When the centaur is shown shooting (Exeter), this symbolizes the soul of Christ departing to deliver souls from Hell.

Crane. The bird acting as sentinel for the flock holds a stone in an uplifted claw to ensure vigilance (Denston, Pl. 11a).

Dolphin. Said to follow music or the human voice. Often shown on supporters with a mermaid in the centre (Pl. 39d).

Dragon. Largest of all serpents and symbol of the Evil One.

Elephant. See p. xxix.

Fox. Shams dead to attract birds (Whalley). The hero of many animal fables.

Frog. Symbolizes the croaking of heretics (Edlesborough).

Hart. See p. xxxv. Appears singly or in hunting scenes.

Hedgehog. Impales fallen fruit on its prickles (New College, Oxford), thus symbolizing the deceits of the Devil.

Hoopoe. Young birds restore the youth of their parents by plucking out their old feathers (Windsor). Example of filial duty.

Hyena. Said to live among tombs and devour corpses. Is compared to those who worship false idols (Carlisle, Pl. 11b).

Ibis. Bird that lives on the water's edge and eats carrion rather than swim out in search of clean food. Shown with snake in its beak at Windsor and pecking a dead man's head at Lavenham (Pl. 11c).

Lion. See p. xxxv. The constant use of the lion in heraldry contributed to its popularity with the carvers.

Ostrich. In describing its speed in running, the Bestiary says the bird has feet like a camel. Usually shown with hooves or cloven feet. Credited with the power of digesting iron, it is sometimes shown with a horse shoe in its beak (Stratford-on-Avon, Pl. 11d).

Owl. Symbolized the Jews who prefer darkness to light. Often shown mobbed by small birds (Norwich, Pl. 12a).

Pard. Hybrid offspring of panther and lioness. Said to be very bloodthirsty; shown with long tongue extended and also a branching tail.

Parrot. Can only learn if hit with an iron bar. Rarely shown (Pl. 31c).

Peacock. Represented immortality in Roman mythology, and the Bestiary said its flesh was incorruptible (Pl. 30. a).

Pelican. Always shown feeding its fledglings with blood from its own breast. Never represented naturalistically (Pl. 12b, c, d).

Siren. Both the bird-siren and the fish-siren or mermaid occur, the latter being more common. Occasionally the merman is also shown. At Boston sailors are being lured to destruction by the siren's song (Pl. 13a).

Unicorn. An unconquerable beast, symbolizing Christ. In Durham Castle Chapel it tramples on the human-headed Serpent associated with the Fall of Man (Pl. 13b). If a pure virgin sits in the forest the Unicorn will lay its head meekly in her lap and be easily slain. Symbolized the Incarnation and Passion of Christ.

Whale. See *Aspido Chelone.*

Wodehouse. A wild man dressed in skins or with naked body covered in long hair. Often shown fighting with wild beasts.

Wolf. Shown with a thick mane down its spine. Said to bite its own feet to make them tread more quietly (Faversham, Pl. 13c).

Wyvern. A two-legged dragon.

Most scenes of agricultural labour shown on misericords were probably copied from calendar illustrations in books of devotion and are self-explanatory, although the allocation of labours to months varies slightly. Figures holding flowers or branches represent the Rogationtide processions for the blessing of the fields. In autumn the swineherds knocked down acorns to fatten their charges before shortage of fodder forced men to kill off all surplus animals. A scene of feasting (Malvern), or of a man sitting comfortably by the fire (Ludlow), represents one of the dead winter months, and then the annual routine of sowing and reaping is resumed. Scenes of vintage sometimes occur, but there is hardly ever a reference to the all-important care of sheep.

Studies of men at other forms of work are relatively rare. There are ship builders at St. David's (Pl. 2d) and at Wellingborough (Pl. 13d), Great Doddington (Pl. 14a), and in the Victoria and Albert Museum (Pl. 14b) we see carvers at work surrounded by their tools. A shepherd with a sheep under each arm is cleverly foreshortened to fit the form of a corbel in Winchester College Chapel, and some processes of cloth-making are shown on a misericord now returned to Brampton, Hunts. (Pl. 14c). Almost every woman shown in genre subjects has her distaff in hand, but on the whole the wool and cloth trades, on which the economy of medieval England depended, are sparsely illustrated.

It is difficult, when considering the many scenes of daily life shown in the carvings, to estimate the probable proportion of these which were suggested to the carvers by sermon *exempla*. The representation of women seems to reflect the preachers' influence most strongly, for their denunciations of women as monsters who disturb all tranquillity in the home can be paralleled by the many carvings of women beating their husbands (Pl. 14d), and by the hideous hag at Ludlow against whom the little men on the supporters defend themselves with sword (now broken) and buckler. All forms of women's finery were considered as snares of the Devil, but the twin-peaked head-dresses were worst of all, and a devil is shown peering from between these horns on a misericord at Minster-in-Thanet (Pl. 15a). There is also evidence of a negative influence. Although medieval carvers probably thought about courtship and pretty women as much as do their descendants, this is never reflected in their work. The only beautiful woman's face I have seen on a misericord is one of the seven heads of a hydra in New College, Oxford (Pl. 15b), representing the Seven Deadly Sins; the beautiful face is presumably *Luxuria*. Preachers who had difficulty in holding the attention of their congregations naturally fostered belief in the demon Tutivillus, whose special function it was to record the idle words of those who chattered in church (Gayton (Pl. 16b), Enville, and Ely Cathedral) and the mangled phrases of clerics who drowsed over their psalters (New College).

Closely allied to the influence of the pulpit was that of the stage. Tutivillus has an important part in the Towneley Doom Play; and the Dishonest Ale-Wife, who is shown on a misericord at Ludlow (Pl. 15d) being carried off to Hell wearing a peaked head-dress and holding her false measure in her hand, figures in the Chester Plays. The Resurrection misericord under the Dean's stall at Lincoln (Pl. 16a) shows Christ heavily disguised as 'the gardener'; and the demon at Gayton (Pl. 16b), who wears the feathered tights usually associated only with angels, reminds us that 'the Devil in all his feathers' rode before the Butchers in the Midsummer procession at Chester.

Subtle analyses of the Deadly Sins, and of the lesser failings which stem from them, figured in both sermons and plays, and were illustrated in many wall-paintings by lively little scenes of contemporary life. Some misericords may have been based on these painted moralities, but the only certain representations of the Deadly Sins occur on the misericords of Norwich Cathedral. Here Gluttony rides a sow; we are reminded of Spenser's Gluttony, who

> . . . in his hand did beare a bouzing can
> Of which he supt so oft that on his seat
> His dronken corse he scarce upholden can.
> *Faerie Queene*, Canto III.

Wrath rides a wild boar and draws his sword, while Lechery is represented as a man riding a stag and ensnared in the net of his own passions. A misericord at Stratford-on-Avon which shows a naked woman mounted on a hart may be derived from a drawing of the goddess Diana transformed into the Vice of Lechery.[1]

Folk tales and proverbial sayings occur occasionally. At Worcester a naked woman draped in a coarse net, beneath which she holds a rabbit, is shown riding a goat with one foot touching the ground and the other cocked high (Pl. 16c). This is the Clever Daughter of an

---

[1] Drawings of the Deadly Sins portrayed as different types of men and women mounted on appropriate animals occur in a late fourteenth-century manuscript in Paris: Bibl. Nat. MS. franç. 400.

internationally popular folk-tale, who won the boon she craved by ful-
filling the king's conditions that she must come before him neither
naked nor clothed, neither riding nor walking, and bringing a gift and
no gift. In the variant shown here the gift was evidently a rabbit which
escaped as soon as it had been released in the king's presence.

At Bristol a naked woman leading a pack of apes into the jaws of
Hell illustrates the supposed fate of the woman who dies unmarried,
to which Shakespeare refers in both *The Taming of the Shrew* (II. i) and
Much Ado about Nothing (II. i). The apes are the souls of unmarried
men. At Whalley the carving of a goose fixed into the frame devised
for shoeing vicious horses has an explanatory inscription: 'He that
meddles with what man does, let him come here and shoe the goose';
in other words, waste his efforts. Another misericord here is inscribed
in French: 'Think much, say little', but the connection between this
adage and the subject of a woman confronting a wodehouse is mysterious.

The wodehouse played an important part in popular mythology.
With some incidents, such as his conflicts with lions (Pl. 16*d*), scholars
associated complex symbolical interpretations relating it to the struggle
between spirit and flesh, but these are unlikely to have been known to
the carvers. The romance of Valentine and Orson may be illustrated on
a misericord at Beverley, St. Mary's, Valentine being shown as a courtly
youth recognizing in the rugged woodman his long-lost brother who
had been carried off by a bear; but interpretations of this, or of the
many carvings of wodehouses with other figures, should be regarded as
purely tentative. Taken together with various representations of sport—
football at Gloucester, wrestling at Halsall, and bear-baiting at Enville—
and the frequent carvings of jesters, contortionists, and dancers, they
help us to build up a picture of the lighter side of medieval life. Men's
highest aspirations, and their cynicism, their dreams of an ever-widening
world in which almost any strange creature might exist, and their
sardonic commentaries on social abuses at home, are all reflected in the
iconography of British misericords.

ENGLAND

BEDFORDSHIRE

BEDFORD   St. Paul's   *Nine*

North side from west

1 and 2. Missing.

3. Centre carving missing. Supporters: Left, an ape on a leaf. In its right hand a staff on which it leans, round its neck a broad collar to which a small ape on its back holds with both hands. Right, a seated ape (head gone); on its back a young ape.

4. Centre carving gone. Supporters: Left, shield hanging by a strap and buckle from the bracket moulding, charged: *diapered, a cross engrailed with label of three points* (possibly the arms of Mohun, without the three bezants). Right, shield similarly hanging, charged: *three bezants with label of three points.*

5. Centre carving gone. Supporters: Left and Right, leaf.

6. Centre carving much broken. Supporters: Left and Right, lion's mask with protruding tongue.

7, 8 and 9. Missing.

South side from west

1 and 2. Missing.

3. Foliage broken. Supporters: Left and Right, dragons with ribs and vertebrae prominent.

4. Castle with loopholes and a portcullis. Supporters: Left, man in armour with a crossbow, his left foot thrust through its stirrups. Right, wodehouse holding a club and a shield charged: *diapered a cross fleury* (the arms of the town of Bedford).

5. Vine-leaves and grapes. Supporters: Left and Right, three leaves forming a circle.

6. The lower jaw and teeth only remaining of a foliated mask. Supporters: Left and Right, leaf.

7. Bearded head in kerchief (broken). Supporters: Left and Right, leaf.

8 and 9. Missing.

DATE: Probably early 15th century.

LEIGHTON BUZZARD All Saints *Twenty-five*

There are fourteen stalls on each side of the chancel, three on each side being returned. One stall-seat is fixed and two have the carving missing.

North side from west

1. Man's head clean-shaven with curly hair. Supporters: Left, shield charged: *chevron between three crows, one and two* (arms of John Crowner). Right, shield charged: *two chevrons* (arms of Aynel).
2. Rose. Supporters: Left and Right, rose.
3. Woman's head with wimple and gorget. Supporters: Left and Right, leaf.
4. Centre carving broken. Supporters: Left and Right, leaf.
5. Stem between two leaves. Supporters: Left and Right, leaf.
6. Lion's mask. Supporters: Left and Right, leaf.
7. Large leaf. Supporters: Left and Right, small leaf.
8. Woman's head in wimple and gorget. Supporters: Left and Right, leaf.
9. Missing.
10. Man's head. Supporters: Left and Right, square foliated ornament.
11. Centre carving missing. Supporters: Left, leaf. Right, missing.
12. Man's head in a cap. Supporters: Left and Right, leaf.
13. Flower. Supporters: Left and Right, leaf.
14. Man's face with very creased brow and splayed nostrils, wearing a hood with liripipe. No supporters.

South side from west

1. Swan with outspread wings (the badge of Warwick). Supporters: Left, shield charged: *a fess between six cross crosslets* (the arms of Beauchamp). Right, shield charged: *a cross saltire* (the arms of St. Albans Abbey).
2. Dragon. Supporters: Left, shield charged with the arms of Thomas Frowicke, who was Lord Mayor of London from 1435 to 1444, *chevron between three lion-masks couped and langued, two and one; a mullet for difference.* Right, the same without the difference (the arms of Frowicke).
3. Two apes seated facing each other. Supporters: Left and Right, leaf.
4. Woman in wimple and gorget. Supporters: Left and Right, leaf.
5. Two leaves. Supporters: Left and Right, leaf.
6. Rose with sprays on each side. Supporters: Left and Right, large rose.
7. Centre carving missing. Supporters: Left and Right, leaf.
8. Bearded man's head in capote and liripipe. Supporters: Left, shield charged: *on a fess three roundels and in chief a fleur-de-lys for difference: on a fess three torteaux or bezants* (both probably arms of Thorneburgh). Right, shield charged: *checky a chevron* (possibly the arms of Newburgh, which was quartered by Beauchamp).

9. Head wearing a cap. Supporters: Left and Right, leaf.

10. Woman's head. Supporters: Left and Right, leaf.

11. Woman's head with long, flowing hair which is crossed underneath her chin. Supporters: Left and Right, rose.

12. Man's head wearing a hood. Supporters: Left and Right, leaf.

13. Seat fixed.

14. Missing.

Probably the stalls were not originally made for the church where they now are, but came from St. Albans Abbey. Seven of the eight heraldic items have been identified. There are two of the Earl of Warwick, two of Frowicke of South Mymms, one of Thomas Thornburgh, the Steward of the Abbey in 1391, a mutilated shield of the Aynel family and the Abbey, and, on one misericord (South 1), a swan, which was the emblem of the Earl of Warwick. All these people were connected with the Abbey.

The original number of stalls in the Abbey was sixty-eight. The twenty-eight which are now in All Saints show traces of weathering and may have lain in some contractor's yard before they came to the church. The fan-shaped slots in the free ends of the stalls indicate where they have been shortened. At the corners of the stalls are kings' heads, finely carved. It has been suggested that these heads represent King Offa, the reputed founder of the Abbey.

The coat of arms of the Steward of the Abbey fixes the date at the end of the 14th century (S. J. Forrester, *Guide to the Parish Church of Leighton Buzzard*, pp. 22 f.), but see South No. 2.

NORTHILL   St. Mary Virgin   *Three*

There are six stalls with three surviving misericords.

North side from east

1. Plain seat.

2. Fleur-de-lis.

South side from east

1. Double fleur-de-lis.

2. Plain seat.

3. Plain seat.

4. Two plain scrolls back to back.

DATE: *c.* 1405 (Cox and Harvey, *English Church Furniture*, Methuen, London, 1907). The church was made collegiate in 1405 by Sir William Trailly and his son, Gregory (*V.C.H., Bedfordshire*, i, p. 403).

SWINESHEAD   St. Nicholas   *Eight*

There are eight stalls with misericords with simple moulded brackets, believed late fifteenth century (*V.C.H., Bedfordshire*, iii, p. 170) (PLATE 17*a*).

BERKSHIRE

SUTTON COURTENAY   All Saints   *Three*

1. Lion fighting dragon.
2. Head of wide-mouthed lion.
3. Hawk on bird she has killed (PLATE 17*b*).

(These misericords are damaged and the supporters are missing. Ball-flower ornament known to have been on these could fix date as early fourteenth century. The chancel was reconstructed in 1300 (C. E. Keyser, *Berks, Bucks & Oxon A.J.* xxii (1916), p. 37).

WANTAGE   St. Peter and St. Paul   *Seventeen*

In the chancel are nine stalls on each side, three of which on each side are returned. All have misericords except No. 1 on the south side from the east.

North side from east

1. Four large vine-leaves on a common stalk, arranged in a square pattern. Supporters: Left and Right, single similar leaf.
2. Plain shield. Supporters: Left and Right, a spray of three figs.
3. Plain shield. Supporters: Left and Right, vine-leaf.
4. Large indented flower, fully opened. Supporters: Left and Right, vine-leaf.
5. Large pattern of four vine-leaves.
6. Plain shield. Supporters: Left and Right, long branch terminating in vine-leaf.
7. Shield bearing three flagons. Supporters: Left and Right, vine-leaf. (PLATE 17*c*).
8. Double-headed eagle. Supporters: Left and Right, vine-leaf (PLATE 17*d*).
9. A pelican in her piety. Supporters: Left and Right, vine-leaf (PLATE 12*d*).

South side from east

1. Missing.
2. Entwined pattern of vine-leaf, which includes the supporters.
3. Plain shield. Supporters: Left and Right, vine-leaf.
4. Plain shield. Supporters: Left and Right, fruit and vine-leaf.
5. Plain shield. No supporters.

6. Plain shield. Supporters: Left and Right, vine-leaf.

7. Large vine-leaf in square format. Supporters: Left and Right, twig.

8. Entwined twig and vine-leaf in diagonal form. Supporters: Left and Right, pendant twig and vine-leaf.

9. Plain shield. Supporters: Left and Right, full lion-head, with mouth-foliage of a bunch of grapes and vine-leaf.

DATE: 15th century (*V.C.H., Berkshire*, iv, p. 328).

WINDSOR   St. George's Chapel   *Ninety-six*

At the west end are eight returned stalls.

On the north and south sides, divided into two rows on each side, twenty-seven in each upper row and twenty-one in each lower, the latter in two blocks.

South side, Upper Row, the four returned stalls

1. The meeting of Edward IV and Louis XI of France on the bridge at Picquigny on 29 August 1475. The bridge has a wooden barrier across it in the middle. On each side is a king in armour and short surcoat, attended respectively by nine armed men on the right and eleven on the left. The king on the left stretches out his hand to the other. Supporters: Left, the King of France comes out of a castellated gateway preceded by three men. Right: the King of England in the door of his tent, which is surmounted by the banners of St. George. He has crown, orb, and sceptre, and four attendants. (This is the Sovereign's stall. It is much larger than usual, 3 ft. 7 in. across.) (PLATE 1*a*.)

2. Gatehouse, flanked by towers and walls of a city, two watchmen above. Supporters: Left, archer holding an arrow under his chin bending his crossbow, a shield at the side. Right, soldier aiming a hand-gun at the gatehouse.

3. Angel with blank scrolls, one held by two eagles.

4. Jester plays on bagpipes, lady sits with falcon on arm and cat at feet. Man sits on ground, dog comes to him. Supporters: Left, man with pointed shield. Right, man with crutch. Squirrel and nut.

South side

5. Monster holds dragon by a rope. Supporters: Left, curled-up dog. Right, elephant and castle.

6. Two dogs gnaw a bone. Supporters: Left, clothed ape holds up a comb and stands before a fox sitting in a tub and holding a basin; snails. Right, ape with stole, chained by the neck to a clog, blesses a cat crouching before him; snail.

7. Two wyverns biting a tree between them. Supporters: Left, ox-lion with scroll. Right, monster biting his own tail.

8. Fox in gown and hood (in which is a goose) stands in a pulpit holding a goose by the neck and preaches to two other geese. An ape in a bush aims at him with a crossbow. Supporters: Left, man-monster and dragon. Right, wodehouse with spear pointed at the ape.

9. Two men wrestle in a garden. Supporters, craftsmen with hammer and graver, a large covered cup between them.

10. Two lizard-like animals intertwined. Supporters: Left, dog-beast and frog. Right, a dog bites paw of monkey by a palm tree.

11. Two dragons with crossed necks over a skull. Supporters: Left, composite beast. Right, dragons intertwined.

12. All carved foliage.

13. Bearded head and faces among leaves.

14. Man in cloak sitting beside a seated naked woman who is trying to pull the cloak over her (St. Zosimus and St. Mary of Egypt). Supporters: Left, beast, half rhinoceros, half hippopotamus. Right, dog on flower.

15. Four dogs; one eating out of a pot, one biting him, one asleep, and one looking on. Supporters: Left, man brandishing ladle and chopper; dresser, pestle and mortar. Right, human-headed swan.

16. Wodehouse man on unicorn tilting at wodehouse woman on another beast. Supporters: water flowers.

17. Foliate masks. Supporters: Left, dog-like beast. Right, lion.

18. Sea-monster holding fish. Supporters: Left, head of woman. Right, head of paynim.

19. Jester half-length. Supporters: Left and Right, double rose.

20. Cockatrice fighting a beast. Supporters: Left and Right, dog-like beast.

21. Unicorn fighting dragon. Supporters: Left, dog-like beast. Right, wodehouse.

22. Two beasts facing each other. Supporters: Left, heron-like bird preening itself. Right, web-footed bird, possibly an ibis, holding an eel.

23. Apes in a vine picking grapes. Supporters: Left and Right, ape on dog, face to tail, birching it.

24. Rose-bush between ape and wyvern. Supporters; Left, ape and monkey by a tree with a snail in it. Right, human-headed wyvern and dragon by tree.

25. Rose-bush and snails. Supporters: Left, collared hound. Right, hound scratching his head.

26 and 27. Modern.

South Lower Row, West block

1. Three monks or friars; and a fox with a goose, trundled in a wheelbarrow by a demon into hell-mouth. Blank scroll above. Supporters: Left and Right, Saracen in warlike attitude.

2. Turbaned man kneeling with his breeches down, holding a flower. Behind, another man kneels with wallet on back. A scarf passes from the first man round the other's neck. Supporters: Left, monkey on dog, face to tail, birching it. Right, monkey pouring liquid down the throat of a lean dog lying on its back. A monkey with a scarf holds up a urine-flask (a satire on the despised medieval doctor).

3. Lion bites dead dragon's legs. Supporters: Left and Right, wodehouse with club.

4. Wodehouse beats dog who has his foot on another beast. Supporters: Left and Right, water-flower.

5. Four-legged demon, horned and winged, takes food out of a dish on a table, cooking-pot near. On the right an old man with closed eyes ladles food out of the dish with a long ladle and blesses it. Illustration of proverb: he who sups with the devil needs a long spoon. Supporters: Left and Right, man-monster with ragged staff.

6. Man puts a frog into the mouth of a prostrate man held by the head and legs by two others. Supporters: Left and Right, flower.

7. Scenes from the Dance of Death. Death comes to the rich man seated in the centre; on a shelf are flagons; on a table are cups, and below it a chest and coffer. Supporters: Left, Death comes to a labourer who is digging. Right, Death comes to a thresher.

8. Flowers between fox and rabbit (left) and fox and goose (right). Supporters: Left and Right, water-flowers.

9. Dog, head entangled in an overturned trivet and pot, tries to escape from an old man who beats him; a leather bottle lies on the ground. Supporters: Left, sitting man plays pipe to dancing dog. Right, sow plays harp to three dancing piglets.

10. St. George attacks the dragon. Princess kneels with lamb. King and queen look on from a castle. Supporters: Left and Right, snails on a mitre (the badge of Bishop Beauchamp of Salisbury, 1475).

South Lower Row, East block

1. Man with a kid tied on his back creeps along; another feeds a kid on the back of a third. Supporters, Left, pelican in her piety; four nestlings. Right, man and woman in whelk-shells fight.

2. Lion-beast and dog-beast face each other. Supporters, water-flowers.

3. Park paling. Hound chases hare; snail and frog. Supporters, Left, dog scratches his ear. Right, dog bites himself.

4. Pedlar lying with hose undone being robbed by apes, three combs beside him. A hawk's perch with an ape giving away hawk's bells and combs to two others, one of which holds a hawk by the tail; another ape kneels by the man. Supporters: Left, drunken man dancing in top-boots and clutching at a plant. Right, seated jester.

5. Two lion-beasts. Supporters: Left, man-monster and dragon. Right woman-monster and dog.

6. Ape fights wyvern. Supporters: Left, dragon on bird. Right, man-monster crouches under plant.

7. Lion fighting dragon. Supporters: water-flowers.

8. Two men quarrelling over a backgammon board and dice. One is threatened by the other with a dagger which he seizes with his left hand, pinching the side of the face of the first man with his right; a coffer on right with a cat on it; sideboard with flasks on left. Supporters: Left, two boys with hands tied and knees drawn up through them; they hold short sticks and try to hit each other. Right, seated man hands a bag of money to another seated man.

9. Water-plant and snails. Supporters: Left, large leaves. Right, water-plant and snails.

10 and 11. Modern.

North Side, Upper Row

1. Castellated building with gatehouse flanked by towers. Supporters: Left, two men carry on their heads a boat-shaped shield having on its side a dormer window and at the end a wheel for trundling it. Right, man with axe under a similar shield. Such shields were used in sieges. (The Prince's Stall.)

2. Mermaid with mirror and comb on a rock; a building; a moored boat carrying a little banner of St. George in the bow; rocks on left. Supporters: Left, bird eating an eel. Right, otter with fish in its mouth.

3. Man and naked woman seated, practically the same as South Upper 14. Supporters: Left, naked man on a horse, shield of St. George on his back, tilts at a rabbit. Right, couchant antelope with bow and sheaf of arrows; dog pointing at the rabbit.

4. Head with bat's ears and mulberry mouth-foliage. Supporters: Left, a turbaned head. Right, veiled female head.

5. Samson, bearded and long-haired, in a tunic, tight hose, and boots, astride the lion and pulling its jaws apart; right, a woman holding out to him a mace (broken). Trees and two horses in the background. Supporters: Left, seated ape with ring about his middle takes food from another ape; trees. Right, two crested birds (hoopoes) attack a third (young plucking the parent to restore its youth).

6. Foliage and fruit.

7. Man with back towards us and his legs widely outstretched and having each hand on the back of an eagle which is perched on each of his ankles. One form of the Flight of Alexander. Supporters: Left, eagle full face. Right, eagle flies away.

8. Seated ape chained to a small barrel, holding under the chin a foolish-looking dog which is facing him. Supporters: Left and Right, foliage.

9. Oak-leaves. Supporters: Left and Right, double rose.

10. Demi-eagle with scroll. Supporters: Left and Right, flower.

11. Turbaned man holding on to stalks of plants. Supporters: Left, eagle with scroll. Right, lion biting the leaf of a plant.

12. Two monsters. Supporters: Left and Right, flower.

13. Griffin holding down a dog. Supporters: Left and Right, water-flower.

14. Griffin with wings expanded. Supporters: Left and Right, water-flower.

15. Swan with three cygnets swimming. Supporters: Left and Right, eagle with expanded wings.

16. Demi-angel with scroll. Supporters: Left and Right, water-flower.

17. Amphisbaena with coiled tail. Supporters: Left and Right, wyvern with spread wings.

18. Mermaid with comb and mirror. Supporters: Left, winged lion on scroll (for St. Mark). Right, winged ox, scroll in mouth (for St. Luke).

19. Foliage and fruit. Supporters: Left and Right, the same.

20. Long-bodied dog chasing rabbits in a warren. Supporters: Left, fox running away with goose. Right, talbot dog (a mastiff used frequently in heraldry).

21. Head of a demon, dragons issuing from the corners of mouth. Supporters: Left and Right, rayed rose.

22. Merman in tunic and hat, holding buckler and leg of a bull. Supporters: Left, eagle, scroll in beak (for St. John). Right, demi-angel with scroll (for St. Matthew).

23. Bearded face between leopards. Supporters: Left and Right, large, round leaf.

24. Demi-angel with plain shield. Supporters: Left and Right, angel in clouds with plain shield.

25. Owl with feet on a mouse, mobbed by two birds in bushes. Supporters: Left and Right, bird mobbing the owl.

26 and 27. Modern.

North Lower Row, West block

1. Eight men in armour fighting with a large bird which stands on one of them and bites the toe of another prostrate. Supporters: Left, dog and toad. Right, man lying down resists a tiger-like beast.

2. Eagle or falcon attacks rabbit in a warren. Supporters: Left, birds on a plant. Right, parrot and swan bite leaves of a plant.

3. Dog-like beast with scroll, and lion-like beast. Supporters: Left and Right, five water-flowers.

4. Flowering plant with snails. Supporters: Left and Right, flower.

5. Wodehouse fighting horned dog-like beast. Supporters: Left, dog. Right, leopard.

6. Manticora. Supporters: Left, man–dog in a vine. Right, winged monster.

7. A reclining demon evacuates a man in an apron. In the apron are two objects which another demon seizes. (Perhaps a fraudulent ale-seller.) Supporters: Left, seated man drinks from a churn-like vessel; chopper and basin in front; behind him is a winged demon, its forepaws on his head. Right, winged demon drinks from bottle.

8. Bear-like beasts bite a man's arm. Supporters: Left and Right, double rose.

9. Eagle-monster fights another monster. Supporters: Left and Right, couchant hind.

10. Angel in clouds with scroll. Supporters: Left, lion eats dead monkey. (This, according to the bestiary, was the specific medicine for a sick lion.) Right, lion and bear in conflict.

North Lower Row, East block

1. Friar evacuates a demon. Another friar and demon on right. Supporters: Left, ape drags dog by tail; it has a bone and yelps. Right, seated clothed ape plays bagpipes. Another ape blows into the chanter.

2. Rayed rose ensigned, with crown between lions, the crest of the house of March. Supporters: Left and Right, water-flower.

3. Kneeling man fights dragon with club. Supporters: Left, a lion-like beast. Right, dog-like beast.

4. Naked boy seized by dog-monster and wyvern. Supporters: Left and Right, lion.

5. Tusked antelope running. Supporters: Left, a post-windmill with three sparrows carrying sacks of corn to it. Right, alehouse with bush-and-ring sign projecting from the gables. In front a large bird with a napkin or empty sack about its neck holds out a bowl to three smaller birds; tree behind.

6. Lion-face; wyverns issue from the corners of the mouth. Supporters: Left and Right, water-flower.

7. Crouching boy. Supporters: Left and Right, rayed rose.

8. Elephant and castle walking past a town. Supporters, Left, ibis with snake in beak, ostrich with horse's legs and hoofs, horseshoe in beak, another horseshoe on ground. Right, owl in bush, four small birds fly down to mob it.

9. Winged dog-beast and another beast. Supporters: Left and Right, water-flower.

10. Modern.

DATE: (except those described as modern) from 1477 to 1483 (the closing years of the reign of Edward IV). The modern stalls and misericords were carved by Henry Emlyn in the years 1786–90 (M. R. James, *St. George's Chapel, Windsor; the Woodwork of the Choir*, 1933).

BUCKINGHAMSHIRE

AYLESBURY   St. Mary   *Five*

In the chancel are two rows of stalls of four each. On the north is one misericord, a grotesque animal.

On the south from the east

1. Small animal.
2. Human head.
3. Human figure supporting the bracket. Supporters of each are foliage.
4. Only blocked out. The carving is unfinished.

DATE: Late 15th Century (*R.C.H.M., Buckinghamshire*, i, p. 27).

EDLESBOROUGH   St. Mary the Virgin   *Six*

There are six returned stalls.

North to south

1. A seated mermaid suckling lion. Supporters, rayed faces. (PLATE 8*b*.)
2. Dragon. Supporters: Left and Right, frog.
3. Owl.
4. Eagle with two eaglets.
5. Beast with claws.
6. Bat.

DATE: 15th century (*R.C.H.M., Buckinghamshire*, ii, p. 109).

NORTH MARSTON   St. Mary   *Six*

In the chancel are six carved misericords with lierne vaulting on foliated corbels.

DATE: 15th century (*R.C.H.M., Buckinghamshire*, ii, p. 225).

CAMBRIDGESHIRE

BALSHAM   Holy Trinity   *Ten*

In the chancel on either side are three returned stalls, backing on the screen, and ten against the north or south walls of the chancel.

South side from west

1. Wyvern.
2. Bust of a man with thick wavy hair.

3. Human face.

4, 5, 6, 7, and 8. Missing.

9. Lion with a large head resting on his front paws. The hindquarters are spread slightly and have two tails twisted together.

10, 11, and 12. Missing.

13. The bust of a man with traces of a short forked beard (damaged), holding a shuttle in his left hand and a round convex object with a central, knob (like the bottom of a wooden bowl) in his right hand.

North side from west

1. A male bust.

2. The head and foreparts of a devil with cloven hooves.

3, 4, 5, 6, and 7. Missing.

8. Large face of a man with mouth-foliage.

9. The head and shoulders of a hooded man with long, curly beard (modern). It may have been the work of Canon H. J. S. Burrell, a former vicar who was a noted woodcarver.

10, 11, and 12. Missing.

13. Bust of a girl wearing a round, flat hat. Supporters, stylized leaves.

The stalls were given by ohn Sleford, rector who died in 1401 (*Jour. Brit. Arch. Assoc.*, N.S., xxxvi (1931), p. 246).

CAMBRIDGE King's College Chapel *Sixty-eight*

There are sixty-eight stalls, thirty-four on each side of the chancel of which four on each side are returned.

South side from west

Returned Stalls

1. Pair of winged, two-legged monsters with cloven hooves and horned human heads, only one of each showing, and with long tails ending in flowers. A small head is between them. Supporters: medallions containing a head. Some delicate foliage between the medallions and the monsters covers parts of their bodies. (The Provost's Stall, nearly 4 ft. wide.)

2. Ram's head between two human monsters, with wings, animal hind legs with cloven hoofs; one is bearded. Supporters: Left and Right, lion on a lead held by each monster.

3. Winged human torso with paws for hands holds two scrolls against its chest. Supporters: similar creatures with bird's claws treading on a wyvern—a dragon. The one on the left steps on his dragon with his left claw and with the other holds the central of three bird's heads on long necks issuing from the mouth of a horse; the one on the right holds a horse by a halter.

4. Winged, goat-headed monster with female breasts. Supporters: Left, the back view of a naked woman (?) holding a wyvern by a halter and waving a snake in the air. Right, a nearly naked man with a sword, holding a snake.

South side from west

1. Simple foliage. Supporters: Left and Right, three trefoiled leaves.
2. Simple foliage. Supporters: Left and Right, foliated spirals.
3. Similar to No. 2.
4 to 11. Simple foliage. No supporters.
12. Foliage with leonine face in the middle.
13 to No. 21. Foliage.
22. Rose on a shield, surmounted by a crown. Supporters, fine foliate scroll containing the upper part of a face.
23 to 29. Foliage.
30. Foliate mask.

North side from west
Returned Stalls

1. Ram's head with delicate foliage between two monsters, whose upper parts are human and hindquarters animal with cloven hooves, holding ribbon scrolls which go out to the supporters' medallions. Supporters: Left, back view of a man wearing only a flowing cloak on a horse and holding a baton in his left hand. Right, front view of the same. (The Vice-Provost's Stall, wide like the Provost's.)
2. Lion's mask holding in its mouth the tails of two birds with webbed feet and fantastic animal heads. Supporters: Left, a fish-head. Right, a horse-head.
3. Plain shield held by two animal-headed birds. Supporters: Left and Right, moustached mask.
4. Heavy foliage between two baby faces surrounded by scrolls.

North side from west

1. Foliage.
2. Fine foliage.
3. The same.
4. Foliage with a head in the middle.
5 to 9. Foliage.
10. Winged leonine head.
11. Foliage.
12. Foliage.

13. Winged head slightly turned to the right, with horn and animal on left side only.

14 to 19. Foliage.

20. Winged head.

21. Foliage.

22. Elaborate foliage with fine foliated scrolls.

23 to 25. Foliage.

26. Foliage with a minute winged head at the base.

27 to 30. Foliage.

DATE: 1533–8 (*R.C.H.M.*, *City of Cambridge*, i, p. 131).

CAMBRIDGE   Jesus College Chapel   *Forty-two*

In the nave, built into the front benches, together with other old woodwork, are six misericords. They are all alike, the centrepiece being a group of fruit and seed-pods in foliage; the supporters are rosettes (*c.* 1500).

In the chancel there are eighteen misericords on each side, of which three on each side are returned.

They are all alike, having a plain moulded bracket, and supporters of simple flowers copied by Pugin, 1849–53, from original design of *c.* 1500 on fragments preserved in the Master's Lodge (*R.C.H.M.*, *City of Cambridge*, i, p. 90).

CAMBRIDGE   Pembroke College Chapel   *Thirty*

They are all alike, the motif being acanthus leaves.

DATE: *c.* 1665 (*R.C.H.M.*, *City of Cambridge*, ii, p. 154).

CAMBRIDGE   Peterhouse Chapel   *Two*

In the chancel, flanking the entrance, for the Master and Vice-Master.

North side

Master's Stall. A lion's head. Supporters: Left and Right, bird and flower.

South side

Vice-Master's Stall. A cherub head. Supporters: Left and Right, female bust and flower.

DATE: presumed *c.* 1632 (*R.C.H.M.*, *City of Cambridge*, ii, p. 159).

CAMBRIDGE   St. Clement's Church   *One*

In the chancel is a single sixteenth-century misericord, probably of foreign origin. It forms the seat of a nineteenth-century chair. The carving consists of a bracket covered with acanthus leaves in low relief, and emerges from the centre of a stylized flower below it. Supporters: Left and Right, plain volutes. See *R.C.H.M., City of Cambridge*, ii, p. 271.

CAMBRIDGE St. John's College Chapel *Forty-four*

There are twenty-two stalls on each side of the chancel, with misericords, mainly alike, but with a few variations as listed below.

North side from west

1 to 8. Foliated bracket. Supporters: Left and Right, foliage and flower.

9. Foliated bracket. Supporters: Left and Right, shield charged with a pomegranate.

10 to 13. Foliated bracket. Supporters: Left and Right, foliage and flower.

14. Crowned Tudor rose. Supporters: Left and Right, foliage and flower.

15. Foliated bracket. Supporters: Left and Right, plain shield.

16 to 22. Foliated bracket. Supporters: Left and Right, foliage and flower.

South side from west

1. Eagle holding a scroll. Supporters: Left and Right, foliage and flower.

2. Mask amid foliage. Supporters: Left and Right, foliage and flower.

3 to 8. Foliated bracket. Supporters: Left and Right, foliage and flower.

9. Shield amid foliage. Supporters: Left and Right, foliage and flower.

10 to 13. Foliated bracket. Supporters: Left and Right, foliage and flower.

14. Shield amid foliage. Supporters: Left and Right, foliage and flower.

15. Shield charged with a rose. Supporters: Left and Right, foliage and flower.

16. Fleur-de-lis amid foliage. Supporters: Left and Right, rose.

17 and 18. Foliated bracket. Supporters: Left and Right, foliage and flower.

19. Foliated bracket. Supporters: Left and Right, male head.

20. Bat in foliage. Supporters: Left and Right, foliage and flower.

21 and 22. Foliated bracket. Supporters: Left and Right, foliage and flower.

DATE: Probably 16th century, possibly 1510–25, as indicated by pomegranate badge of Katherine of Aragon.

ELY The Cathedral *Sixty-five*

In the choir there are eighty-four stalls, twenty-four in the North upper row, nineteen in the North lower row, twenty-three in the South upper, and eighteen in the South lower, all having misericords, nineteen of which are modern.

North Side from west, upper row

1. Two demi-angels. Supporters: Left and Right, leaf (modern).
2. Two grotesque faces in foliage. Supporters: Left and Right, leaf.
3. Stag. Supporters: Left, huntsman winding his horn, carrying bow on right shoulder and a quiver of arrows. Right, stag.
4. Man in long cloak leaning forward and clasping his knees. Supporters: Left and Right, leaves.
5. Man with two hounds in leash, a hare slung over his back. Supporters: Left, boy with hound. Right, hare running into foliage.
6. Two lions issuing from foliage. Supporters: Left and Right, vine-leaves and foliage.
7. Man bending forward, hands on knees, supporting the bracket on his shoulders. Supporters: Left and Right, foliage.
8. Woman seated looking through the fork in a tree, her arms are raised, supporting the bracket. Supporters: Left and Right, stag browsing.
9. Bearded man in long tunic leaning forward, hands on knees. Supporters: Left and Right, lion biting itself.
10. Man in a vine picking grapes. Supporters: Left and Right, vine-leaves and grapes.
11. Woman kneeling, hands clasped, confessing to seated man. Supporters: Left, skull wreathed in foliage. Right, foliage.
12. Pelican in her piety. Supporters: Left and Right, flowers and foliage.
13. Man leaning on a sword (or hammer). Supporters: Left and Right, oak foliage.
14. Face in foliage. Supporters: Left and Right, oak foliage.
15. Two wrestlers or tumblers, the upper one wears a cap with ears to it. Supporters: Left and Right, lion and griffin fighting.
16. Man wearing tight-fitting cap and loose jerkin with his horse falling to the ground. His hunting horn lies broken beside him. Supporters: Left, two dogs hunting hinds through a wood. Right, woman in a chapel praying before a small altar.
17. The capture of the unicorn. According to legend this beast could be lured by a virgin.
18. Two women seated side-by-side, hands on knees. Supporters: Left and Right, flowers.
19. Woman striking with her distaff at a fox running away with a goose. Supporters: Left, fox in monk's cowl with pastoral staff in his hand preaching to a cock and two hens. Right, man with flail standing before a crop of wheat.
20. The Temptation of Adam and Eve. The Tree of Knowledge stands in the centre and around it is twined the serpent with a human head. Adam is about to eat an apple and holds another in his hand. Eve looks on.

Supporters: Left, ape and two small quadrupeds in foliage. Right, rabbit-warren with birds and foliage.

21. Seated woman, hands on knees. Supporters: Left and Right, leaves.

22. Man leaning forward (broken). Supporters: Left and Right, oak-leaves and acorns.

23. Two hooded, bearded men throwing dice. Supporters: Left, woman seated on a bench, holding a spray of flowers, a barrel beside her. Right, man in long tunic carrying a cup in one hand and a bottle in the other.

24. Man kneeling on one knee and supporting the bracket with his hands. Supporters: Left, man playing a viol. Right, dog lying curled up.

South Side from west, upper row

1. Two demi-angels supporting a shield (modern).

2. Two monks seated on a bench. Supporters: Left, lion's mask from which issues foliage. Right, birds in foliage.

3. Noah looking out of the Ark, which is three-tiered. Supporters: Left, raven on carcass of ox. Right, the dove flying to Noah with the olive-branch. (PLATE 18a.)

4. Seated woman, leaning forward, hands raised to each side of her face. Supporters: Left and Right, house in oak-foliage.

5. Ape, with drapery over his shoulders and with long fingers to hands and feet, supporting the bracket with back. Supporters: Left and Right, winged dragon, the tails being a prolongation of the bracket moulding.

6. Woman seated in a chair, her hands resting on the heads of two hounds standing one on each side of her. Supporters: Left and Right, ape in foliage.

7. Man grimacing, hands on knees and legs bent up behind him. Supporters: Left and Right, oak-leaves.

8. Man with his arms round two monsters with serpents' bodies. Supporters: Left, centaur playing pipe and tabor. Right, female centaur playing dulcimer. Both supporters in foliage.

9. Seated long-haired, bearded man, legs crossed, with hands on knees. Supporters: Left and Right, oak-leaves.

10. Man and woman, both seated; man crosses right foot on to left knee.

11. Seated man, extended arms supporting the bracket. Supporters: Left and Right, foliage.

12. Man squatting, arms under chin, head supporting the bracket. Supporters: Left and Right, lion biting itself.

13. Seated king and queen in voluminous drapery. Supporters: Left and Right, three birds with their heads to the centre carving.

14. Crowned king seated on canopied throne. Supporters: Left and Right, figure kneeling in adoration.

15. Jester (body gone) standing in water. Supporters: Left, child riding a dog. Right, dog taking a child out of the water in its mouth.

16. Samson astride the lion, pulling its jaws open. Supporters, foliage.

17. Woman nursing child whose arms are round her neck. Supporters: Left and Right, foliage.

18. Demon opening a man's mouth, holding his beard, and trying to pull out a tooth. Supporters: Left and Right, foliage.

19. Squatting man, one arm raised above his head, the other supporting it. Supporters: Left and right, ape in foliage.

20. Bear beneath a tree in which are two apes. Supporters: Left and Right, ape in foliage.

21. Monk and nun.

22. Seated man leaning forward, his hands behind him. Supporters: Left and Right, foliage.

23. Two men seated, their heads resting on their hands. Supporters: Left and Right, foliage.

North side from west, lower row

1. The daughter of Herodias receiving the head of St. John the Baptist from the gaoler; the prison is in the background. Supporters: Left, Herod, Philip, and Herodias seated at a table, in front of which the daughter dances. Right, the mother, crowned, receiving the head in a charger from the daughter.

2. Owl perched in a tree, holding a mouse with its foot. Supporters: Left and Right, foliage in which are small birds.

3. Man fallen down under trees, he holds a billet of wood in each hand. Supporters: Left, man blowing horn. Right, two men armed with swords and bucklers.

4. Crowned king resting his head on his right hand, his left grasping the skirt of his mantle. Supporters: Left and Right, leaves and grapes.

5. Adam and Eve being driven out of the Garden of Eden by the angel with a large sword. Supporters: Left, Adam and a son digging. Right, Eve spinning; cat playing with the yarn (PLATE 18b).

6. Man seated, hands on knees (modern). Supporters: Left and Right, leaves.

7 and 8. Modern.

9. Seated bearded man holding a scroll in front of him. Supporters: Left and Right, dragon in foliage.

10, 11, 12, 13, 14, 15, and 16. Modern.

17. Two women grinding corn, surrounded by cooking utensils. Supporters: Left and Right, leaves.

18 and 19. Modern.

South Side, from west lower row

1. King, fully armed, riding and aiming a blow at a figure with a crutch behind him (all head, no body). (One of the hind legs of the horse has been broken off.) Supporters: Left, Christ in the act of benediction (head and orb gone); two angels adoring on either side swing censers, background diapered. Right, bishops in mitres exorcizing a female spirit out of a nude figure.

2. Two seated women; left one wears a chaplet and carries a rosary; the other has a book. The devil pokes his head between them and puts his arms round their necks. Supporters: Left and Right, small devil with scrolls in foliage. (Devil listening to chatterers in church.)

3. Man and woman riding on a horse; she holds its tail, he grasps its mane. The horse has knocked down two people over whom it tramples. Supporters: Left, two men. Right, two women.

4. Two men, wearing long, loose gowns wrestling. Supporters: Left and Right, leaves.

5. Ram under two oak-trees. Supporters: Left and Right, oak-leaves.

6, 7, and 8. Modern.

9. Old man wearing loose cap kneeling and supporting bracket with his left hand, Supporters: Left and Right, leaves.

10. Modern.

11. Bearded man squatting, head on one side. Supporters: Left and Right, ivy-leaves and fruit.

12. Modern.

13. Seated bearded man, hood drawn over head, bending forward. Supporters: Left and Right, ivy-leaves.

14. Knight, fully armed with vizor to his helmet, sword, and battle-axe, kneeling on one knee, his body supporting the bracket. Supporters: Left and Right, leaves.

15. Seated man. Supporters: Left and Right, leaves.

16. Man and woman seated on the ground: he has his right thumb in her mouth; she strikes him in the face and kicks his knee. Supporters: Left and Right, grotesque lion with foliated tail.

17. Kneeling man, one hand behind head, the other on hip, supporting the bracket. Supporters: Left, two rams fighting. Right, eagle carrying off a lamb.

18. Bearded man in a cave or cell, with an arrow in his knee, stooping and caressing a hind, and carrying a rosary in the other hand. (The legend of St. Giles.) Supporters: Left and Right, archer in foliage shooting at the hind (PLATE 2*a*).

The stalls were designed by Hurley, 1339–40, and seem to have been finished in 1340–1 (*V.C.H., Cambridgeshire*, iv, 64).

FORDHAM   St. Peter and St. Mary Magdalen   *Twelve*

North side from west

1. Foliage. Supporters: Left and Right, foliage.
2. Grotesque human-headed monster with webbed feet. Supporters: Left and Right, foliage.
3. Bull's head. Supporters: Left and Right, rose.
4. Similar monster to No. 2 but with a lion's face. Supporters: Left and Right, sunflower.
5. Bull's face. Supporters: Left and Right, rose.
6. Lion's head with protruding tongue. Supporters: Left and Right, vine-leaf.

South side from west

1. Shield uncharged. Supporters: Left and Right, foliage.
2. Grotesque monster, winged, with webbed feet. Supporters: Left and Right, rose.
3. Lion's mask. Supporters: Left and Right, sunflower.
4. Lion's mask with protruding tongue. Supporters: Left and Right, foliage.
5. Shield charged: *a fess and six fusils* (the arms of Faconberge). Supporters: Left and Right, leaf.
6. Flower. Supporters: Left and Right, foliage.

DATE: Early 14th century. (Cox and Harvey: *English Church Furniture*, Methuen, London, 1907, p. 259, say *c.* 1350.)

GAMLINGAY   St. Mary   *Four*

There are six misericords but the carving of two has been cut away.

1. Animal head with tongue protruding and large pointed ears, punctured all over. Supporters: Left and Right, rose. The seat-shelf has a straight front.
2. Hooded, squatting figure with hands raised. Supporters: Left and Right, conventional foliage.
3. Squatting ape with its hands behind its ears. Supporters: Left and Right, conventional foliage.
4. Mass of vine-leaves and grapes. Supporters: Left and Right, conventional foliage.

DATE: Mid-15th century. The chancel is recorded as having been built in 1442–3, and the woodwork is consistent with its having been inserted immediately (*R.C.H.M., Cambridge*).

GREAT EVERSDEN   St. Mary   *Two*

1. Shield bearing the arms of Beauchamp, *a fess bewteen six cross crosslets.* Supporters: Left, lion mask with protruding tongue. Right, a rose (PLATE 18c).

2. Elaborate foliage design. Supporters: Left, a circular pattern of radiating-branch foliage. Right, a shield bearing the arms of Bardolph, *bordure engrailed, three cinquefoils.*

DATE: 15th century.

N.B. Lysons does not mention either family in connection with this parish. The stalls are said to have come from Queens' College, Cambridge (*The Times*, 24 April 1963).

ISLEHAM   St. Andrew   *Eight*

South side

1. Bishop wearing a mitre.
2. Priest.
3. Noble wearing a coronet.
4. Mask.

North side

1. King.
2. Queen (with stylized hair).
3. Commoner (wearing a soft hat).
4. Youth.

The supporters are all stiff leaves.

DATE: *c.* 1450.

There is a motif on the bishop's mitre and on the noble's coronet which also occurs on a bench-end bearing the arms of Margaret Bernard, who inherited her father's estates in 1451.

LANDBEACH   All Souls   *Four*

(On the north and south sides.) There are four stalls in two pairs. They were originally returned stalls.

North from west

1. Plain shield. Supporters: Left and Right, lizard.

2. Arms of Bishop Arundel, *bordure engrailed; quarterly, one and four checky* (Warenne), *two and three lion rampant* (Fitzalan). Supporters: Left and Right, cinquefoil (PLATE 18d).

South from west

1. Plain shield. Supporters: Left and Right, cinquefoil.

2. Arms of Bishop de Lisle of Ely (1345–61), *bordure, a fess between two chevrons.* Supporters: Left and Right, lizard.

The stallwork and woodwork is very similar to the woodwork in Jesus College, Cambridge, whence it came in 1789–92.

MILTON   All Saints   *Four*

Seats fixed. The carvings consist of two scroll figures.

The provenance of the stalls is not known. Keatinge Claye says that they came from Ely but gives no authority for this statement (W. K. Clay, 'Histories of the four adjoining parishes of Landbeach, Waterbeach, Horningsey, and Milton', *Camb. Antiq. Soc. Procs.* vii, 1869). Another source affirms that they came from King's College, Cambridge (*The Times*, 24 April 1963), and as the living is in the gift of King's College, where the altar rails came from, this is not unlikely.

ORWELL   St. Andrew   *Eleven*

On each side of the chancel there is a row of eight stalls, with eleven misericords remaining. All but four have been nailed up.

North side from east

1. Geometrical design.

2. Floral.

3. Shield.

4. Foliage.

5. Floral.

6. Geometrical.

7 and 8. Foliage.

On the south side the three carvings are of foliage. There are no supporters.

DATE: Probably 15th century.

OVER   St. Mary   *Six*

South from east

1. Human face. Supporters: Left and Right, conventional leaf.

2. Conventional carving. Supporters: Left and Right, Tudor rose.

3. Shield charged with *three rams' heads caboshed* (arms of Ramsey family). Supporters: Left, shield charged with *chevron between three lambs' heads erased* (arms of a family of Ramsey). Right, shield charged with *an escallop between three crosses crosslet botony fitchy* (variant of arms of Walsingham, who intermarried with a branch of the Ramseys).

4. Human face. Supporters: Left and Right, conventional leaf.

5. Ram's face. Supporters: Left and Right, conventional leaf.

6. Ram's head. Supporters: Left and Right, bullock's face (the continuation of the moulding going round and under their chins).

The moulding of the misericords is four-tiered.

Gardner's Directory, 1851, p. 353, states that the stalls were erected by John Colynson, vicar, d. 1481, but local tradition is that they came from Ramsey Abbey. They bear evidence of having been moved, and the Abbey was the patron of the living, but the arms on the misericords are not those of the Abbey.

DATE: 15th century (G. C. Druce, *J. Brit. Arch. Assoc.*, N.S., xxxvi. 250).

SOHAM　St. Andrew　*Ten*

North side from west

1. Head of a jester in a cap with long ears.

2. Man's face with protruding tongue.

3. Woman's head in wimple and gorget.

4 and 5. Broken.

South side from west

1. Monk's head in a medallion.

2. Woman's face, laughing, hair in a net.

3. Man's head, three-quarter face.

4. Woman's head.

5. Bearded man's head.

There are no supporters.

DATE: 15th century. The screen was erected in the early fifteenth century. J. H. Olorenshaw states that traces of colour on the chancel walls are 15th century, and this may help to date the erection of the stalls (*Notes on the Church of St. Andrew, Soham*, 1905, p. 9).

CHESHIRE

BEBINGTON　St. Andrew　*Five*

From the east

1. Pelican in her piety. Supporters: Left and Right, ornamental leaf.

2. Bearded man's face. Supporters: Left and Right, acorns and oak-leaves (damaged).

3. Dolphin. Supporters: Left and Right, dolphin.

In the vestry of this church are two misericord seat-brackets. The carvings on them are:

   1. Bull's head.

   2. Sow with litter.

DATE: 15th century.

CHESTER   The Cathedral   *Forty-four*

The stalls were first fitted into the Abbey Church in 1390 (A. Wolfgang, *Trans. Lancs. & Ches. Hist. Soc.* lxiii, N.S., 27 (1911), p. 81).

All with the exception of five are the original ones. It is said that the five were destroyed in the last century by a Dean who considered these misericords very improper.

North side from west

1. Pelican in her piety.
2. Knight in full armour, mounted; lance over left shoulder, shield charged with St. Andrew's Cross over right. The armour is of the time of Richard II.
3. Four-winged seraph holding emblems of the Passion. Supporters: Left and Right, oak-leaves.
4. Griffin. Supporters: Left and Right, thorn-leaf.
5. Subject uncertain.
6. Scene from the legend of St. Werburgh—the restored goose. Supporters: Left, the culprit detected. Right, the culprit confessing.
7, 8, 9, and 10. Modern.
11. Mask. Supporters: Left and Right, mask.
12. Griffin and hog fighting. Supporters: Left, goat. Right, goat scratching its neck with hind leg.
13. Husband on his knees at the foot of his wife who holds the tippet of his hood with one hand and belabours him with some implement held in the other.
14. Fox on his back with tongue out shamming dead to catch birds, birds pecking at tongue. Oak and black elder trees, rabbits at the entrance of their burrows at the roots. Supporters: Left, fox, carrying off duck. Right, lion startled by the sound of birds.
15. Two herons. Supporters: Left and Right, man's head with heron's body, and a dragon.
16. Seated king. Supporters: Left and Right, griffin, with one foreleg on the seat.
17. Angel seated playing a cittern. Supporters: Left and Right, angel in clouds.

18. Monster with head and forelegs of lion and two dragons' bodies. Supporters: Left and Right, head.

19. Tristram and Iseult. King Mark above looks down on them through foliage. Supporters: Left, squire with sword under his arm. Right, waiting-maid with pet dog in one hand (PLATE 6d.)

20. Wodehouse seated on prostrate man. Supporters: Left and Right, wode-house.

21. Knight in armour on a galloping horse leaning backwards dropping behind him a round object; with his left hand he holds a cub. Supporters: Left, tigress seizing ball; ight, Rtigress crouching.
This refers to the medieval idea that a hunter who captured a tiger cub should, when pursued by a tigress, drop a crystal ball so that the tigress, seeing her reflection in it, would think it was the cub (PLATE 5b).

22. Monster with lion's head and bat's wings. Supporters: Left and Right, double fleurs-de-lis.

23. Wodehouse with club riding lion with chain round its neck. Supporters: Left and Right, animals.

24. Stag-hunt. (Knight with servant leading hound.) Supporters: Left, squire bringing up horse at gallop. Right, hound chasing a stag.

25. King's head crowned. Supporters: Left and Right, medallion head with collar.

26. Lion mask. Supporters: Left and Right, lion mask.

South side

27. Mask with mouth-foliage. Supporters: Left and Right, smaller mask.

28. Richard Cœur de Lion, as in popular legend, pulling the heart out of the lion, the keeper with sword under arm looking on. Supporters: Left and Right, bird resembling gull, perhaps to show that the event occurred over the sea.

29. Lion and dragon fighting. Supporters: Left and Right, wodehouse on animal.

30. Fox in monk's costume making an offering to a nun. Two nuns watching amongst the trees.

31. Winged figure rising from a shell and fighting with dragons. Supporters: Left, two figures, half human, half animal, fighting. Right, deacon with stole over left shoulder, holding a cock.

32. Man's head on two animal bodies.

33. Lion's head crowned on two bodies. Supporters: Left and Right, monster.

34. Man and woman seated; foliage around.

35. Virgin and child with angel on each side. Supporters: Left and Right, pelican in her piety.

36. Wodehouse on a lion with chain around its neck. Supporters: Left and Right, lion.

37. Seated man with round cap. Supporters: Left and Right, rose.

38. Sow and young pigs in a wood; man looking at them through branches.

39. Man leading a lion and holding a club. Supporters: Left and Right, lion.

40. Wrestlers. Marshals on each side with batons. Spectators looking through trees.

41. The capture of the unicorn. Supporters: Left and Right, wyvern.

42. Head on two bodies. Supporters: Left and Right, foliage.

43. Knight fully armed, on his back; griffin standing over him. Supporters: Left and Right, dog.

44. Foliage with roses.

45. Falcon with duck in its claws. Supporters: Left and Right, falcon.

46. Sir Yvain. Supporters: Left and Right, head.

47. Grotesque animals.

48. Coronation of the Virgin. Supporters: Left and Right, angel playing cittern.

MALPAS   St. Oswald   *Three*

Three stalls remain from the fifteenth century although Dr. Ormerod a little more than a century ago described twelve ancient oak stalls in the church. F. H. Crossley (*Lancs. & Cheshire Hist. Soc.* lxviii (1916), p. 104); T. C. Hughes (*Lancs. & Cheshire Arch. Soc.* 12. 1894).

1. Fight between two armed knights, one already vanquished.

2. Mermaid with glass and comb (much broken).

3. Monster with double body. Supporters: Left and Right, single pendant leaf.

The other six stalls in the chancel are modern reproductions.

NANTWICH   St. Mary   *Twenty*

Nantwich was a salt-town governed by the powerful guild of Holy Cross. The church was made collegiate between 1327 and 1333. During a minor restoration in 1964, Captain P. N. Corry, the librarian of Nantwich parish church, found what is thought to be the fourteenth-century numbering on the stalls, and they have been resited in this order.

North side from west

1. Lion and wyvern fighting. Supporters: Left and Right, bat-like grotesques.

2. Letters IHC within entwined band and thorn sprays. Supporters: Left, monogram MR beneath crown. Right, MERCI beneath crown. All letters Lombardic.

3. Devil pulling woman's mouth open for lying. Supporters: Left and Right, deer browsing on leaves.

4. St. George and the dragon. Supporters: Left, owl. Right, bird.

5. Man taking cock to cockfight. Supporters: Left and Right, leaves.

6. Vine with grapes. Supporters: Left and Right, vine and grapes.

7. Rose-bush with five roses. Supporters: Left and Right, double rose.

8. Woman in widow's neckcloth reading book. Supporters: Left, falcon. Right, begging dog.

9. Dragon attacking winged figure emerging from conch-shell. Supporters: Left and Right, leaves.

10. Samson riding lion. Supporters: Left, dog. Right, cockatrice.

South side from west

1. Griffin atop prone man in armour. Supporters: Left and Right, dodo-like grotesque.

2. Fox shamming dead to attract birds which fly overhead. Supporters: Left, fox with spoils. Right, fox with bow and arrows. Both in friar's garb.

3. Wrestling match. Supporters: Left and Right, winged grotesque.

4. Mermaid with comb and mirror. Supporters: Left and Right, dolphin.

5. Crowned head with curled forked beard. Supporters: Left and Right, beardless head in profile.

6. Two wyverns chained face to face. Supporters: Left and Right, wyvern.

7. Woman beating man with ladle. Supporters: Left, a boar. Right, dog with his head in stew-pot.

8. Pelican in her piety. Supporters: Left and Right, bird holding prey in its talons.

9. Capture of the unicorn. Supporters: Left and Right, leaves.

10. Hunters skinning a stag. Supporters: Left and Right, dog watching.

F. H. Crossley, *Lancs. & Chesh. Hist. Soc.*, lxviii (1916), p. 85, firmly refutes a local legend that the stalls came from either Combermere or Vale Royal Abbeys.

DATE: Late 14th century (F. Bond, *Misericords*, 1910, p. 226).

CORNWALL

BODMIN   St. Petroc with St. Leon   *Three*

The lectern of this church has been built up from old woodwork, including screen panels, and the upper part contains three misericords.

PROBABLE DATE: Late 15th century. Two of the subjects show pronounced Italianate influence. The church was rebuilt between 1469 and 1472 and refurnished in 1475 according to parish records. (*Bodmin Parish Church*, B.P.C., London, 1916, p. 11.)

1. Two gowned figures with flowing hair sit facing each other in earnest discussion. Each has the right hand raised and the left hand rests on a closed book on the knee. Behind each figure is the more flatly carved shape of a battle-axe head, but the significance of this is not apparent. The right hand of one figure has five fingers and a thumb (PLATE 19a).

2. Fruit, somewhat similar to a pomegranate, is fully opened, and is surrounded by flat ribbon foliage. A long, curled stalk ending in a knob or knot lies below.

3. Fruit similar to that in No. 2 above, and also having a long curled and pointed stalk, is supported by two winged figures facing outward. They have arms and hands, but animal haunches and hind feet with long tail curled between their legs. The figure on the left appears to have some object in its mouth.

ST. BURIAN   St. Buryan   *Four*

There are four stalls with misericords, two each on the north and south sides of the chancel. They were originally returned stalls. The seats are now fixed, making identification difficult, but they are carved with plain shields.

DATE: 15th century, when the church was rebuilt. There were the Dean and three prebendaries in 1803 (*Polwhele's History of Cornwall*, London, 1803, Bk. II, p. 130).

ST. GERMAN'S   St. Germanus   *One*

There is a chair built into the wall of the chancel with a misericord showing a hunter carrying a crossbow over his shoulder with game slung on it and preceded and followed by his hounds. Locally it is called Dando and his dogs. The dating is uncertain. See J. Furneaux, 'A paper on St. German's Priory Church, Cornwall', in *Exeter Diocesan Architectural Society Trans.* iii (1899), pp. 82–9.

CUMBERLAND

CARLISLE   The Cathedral   *Forty-six*

The Dean's stall is on the north side of the choir entrance and the Bishop's on the south.

North side from west

1. Dragon-like beast swallowing a man in a kilt head first, possibly Judas in the jaws of Satan, as described by Dante. Supporters: Left and Right, dog with bells on its collar.

2. Bird with young birds about it. Supporters: Left and Right, leaf.

3. Dragon holding an animal in its claws. Supporters: Left and Right, lion.

4. Four-legged grotesque beast with human head and hands. Supporters: Left and Right, winged dragon with a second head on its tail.

5. Fight between dragon and elephant. Supporters: Left and Right, leaf.

6. Winged figure playing on a tabor. Supporters: Left and Right, leaf.

7. Dragon devouring bird. Supporters: Left and Right, flower.

8. Coronation of the Virgin. Supporters: Left and Right, rose.

9. Griffin biting its wing. Supporters: Left and Right, griffin biting its wing.

10. Pelican in her piety. Supporters: Left and Right, flower.

11. Lion and dragon fighting. Supporters: Left and Right, dragon (PLATE 10*b*.)

12. Griffin biting its wing. Supporters: Left and Right, web-footed bird.

13. Two dragons joined together by the ears. Supporters: Left and Right, leaf.

14. Two storks feeding out of a sack. Supporters: Left and Right, leaf.

15. Hairy, grotesque man with wings seated on the ground. Supporters: Left and Right, leaf.

16. Angel in clouds playing a musical instrument with a plectrum. Supporters: Left and Right, leaf.

17. Two eagles with necks crossed, one head broken off. Supporters: Left and Right, dragon.

18. Double-headed eagle with a chain round its neck. Supporters: Left and Right, flower.

19. Fox and goose. Supporters: Left and Right, leaf.

20. Two dragon bodies with human head in common. Supporters: Left and Right, flower.

21. Angel in clouds, playing an instrument. (The instrument has been broken.) Supporters: Left and Right, rose.

22. Man seated on the ground with eagle on each side plucking on his beard. (One bird's head is broken off.) Supporters: Left and Right, bird with human, hooded head.

23. Dragon. Supporters: Left and Right, lion with human head.

South side from west

1. Two angels in the clouds holding some object between them. Supporters: Left and Right, monster with legs and body of bird, head of beast, and tail of dragon.

2. Dragon biting his wing. Supporters: Left and Right, lion.

3. Bird struggling with an animal. Supporters: Left and Right, leaf.

4. Two beasts with a single grotesque human head. Supporters: Left and Right, leaf.

5. Winged dragon, elaborately carved. Supporters: Left and Right, leaf.

6. Winged serpent. Supporters: Left and Right, cockatrice.

7. Two smooth animals with a single grotesque head. Supporters: Left and Right, flower.

8. Woman seizing a man by the beard and about to strike him with a domestic weapon; the man has apparently just dropped a poker. Supporters: Left and Right, flower.

9. Griffin with a man's head. Supporters: Left and Right, leaf.

10. Dragon half hidden in foliage. Supporters: Left and Right, leaf.

11. Grotesque face with open mouth with a bird on either side pecking at his tongue. Supporters: Left and Right, bearded man's head with loose cap.

12. Fox and goose. Supporters: Left, ibis, Right, ibis holding an eel or serpent.

13. St. Michael (human figure with wings) slaying the dragon. Supporters: Left and Right, leaf.

14. Wodehouse seizing a dragon by its mouth. Supporters: Left and Right, lion with grotesque head.

15. Angel holding a shield by bands over the shoulders. Supporters: Left and Right, flower.

16. Angel in clouds playing on an instrument with plectrum. Supporters: Left and Right, winged lion.

17. Pelican in her piety. Supporters: Left and Right, pelican.

18. Hyena killing (or eating) a man. Supporters: Left and Right, flower. (PLATE 11b).

19. Man in hood and sleeved tunic attacked by dragons. Supporters: Left and Right, grotesque lion mask.

20. Two dragons held by a man in a tunic. He has Tudor roses on his cap and belt. Supporters: Left and Right, simple flower.

21. Fight between dragon and beast. Supporters: Left and Right, dog.

22. Mermaid with a mirror. Supporters: Left and Right, leaf.

23. Lion and dragon fighting. Supporters: Left and Right, winged lion.

Bishop Strickland (1399–1413) erected the stalls. R. and K. Henderson, 'The Carvings on the Miserere Stalls in Carlisle Cathedral', *Trans. Cumb. Westmorland H. & A. Soc.* xii (1893) 103–4.

GREYSTOKE   St. Andrew   *Twenty*

In the choir are ten stalls on each side, three on each side being returned.

North side from east

1. From each end of the bracket a shaft leads down to a small spade-shaped leaf.

2. Two small, scroll-like shafts intertwined and tied at their intersection by a bow of ribbon. They terminate in arrow-heads (PLATE 19*b*).

3. Triple shafts or stalks radiating downward, the outer two curling upward, and all ending in arrow-heads.

4. Two shafts depending from the bracket-ends. They meet and curl outwards in scroll form, ending in arrow-heads, and are tied by a bar at their intersection.

5. Four shafts or stalks, curving down independently, and ending in simple leaves, the outward or supporting pair having trefoil ends.

6. Uncharged shield. Supporters: Left and Right, shaft extending downward and ending in small circlet.

7. One man holds a horse's head, with his hand over the horse's eyes; a second man appears to be holding the tail (but might be holding up a hind hoof); a third man leans over from behind applying a tool to the horse's body. This subject is generally called 'shoeing the horse', but more resembles clipping or currycombing it. All men have long pointed shoes. Supporters: Left and Right, large circular double flower. 15th century. (PLATE 19*c*.)

8. Deeply cut design of vine-leaves. Supporters: Left and Right, similar leaves branching from main design. (15th century.)

9. St. Michael and the Dragon. Supporters: Left and Right, head of wodehouse in vine-leaf circle. (15th century.)

10. Pelican in her piety. Supporters: Left and Right, male head with long hair. (15th century.)

South side from east

1. At each end of the bracket a scroll pendant and divided, each end curling outward and ending in a simple spade point.

2. Pendant scrolls dividing and their inner branches meeting at the centre.

3. Similar design to No. 2 above, but the inner branches curl upward after meeting, and part again, ending in arrow-head form.

4. Pendant scrolls branching, the ends form simple lobes. They enclose a small shield charged with *a chief; beneath, a bordure*.

5. Two scrolls curving downward and, after meeting, outward to end in a simple leaf.

6. At each end of the bracket a pendant shaft, dividing, with both branches ending in a trefoil. The inner branches meet at a common centre.

7. Shield charged with the Howard coat of arms, as owners of Greystoke Castle, *a bend between six cross crosslets fitchy*. The shield is surrounded by pendant and curved scrolls ending in simple leaf (the Duke of Norfolk is also Baron Greystoke).

8. The capture of the unicorn. A maiden seated with the beast's head in her lap. A hunter attacks it from rear. Supporters: Left and Right, elaborate design of four vine-leaves in square format. (15th century.)

9. Variant of Nos. 1 and 2.

10. Shield charged *bordure; within, a saltire*. It is flanked by intertwined scrolls springing from corbel bases and ending in simple leaf. Supporters: Left and Right, head with flowing hair. (15th century.)

It will be seen that the misericords are of different periods, six from the late 14th or early 15th century, as indicated. The remainder appear to be from the seventeenth century and may be of continental orign. It has been established that there was a restoration of the chancel in 1660, and it is probable that a recusant branch of the Howard family returned from the Continent and incorporated carvings of Flemish design in the stalls. A college of secular canons was confirmed by the Pope in 1382 (*V.C.H., Cumberland*, ii, p. 206).

DERBYSHIRE

BAKEWELL   All Saints   *Three*

1. Dragon with a human head. Supporters: Left, a woman's head. Right, a man's head in a cap.

2. Two grotesque sitting animals. Supporters: Left and Right, conventional foliage.

3. Winged dragon. Supporters: Left, a grotesque with a human head. Right, a mermaid holding a mirror.

DATE: 14th century.

CHURCH GRESLEY   St. George and St. Mary   *Ten*

In the church there are ten stalls with misericords. These were formerly in the chancel, five on each side. They are now situated as follows: a set of three in the chancel, a set of two and a set of three on the wooden floor at the west end of the church, and a set of two at the north-west corner of the church.

There has been some doubt as to the origin and authenticity of these stalls and misericords, but they came from Drakelow Hall, near Gresley, the family seat of the Gresley family until 1931. The stalls were given to the church in that year. (Information from the incumbent, Revd. K. R. Upton.)

The stalls themselves and the misericords are contemporary, though there is a possibility that they may have been matched up at some time. They are of mid-seventeenth-century date, and the stall carvings are identical with those in the Church of St. Jacobus, Antwerp, carved by Quellin in 1660.

Whatever their true origin, the stalls and the misericords are beautifully carved in a continental style, and constitute a noteworthy, if not unique, group. The misericords have no supporters.

Block of three in chancel, from left to right

1. Full-face leopard head, with formalized crest and mane.
2. Formal leaf design, with four lobes, possibly hawthorn, in curved pattern radiating from a central node.
3. Formal large scallop-shaped leaf design, folded over towards the centre (PLATE 19*d*).

Block of two at west end

4. Formal circular pattern of leaves in curved scroll shape. Could be oak-leaves.
5. Formal curved scroll-pattern of leaves with heart-shaped design at centre.

Block of three at west end, from left to right

6. Full-face animal head, with formalized mane and hair. The whole forms an almost circular design.
7. Formal twin leaf patterns springing from a common centre, and folded over to meet at centre in two scallop shapes.
8. Head of putto, with long flowing hair and wings folded across beneath the chin. The whole is framed in a pattern of leaves resembling hawthorn. (PLATE 19*e*).

Block of two at north-west corner of church

9. Formal fan-shaped design of leaves with two lobes at rear in scroll form.
10. Circular scroll-shaped pattern of leaves and fruit resembling hawthorn.

TIDESWELL   St. John the Baptist   *Two*

There are two carved misericords in the single stalls on either side of the entrance to the chancel. In 1883 they were in the Lady Chapel in the North Transept (Preb. R. D. Andrew, 'Notes on Tideswell Church, Derbyshire', *Arch. Soc. Trans.* v, p. 122).

1. Figure grasping the beaks of a wyvern and a basilisk.
2. Crowned angel with outstretched wings, holding a shield on which is a plain cross. Supporters in each case are roses encircled by their stems.

Cox and Harvey, *English Church Furniture*, date these as 15th century.

There are also a few plain stalls with uncarved misericords said to be 14th century. A Chantry for the Guild of St. Mary was founded in 1392 under a charter of Richard II.

DEVONSHIRE

BOVEY TRACEY   St. Peter and St. Paul   *Three*

Three of the choir stalls have carved misericords.

1. Man's head with forked beard.
2. Foliage.
3. Fox carrying off a goose. Supporters; Left and Right, a cock.

The dressing of the man's hair, the raised veins, and the more natural wave in the leaves of the foliage suggest that the date is early fourteenth century, but G. C. Druce, *Jour. Brit. Arch. Assoc.*, N.S., xxxvi, p. 251, says they are fifteenth century, stressing that the seat-ledge has three straight faces, a style unlikely much earlier.

COCKINGTON   St. George and St. Mary   *Three*

North wall of chancel

1. Tonsured head. No supporters.

DATE: Late 13th or early 14th century. This may have come from Torre Abbey, which acquired the church in 1236.

In the sedilia

1. St. Matthew. Supporters: Left and Right, acanthus-leaf forming a lozenge pattern.
2. St. Luke, seated and writing his Gospel. He is flanked by two winged oxen, his symbol, that on the left being rampant, and the words *Sanctus Lucas* are inscribed above him. Supporters as for No. 1.

DATE: 15th century. They were brought from Tormohun church in 1825. Tormohun was the mother church of Torquay, and is perpendicular in style.

EXETER   The Cathedral   *Fifty*

The misericords in this cathedral are the oldest complete set in Britain. There is no written record of their date, but there is a local tradition that they were carved between 1238, when Bishop Bruere returned from the Holy Land, and 1244, when he died.

The Fabric Rolls of the Cathedral were begun by Bishop Bronscombe in 1279 and continued by his successors up to 1439, but they have no entry of the original erection of the stalls, which may have been finished before the records began or may have been a private donation. The stalls seem almost entirely the work of one hand, and must have been carved over a long period. Some might well have been carved earlier than 1230, but there are some that from stylistic evidence can hardly be earlier than 1260. Nos. 1 and 43 are later. They have all been cut to fit into their present position, and this mutilation may have taken place in *c.* 1684, the date of the new pulpit. There are new pews of that date in the choir. On several of the misericords is cut a device of two concentric circles, which may be a mason's mark. (K. M. Clarke, 'The Misericords of Exeter Cathedral', *Devon and Cornwall Notes and Queries*, xi, part II, 1920, pp. 1–54.)

The earliest consist of good examples of the stiff leaf ornament.

South side

1. Lion and dragon fighting. No supporters. (The Dean's stall: 1250–60.) In 1920 there were mask supporters of a later style than the estimated date suggests.

2. Stiff leaf decoration. Supporters: Left and Right, dragon. (1220–30.)

3. Oak-leaves and acorns which spring from a satyr's mask. A favourite Decorated subject. Supporters: Left and Right, beetle curled up amongst leaves. Beautifully carved (1260–70).

4. Bird sirens, classical in style (1250–60), with fleur-de-lis between them.

5. Maple-leaves (1260–70).

6. Bird sirens in quite different style from No. 4. Early English (1240–50).

7. Bird with human head and trefoil tail, perched on branch of trefoil leaves.

8. Decoration. Supporters: portrait heads of a man (Left) and a woman (Right) (1220–30).

9. Female centaur.

10. Decoration. Supporters: Left and Right, portrait head.

11. Crowned knight fighting a leopard. Supporters: Left, head of a man wearing a hood. Right, head of a woman with a head-dress and gorget (1230–40).

12. Decoration (1240–50).

13. Knight stabbing a dragon, whose head he forces backward. Supporters, trefoil leaves.

14. Branch springing from dragon's mouth (1240–50).

15. Kneeling man with pipe and tabor. Supporters: Left and Right, dragon.

16. Decoration (PLATE 3*b*).

17. Male centaur transfixes with an arrow a dragon forming a supporter. The only example where a supporter forms part of the main subject. (1250–60).

18. Chevalier au Cygne. The twelfth-century romance of the Knight of the Swan (on which Wagner based *Lohengrin*) was widely known and many noble families claimed the knight as their ancestor (PLATE 4*a*).

19. Decoration.

20. Decoration.

21. Decoration.

North side

22. Decoration with animal-head in centre (1250–60).

23. Basilisk and asp (1260–70).

24. Decoration.

25. Mermaid with fish in each hand (one broken). The fish in the hand of the mermaid signifies the soul in the grip of earthly passion (1250–60). (PLATE 3*c*.)

26. Decoration.

27. The elephant. It has been suggested that the carver had seen an elephant which in 1255 was given by Louis IX to Henry III and carved it from memory. Supporters, the head of a man and a woman, presumably his wife, wearing a fashionable and costly head-dress and gorget with her hair in a net. Possibly the donors. (1250–60.) (PLATE 4*c*).

28. Man putting a weight (1230–40).

29. Decoration, fleur-de-lis.

30. Man on all fours, crowned, with hoofs instead of feet, a saddle-cloth on his back on which is a saddle with stirrups. He has a tail which is held erect and is a snake. This fits the description of the locust of the Apocalypse (Rev. 9: 7–10). Alternatively identified as Aristotle (PLATE 3*d*).

31. Animal mask with foliage issuing from mouth. Supporters, masks with foliage issuing.

32. Siren with two bodies.

33. The wicked soul cast into hell (a head surrounded by flames).

34. Decoration.

35. Lion.

36. Two fish. Supporters: Left, head of a man who wears the hood of a citizen. Right, head of a woman who wears a hood and wimple. Possibly the donors.

37. Decoration.

38. Merman and maid lifting a tabor under which is a mask. Supporters, Left and Right, maple-leaf. (1260–70.)

39. Wodehouses.

40. Decoration.

41. Two doves facing each other, in foliage. Supporters: Left and Right, leaf.

42. Hands and arms in gloves, holding a trefoil leaf beneath the shelf.

43. Man seated wearing a jerkin with square buttons, and a dagger in his belt. His right hand supports the shelf, his left supports his head. Supporters: Left and Right, stiff leaf. The seat has a straight front. (15th century.)

44. Two doves facing each other with a leaf between them. Supporters: Left and Right, natural maple-leaf with a strawberry leaf as a central ornament. (c. 1270.)

45. Decoration.

46. Decoration.

47. Bearded portrait head in Early English foliage. Supporters: Left and Right, similar head in foliage. Miss K. M. Clarke (*Devon and Cornwall Notes and Queries*, xi, pt. II, 1920) asserts that these are heads of bishops copied from tombs in the Cathedral.

48. Decoration.

49. Decoration.

50. Decoration. Supporters, birds.

Unless otherwise stated above, the supporters and also the main subjects, where decoration is the motif, consist of varying designs of typical Early English trefoil foliage.

KINGSBRIDGE St. Edmund *One*

There is in this church a double stall with two misericord seats; one misericord is carved, the other has a plain bracket. The carved misericord is of an angel. The head is missing.

DATE: 15th century. Origin unknown. There are other fragmentary pieces of 15th-century carved panels in the church fittings.

OTTERY ST. MARY St. Mary the Virgin *Twenty*

The original church was transformed into a collegiate church modelled upon Exeter Cathedral by John de Grandisson, Bishop of Exeter. The work was completed about 1342.

Twenty of the old choir stalls remain; twelve in the chancel and eight in the Lady Chapel.

The carved misericords show either Bishop Grandisson's arms (*Paly of six, a bend charged with a mitre between two eagles*), or a female head with a short fringe and a long, thick curl on either side of the face. This may be intended to represent the Bishop's sister Katherine, first Countess of Salisbury.

Elsewhere throughout the church the Bishop always introduces her arms as a pendant to his own, which are *Paly of six argent and azure, a bend gules charged with a mitre argent between two eagles displayed or.*

DORSETSHIRE

MILTON ABBAS St. James the Great and other Saints *Twelve*

There are forty misericords in this abbey but only twelve are originals; the remainder are modern copies.

The misericords are all of the same very plain design; a corbel running down to a point. The date 1498 appears on the screen together with the rebus of Abbot Milton, and the misericords may be contemporary.

SHERBORNE The Abbey *Ten*

There are now ten stalls with misericords in the choir, five on each side. They were originally installed after a disastrous fire which occurred in 1436, and it is thought that the number was then greater. All were again removed at a later date, as British Museum, Add. MS. 29931, ff. 28–9, states: 'Carvings on the underparts of the seats which were once in the choir, now thrown by in a north chapel.' The manuscript describes two which do not form part of the present set:

'Five birds hanging an animal (perhaps fox); on either side a monk.'
'Hunter blowing his horn; dexter, the stag; sinister, the hounds.'

The examples now in position are as follows:

North side

1. Bust of man with hood, surmounted by foliage. Supporters: Left and Right, stiff leaf foliage.
2. Man grimacing and pulling his mouth sideways with his hands. He has flowing drapery. No supporters. (PLATE 20*a*.)
3. The Last Judgement. Christ sitting on the vault of heaven and showing the wounds in his hands and feet. Supporters: Left and Right, the dead rising from their graves and holding out their hands in entreaty.
4. Foliate mask with elaborate foliage. Supporters: Left and Right, foliage.
5. Foliage design. Supporters: Left and Right, foliage.

South side

1. Legend of St. Margaret. A girl with flowing hair and a circlet on her forehead kneels in prayer with hands together on the body of a dragon. Supporters: Left and Right, foliage. (PLATE 1*d*.)
2. Chained monkey. Supporters: Left and Right, foliage.
3. Man, with boy, holding book, prone across his knee. He uncovers the boy's bottom with his left hand and with his right raises a birch to strike. Supporters: Left, two boys seated with books. Right, boy seated with legs crossed. (PLATE 20*b*.)

4. Boy on one knee drawing a bow and shooting left. Supporters: Left, a boy holding a bow and riding an elaborately draped hobby-horse. Right, boy riding a lion. (PLATE 20c.)

5. Woman beating a man. Supporters: Left and Right, foliage.

WIMBORNE   St. Cuthberga   *Thirteen*

All the carvings are of foliage or leaves and fruit, lightly stylized and covering the whole of the spaces beneath the brackets, there being no supporters. The brackets are heavy.

DATE: 1608. There were originally eighteen, erected in 1608 when the church was repaired after the spire had fallen (C. Mayo, *History of Wimborne Minster*, 1860, p. 43).

DURHAM

BISHOP AUCKLAND   St. Andrew   *Twenty-eight*

Otherwise known as the South Church. There are twenty-eight misericords, two carved with shields charged with *a Saint George's Cross surmounted by a coronet* (the arms of Bishop (later Cardinal) Langley, 1406–37). The remainder are well carved with conventional roses and foliage.

BISHOP AUCKLAND   The Castle Chapel   *Six*

North

1. The arms of Bishop Cosin (1660–72).

2. Lion.

3. Fruit.

South

1. The arms of Bishop Cosin.

2. Eagle.

3. Fruit.

The supporters of each misericord are: Left and Right, rose.

DATE: *c.* 1660.

BRANCEPETH   St. Brandon   *Fourteen*

There are fourteen stalls with misericords in the chancel, seven on each side, of which two on each side are returned. They are attributed to John Cosin, who was Rector here from 1626 to 1633, later becoming Bishop of Durham in 1660 (see Bishop Auckland, Durham Cathedral, and Sedgefield).

The misericords on the four returned stalls, however, appear to be of later date. They have been made in two separate sections, the lower being integral with the seat and the upper having been screwed into position. This, however, may have been done at some restoration. The remaining misericords have also been carved separately and screwed under the shelves, but are probably correctly dated.

Returned Stalls. An elaborate spray of foliage spreading from the centre base, at which is a fully open flower. The whole resembles buttercup and foliage. The small supporters at each end of the bracket are similar leaves. At the lower corners of the seat are small flowers deeply recessed in a circle. These stalls are wider than the rest.

Side stalls. An angular vaulted corbel rising from a multi-moulded base, which is identical with part of the ornament on the Carolean pulpit, installed at the same time. The front of the vaulting is deeply incised with simple formal ornament.

DARLINGTON St. Cuthbert *Eighteen*

North side from east

1. Lion's head with protruding tongue. Supporters: Left and Right, stem with four-lobed leaves with berries in centre.

2. Stout, nude man wearing boots, unlaced, apparently asleep, supporting the bracket with head and shoulders. Supporters: Left and Right, triple-lobed leaf. This is thought by some to refer to Bishop Langley (lang-lay) but a more likely theory is that it refers to St. Godric, who lived an ascetic life in the neighbourhood. This misericord and the subjects of South 2 and 4 (q.v.) bear some resemblance to alleged incidents in the life of St. Godric.

3 to 7. Modern.

8. Angel holding book, edges to the front. Supporters: Left and Right, triple-lobed leaf.

9. Modern. (Dean's Stall.)

South side from east

1. Monster with bearded human head, winged and clawed, possibly a sphinx. Supporters: Left and Right, triple-lobed leaf.

2. Nude little man wearing laced boots, and bearing two large bunches of flowers. (See note to North 2 relating to St. Godric.) Supporters: Left and Right, large double flower with berries.

3. Eagle regardant (see note below). Supporters: Left and Right, triple-lobed leaf.

4. Nude little man wearing boots, one laced, the other unlaced, having a ragged staff on his right shoulder, and leading a bear by a chain. Supporters: Left and Right, grotesque mask fringed with leaves. (PLATE 20*d*.)

5. Demi-angel holding open book. Supporters: Left and Right, double roundel.

6. Griffin with outspread wings. Supporters: Left and Right, triple-lobed leaf.

7. Large head of man with long, curly hair, beard, and moustache. Supporters: Left and Right, rosette set in four-lobed leaf.

8. As for 7 above but head larger, and design of supporters more formal.

9. Crowned king holding in his hands two sceptres, and having a broad collar with engrailed border round his neck. On each side is a griffin sejeant gorged. Supporters: Left and Right, triple-lobed leaf. This seems likely to be an example of Alexander's Flight. (PLATE 21a.)

The misericord seats, which are of solid oak, are remarkably thick (5 in.). They were installed during the time of Cardinal Langley (1406–47), probably before 1430. This is demonstrated by the presence on the stalls of his device or badge, *an eagle regardant*, and his coat of arms, the same as that in the Galilee at Durham. Some time between 1838 and 1840 three of the stalls on the north side and the two returned ones on the west were destroyed by an Irish sub-curate with his own hands to make room for a large family pew. They were replaced when the chancel was restored in 1864–5.

DURHAM The Castle: Bishop Tunstall's Chapel *Fourteen*

There are twenty-two stalls; nine on the north side and five on the south have misericords.

North side from west

1. Man, wearing a short tunic and cap, wheeling a woman in a barrow. She holds a scourge in her right hand and holds on to the barrow with her left. Supporters: Left and Right, rose.

2. Pig playing bagpipes; two young pigs dancing. Supporters: Left and Right, rose.

3 and 4. Missing.

5. Unicorn with long tail curled under its hind leg and ending in three tufts across its haunch. Supporters: Left and Right, rose. (PLATE 13b).

6. Man, holding a shield, fighting a winged and cloven-footed dragon. Supporters: Left, mask. Right, mask with protruding tongue (broken).

7. Child issuing from a whelk-shell (left arm broken off) holding some object. A dragon is about to attack it. Supporters: Left and Right, foliage.

8. Central carving missing. Supporters: Left and Right, rose.

9. Grotesque monster. Supporters: Left and Right, foliage with flower.

10. Central carving missing. Supporters: Left and Right, foliated ornament.

11. Foliage. Supporters: Left and Right, rose.

South side from west

1. Man on a horse attacking a dragon with a spear. Supporters: Left and Right, flower.
2. Chained and muzzled bear. Supporters (new): Left and Right, foliage.
3 and 4. Missing.
5. Foliage. Supporters: Left and Right, rose.
6. Eagle. Supporters: Left and Right, small eagle.
7, 8, 9, and 10. Missing.
11. Eagle-headed monster. Supporters: Left and Right, rose.

These were originally in Auckland Castle, having been placed there in 1508–22 in the time of Bishop Ruthall, whose arms appear on a bench-end.

They were removed to the Chapel in the time of Bishop Tunstall. In the accounts the following entry appears: 'To Robert Champnere 17 days in taking downe of the stalls in the Highe Chapell and sortynge of them and dythinge of them and dressinge of them and helpinge to convey them to Durham 39s. viiid.' (E. Phipson, *Choir Stalls and their Carvings*, p. 91). Revd. J. S. Purvis (*Archaeologia*, 85, p. 108) asserts that they were in imitation of the Ripon models.

DURHAM   The Cathedral   *Thirty-seven*

Of the thirty-seven misericords in this Cathedral, thirty-six are in the choir, and the remaining stall is in the Durham Light Infantry Chapel (it was formerly in St. Oswald's Church) and is of an eagle.

In the Choir, north side from east

1. Eagle.
2. Winged monster.
3. Head between foliage.
4. Similar monster to No. 2.
5. Wolf-like monster.
6. Figure of boy ending in foliage; on each side a cornucopia.
7. Figure of a child issuing from foliage, the base of which ends in an eagle's head.
8. Foliated figure with hand in mouth; foliage round it.
9. Ape with apple.
10. Crab.
11. Squirrel with nut.
12. Similar to No. 6.
13. Crab.

14. Similar to No. 6.

15. Peacock with expanded tail.

16. Mermaid between dolphins.

17. Lion with large mane.

18. Uncharged oval shield, supported by two lions.

South side from west

1. Lion passant regardant.

2. Demi-figure of a man issuing from foliage and blowing a conch-shell.

3. Winged scaly animal.

4 Horse lying down.

5. Man offering round object to open-mouthed monster.

6. Winged boy surrounded by foliage and fruit.

7. Human-headed monster between two dragons.

8. Human-headed foliated monster with foliage.

9. Boy with fruit.

10. Winged dragon.

11. Mermaid between dolphins (similar to North 16).

12. Squirrel and nut.

13. Merman and mermaid.

14. Figure of boy issuing from foliage and cornucopia.

15. Mermaid on a dolphin.

16. Squirrel with nut and fir cones.

17. Child chased by lion.

18. Uncharged oval shield, supported by two lions (similar to North 18). These misericords are without supporters.

These stalls and misericords were placed in the Cathedral by Bishop Cosin. They are believed to be the work of James Clement, carver of Durham, who died in 1690. They replace stalls and misericords which were destroyed by Scots prisoners in 1650.

The date of the misericord in the Durham Light Infantry Chapel is probably 14th century.

LANCHESTER All Saints *Six*

There are six stalls with carved misericords; one has a grotesque head and the others foliage or are broken.

DATE: 15th century.

SEDGEFIFLD   St. Edmund   *Six*

The six returned stalls have a slight geometrical carving. Their date is during the bishopric of Bishop Cosin, 1660–72.

STAINDROP   St. Mary   *Seventeen*

There used to be ten misericords on each side of the chancel with two returned stalls on each side; now, on the north side the two westernmost and the five easternmost are replaced by ordinary seats of recent date. They were probably destroyed in the early nineteenth century. Many of the others are fixed. The carvings are either acanthus leaves or Tudor roses in a diamond setting.

J. F. Hodgson, 'The Church of Auckland St. Andrew', *Arch. Aeliana*, 2nd Series, xx (1899), 150.

DATE: Early 15th century. The college was founded by Ralph, Earl of Westmorland in 1408. (*V.C.H., Durham*, ii, p. 129.)

ESSEX

BELCHAMP   St. Paul's   *Ten*

The carvings all consist of plain vaulting, at the base of which are motifs as detailed below.

North side from east

1. Group of fruit and leaves resembling strawberry plant. Supporters: Left and Right, four-petalled rose.

2. Same as No. 1. Supporters: Left and Right, rosette.

3. Base of moulded corbel. Supporters: Left and Right, rosette.

4. Plain shield, similar to example in St. Peter's, Sudbury, Suffolk, not far distant (q.v.). Supporters: Left and Right, acanthus-leaf.

5. Large rosettes. Supporters: Left and Right, rose.

South side from east

1. Plain shield. Supporters: Left and Right, three-lobed leaf with curled tips.

2. Moulded corbel. Supporters: Left and Right, large rose.

3. Foliate mask with upraised arms. Supporters: Left and Right, triple acanthus-leaf.

4. Triple-lobed leaf with curled tips. Supporters: Left and Right, pendant fruit and leaf.

5. Faceless winged creature (unidentifiable). Supporters: Left and Right, pendant fruit and leaf.

DATE: 15th century. (*R.C.H.M. Essex, North West*, p. 17). The local tradition is that they came from Clare Priory, close by, after the Dissolution.

CASTLE HEDINGHAM   St. Nicholas   *Five*

South side from east

1. New stall.
2. New stall.
3. Head of negro. Supporters: Left and Right, leopard's head.
4. Three shields charged with St. George's Cross.
5. Fox with a monk hanging head down on his back; demon in background. Supporters: Left, a fox with what appears to be a trumpet. Right, a leopard's head.
6. Large leaf foliage. Supporters: Left and Right, leopard's head.
7. Three plain shields.

DATE: First half of 15th century, except No. 5 which may be late 14th century (*R.C.H.M., Essex, North West*, p. 51).

GLOUCESTERSHIRE

BRISTOL   The Cathedral   *Twenty-eight*

Twenty-eight misericords now remain, several having been removed for various reasons in the nineteenth century. All have supporters of complicated formal flower pattern, in some of which, as indicated below, human or animal heads have been incorporated. The present order of the carvings differs from that given in earlier descriptions, doubtless because of errors in replacement during renovations, etc.

Numbers North 1, 2, 3, 5, and 9, and South 3 are taken from the 'History of Reynard', an old folk-tale which was printed by Caxton in 1481. It is published in the *English Scholar's Library of Old and Modern Works* edited by Arber, and is taken from the French 'Roman de Renard'.

North side from west

1. In the carpenter Lanfert's yard Bruin is enticed by Reynard with the promise of honey in a cleft in an oak held open by a wedge, and is caught when the wedge is removed, and is then attacked by Lanfert and his friends. Supporters, inverted flowers.

2. Tybert the cat is persuaded by Reynard to go into the priest's barn to catch mice and is caught in a gin. The priest Martynet and Dame Julok are also shown in the carving. Supporters: Left, face in flower. Right, recumbent face in flower.

3. Reynard is being led to the gallows before Noble the lion and his queen. Reynard escapes by flattering Noble. Tybert climbs the gallows to make a knot; Bruin watches Reynard in case of escape. Isegrym the wolf gives

advice. A bird, a rabbit, and another animal are also shown. Supporters, on flowers: Left, head in flat cap. Right, ape playing pipe. (PLATE 9*d*.)

4. Pedlar lying asleep while apes rifle his pack. Supporters: Left and Right, pendant flowers.

5. Fox preaching to geese. A frequent subject, which is mentioned in 'The Shifts of Reynardine', a seventeenth-century pastiche, probably compiled from older traditional stories. Supporters: Left and Right, flower; in the right one, a fox emerging.

6. Pig about to be killed, held on a bench by two men. Under the bench are two rabbits, one looking out of its hole, the other disappearing into it. (This is said to be the only example of a carving of a rabbit entering a hole.) Supporters: Left and Right, rosette with face at centre.

7. Stag, shot in the flank by an arrow, looks round while a hunter and dog approach. Supporters: Left and Right, flower; a dog emerging from that on the left.

8. Ape riding a horse, with a half-filled sack for saddle, followed by nude man holding the horse's tail and waving a stick. Below, rabbits in burrows. Supporters: Left and Right, flower.

9. Fox being hanged by geese. Supporters: Left, rosette having in centre a woman's head; Right, rosette having in centre a bearded man's head.

10. Spray of conventional foliage. Supporters: Left and Right, flower.

11. Mermaid holding up her hands palms upward, between a human-headed creature with wings and claws, who is holding her tail, and a wyvern. Supporters: Left, hooded head in a flower. Right, ape with flask in a flower.

12. Adam and Eve (holding apple) and a human-headed serpent. Supporters: Left and Right, large rosette.

13. Samson holding the lion's jaws, a second lion in background. Below left, a rabbit looks out of its hole. (This detail was often used to fill a vacant space.) Supporters: Left, woman in gown and wimple, holding her head bent to one side. Right, man with long hair and beard, wearing full robe and flat cap.

14. Two nude men wrestling, grasping each other by a neck-band; a third, also wearing a loose neck-band, stands with his hand on the shoulder of one combatant and points at his leg. Supporters: Left, flower with nude man; Right, flower with fox.

South side from west

1. Mounted woman bringing a sack of corn to a post-mill. Supporters, on flowers: Left, head with curly hair. Right, bearded head with cap and liripipe.

2. Man riding face to tail on a horse, another man at his side. Supporters, on flowers: Left, bearded head in cap. Right, boar.

3. Tybert the cat, Dame Julok, and the priest, who, leaping from bed to catch the raider, is clawed by the cat. On the right Reynard watches from a bush. Supporters: Left and Right, rosette with heads in centre, that on the left with protruding tongue.

4. Woman seated at a lectern on which is a book. In right background a building. Supporters: Left and Right, large rosette.

5. A large slug beneath a tree, with corded pack on its back, being led on a leash by a man, while another man behind raises a double-thonged whip. (Sky Slug was the Somerset nickname for a slow horse.) Supporters: Left and Right, pendant flower.

6. Man with long sword fights a long-tailed beast with sword and round shield, whilst on left another beast holds a shield and watches. Supporters: Left, flower with beast crouching. Right flower.

7. Dragon with second head in its belly driving three nude figures. Supporters: Left, flower with large head in hood with protruding tongue. Right, ape with lute. (PLATE 21*b*.)

8. A devil in the jaws of hell receives a nude woman leading four leashed apes. Supporters: Left and Right, flower; from the left one small animal emerging.

9. Bear-baiting. Muzzled, tethered bear approached from each direction by man with a wheelbarrow and dogs. Supporters: Left and Right, rosette with lion mask at centre with protruding tongue.

10. Two bears dance to a drum beaten by an ape. Supporters: Left and Right, flower.

11. Woman throwing a bowl at a man who lifts the lid of her cooking pot. Supporters: Left and Right, double rose.

12. Man holding a long fork (broken) and riding a sow meets a woman holding a broom and riding a bird (goose?). Behind her is another broom. (A satire on tournaments.) Supporters: Left and Right, bearded head in flower.

13. Two nude figures sitting cross-legged tailor-wise on a bench facing each other (the arms of one are missing); under the bench is a small bush. Supporters: Left and Right, flower.

14. Man, mounted on a boar, tilting with a pole at a large, full sack held by a large dog-like beast. (Tilting at the quintain.) Supporters: Left, flower with large head in loose cap. Right, flower with triple head under one cap or hood. (These are three separate faces and not the usual design of one face with four eyes and three noses.)

Nos. North 8, North 11, South 2, and South 7, are all copied from marginal ornaments used by early Parisian printers such as Simon de Vostre and Thielman Kerver.

DATE: 1520. R. H. Warren (*Archaeological Journal*, xviii (1861), p. 273) states they were erected by Robert Elyot, Abbot of St. Augustine's, 1515–26, whose initials appear several times on the stalls.

DUNTISBOURNE ROUS St. Michael *Five*

In the chancel are five misericords, all with the same carving of a grotesque bearded head, with supporters: Left and Right, vine-leaf. Whether they are an importation from another church, or were originally installed here, is not known. There are several possibilities; (1) Sir Roger le Rous founded the church and may have established a chantry; (2) after his death in 1294 the ownership is not known, but Duntisbourne Abbots, nearby, belonged to the Abbey of St. Peter, Gloucester, until dissolution in 1540. There are no stalls in that village church, and they may have been transferred here; (3) *Bristol and Glos. Arch. Soc. Trans.* xii, p. 2, suggests that the stalls were imported, but without substantiation; (4) information from the late W. I. Croome was that excavation of Cirencester Abbey in 1965 disclosed the position of choir stalls demolished in the early fourteenth century and rebuilt. His theory was that the Duntisbourne Rous stalls, if of this period, came from the Abbey, because the church is too small to have several canons or chaplains. The seats appear to be late thirteenth or early fourteenth century.

FAIRFORD St. Mary *Fourteen*

North side from east

1. Fox running off with duck, which lies across his back. Two more ducks in panic, one in rear pecking at the fox's tail. (PLATE 21c.)

2. Demi-angel holding an uncharged shield.

3. Hawk killing duck, which it has seized by the neck. (PLATE 21d.)

4. Man and woman seated, drinking from barrel between them. They are each holding their heads with one hand. (PLATE 22a.)

5. Grotesque lion mask with protruding tongue.

6. Youth and girl teasing each other, sometimes described as a quarrel over a shoe.

7. Domestic scene. Woman spinning. Meanwhile a dog steals unnoticed from a pot over the fire. (PLATE 22b.)

South side

8. Two seated women plucking a fowl on a platter between them.

9. Two wyverns with tails interlaced. Their mouths are open, showing teeth and tongue.

10. Man in crouching position, clasping his shins, with two dogs, one on each side of him, leashed. He wears a close-fitting cap and quilted, belted tunic. Possibly a hunter or poacher.

11. Two men still hungry, sitting facing each other, examining empty platter and flagon.

12. Reapers in short smocks, with wheatsheaf between them.

13. Heavily built man, lying asleep with head on pillow beside small table on which is an empty platter. (PLATE 22c.)

14. Woman beating a man with a wooden scoop whilst holding him by the hair. (PLATE 14d.)

The supporters are all similar, consisting of a formalized vine-leaf.

DATE: Late 15th century. Cox and Harvey, *English Church Furniture*, p. 259, suggest 1460, but F. Bond, *Misericords*, p. 227, says 1490, and this seems more likely, having regard to other estimates of the date of building of the church. The design of the shelf above the carving shows the return to simpler moulding typical of the late fifteenth or early sixteenth century.

GLOUCESTER   The Cathedral   *Forty-six*

South-west to north-west

1. (Modern). The Adoration of the Magi.

2. Two dragons fighting.

3. Knight slaying giant. Armed knight wearing a hauberk covered with a short surcoat open in front and a camailed basinet with the ventaille or visor raised; on his left arm is a heart-shaped shield; his right hand holds a sword with which he strikes a blow at the neck of the giant. He wears plate armour, shoulder roundels, a narrow belt, sollerets pointed and dagged, and no spurs.

The giant's head and neck are covered with hood and liripipe, he wears a belted tunic with narrow sleeves that reaches to his knees, sharply pointed shoes, and a long beard. His back is turned to the knight and he holds a club in both hands. Behind the knight is his charger, saddled and bridled.

4. Samson lies asleep in a long, loose robe. Delilah, a tiny figure, is cutting off a lock of his hair with a pair of shears. Above are four roses.

5. Bear sitting in collar and chain; on the right a dog sitting in collar; on extreme right a terror-stricken keeper wearing a cap and jerkin and holding a stick.

6. Two hooded men facing each other; one has a sword, the other is grasping the sword arm.

7. (Modern.) Coronation of the Virgin. Copied from Chester.

8. (Modern.) Two griffins segreant. Rising between their wings is a crowned man with wavy hair holding in each hand a staff with a boar's head on top at which the griffins are pecking.

9. Owl with two birds on each side with their beaks open.

10. Lady in a garden, standing and wearing a large hood and a long robe with wide, hanging sleeves; at her feet a dog looking up at her.

11. Two monsters: one on right with human hands, three-clawed feet, and a man's face under a conical cap; the other has a woman's face hooded and four three-clawed feet; both have lion's tails.

12. Knight galloping. Near the horse's head a winged and horned demon.

13. (Modern, copied from Worcester.) The Sacrifice of Isaac.

14. Mermaid supporting with each hand a dolphin.

15. Three shepherds beneath a star, each holding a crook, wearing high boots fastened with buttons and long tunics, and carrying at the girdle two or three implements. The Shepherds on their way to Bethlehem.

16. Pelican in her piety.

17. Monster with hind legs only, large arm, and huge mouth swallowing a man. (Taken from Worcester.)

18. (Modern, copied from Worcester.) Female nude figure covered with a net; with one hand she holds a horn of the goat on which she is riding and with the other she holds a rabbit. It illustrates the very old folk-tale of Queen Disa.

19. (Modern.) Man riding a goat and holding one of its horns; he wears a large hood with liripipe; behind him hangs a rabbit. The man's legs appear to be bare; one foot is in a stirrup.

20. (Modern.) Moses rebuking the Israelites. Supporters, intertwined serpents. (Copied from Worcester.)

21. (Modern.) Man riding a mule. In front a hawk striking a duck on the wing.

22. The flight of Alexander. On each side of the seated King is a griffin, standing on the arm of the chair with his beak near the King's ear. (PLATE 7b.)

23. (Modern, copied from Winchester.) Two dragons joined in one jester's head.

24. (Modern, copied from Chester.) Two angels.

25. Crowned man with head supported by his left hand, wearing cap with hood attached, loose mantle, tunic underneath, and pointed shoes, right hand supporting the bracket and holding staff.

26. King seated on throne; his crown, robe, and wavy hair resemble the effigy of Edward II in the Cathedral.

27. Similar to No. 21.

28. Similar to No. 19.

29. Rudely carved figure of a man and a donkey embracing.

30. At the back some swine feeding in a forest; in the centre an oak tree on which are a squirrel and a bird. Under the tree a boar and a sow eating acorns; on the extreme right a dog.

31. Two fighting four-legged monsters with dogs' (?) heads and lions' tails, with a mane running the whole length of the body.

32. Two youths wearing tight leggings and pointed shoes, jupons to the knee, jagged at the bottom and buttoned down the front, hoods with very long and sharp liripipes, playing with five balls or disks. They may be gambling.

33. Two youths, similarly dressed, playing with a large ball. (PLATE 22d.)

34. Lion fighting dragon.

35. Elephant with two-storied castle on his back; his feet are like a cart-horse's, his tail flowing, and his trunk larger at the end than in the middle.

36. Eagle and fox cub fighting.

37. Winged human figure thrusting a spear through a dragon. It may be St. Michael overcoming the devil.

38. Horseman galloping and blowing a horn. A dog is running under the horse.

39. (Modern, copied from Worcester.) The Temptation of Adam and Eve.

40. Four-footed animal, with curling and semi-human face, riding a heavy-looking horse.

41. Lion stealthily approaching a fox.

42. Man wearing cap with hood attached; right hand supporting the bracket, the other holding a staff.

43. Lion defeating dragon.

44. Dog on his hind legs against a tree looking at a fox in the branches; on the left an archer on right knee shooting at the fox.

45. Lion fighting dragon.

46. Presentation of a youth at an altar above which hangs a lamp. (Possibly the presentation of Samuel at Shiloh, as at Worcester.)

47. Half-recumbent bearded man wearing tight tunic buttoned down the front, military belt, and hood of the time of Chaucer, border of which is embroidered, and supporting the bracket with his right arm.

48. Fox carrying off goose.

49. The Sacrifice of Isaac. (Copied from Worcester.)

50. Dragon.

51. In the centre a vine with leaves and bunches of grapes. On each side a man, the one on the left putting a bunch of grapes into a basket which is held by the other.

52. The Tournament. Two mounted knights wearing complete plate armour and joupons which are elaborately jagged and embroidered, rouellé spurs, and helmets with vizors down. Each has a shield with a notch on the upper side on which a lance is rested. One is defeating the other, and the victor's squire is blowing a trumpet of peculiar shape. (Copied from Worcester.)

53. Duplicate of 42.

54. Man shooting with long-bow at a stag.

55. Very roughly carved figure with hands together in the attitude of prayer.

56. Tree and on each side a boy (damaged). On the right a woman walking towards them with outstretched arms, carrying a small object in her right hand.

57. Two men wearing kilts, otherwise nude, and wrestling.

58. (Modern, copied from Worcester.) Lion and dragon fighting.

DATE: Mid 14th century. O. W. Clark, 'The Misereres in Gloucester Cathedral' (*Bristol and Glos. Arch. Soc. Trans.* xxviii, pp. 61–85).

MICHELDEAN (sometimes incorrectly Mitcheldean)   St. Michael
One

There is a single misericord on view in the church, said to have been fixed at one time in the pulpit. The centre carving, flanked by formal rosettes, bears the arms of Greyndour of Abenhall, a manor in the neighbourhood, *a fesse between six crosses crosslet.* This misericord is probably all that remains of the chantry founded *c.* 1425 by Sir Robert Greyndour (d. 1443), and is typical early fifteenth-century work. It is now mounted on the tower-wall of the south aisle.

TEWKESBURY   The Abbey   *Sixteen*

North side from east

1. Damaged and indecipherable.

2. Woman armed with washing-beetle striking a man lying face upward on the ground. No supporters.

3. Three figures, possibly in combat (badly mutilated). Supporters: Left and Right, rosette.

4. Animal, possibly a hyena (headless), with legs, tail, and hands, apparently devouring corpse, of which one arm and hand remain visible. Supporters: Left and Right, stiff leaf.

5. Merman and mermaid. Supporters: Left and Right, stiff leaf.

6. Man seated and dog with long tail resting head on man's knee. A figure on right is missing. Supporters: Left and Right, leaves in scroll form.

7. Monster with three-toed feet, and a female head and shoulders facing rear. Supporters: Left only, stiff leaf.

8. Amphisbaena with duck's head and outspread wings. Supporters: Left and Right, vine leaf.

9. Griffin. Supporters: Left and Right, stiff leaf.

10. Amphisbaena with serpent's tail and scaly ridged back. Supporters: Left and Right, rose.

11. Two birds, one headless, the other with hooded human head, facing each other. Supporters: Left and Right, leaf with five fronds or petals.

12. Damaged. An animal's head with long ears and protruding tongue remains on right. Supporters, as for No. 11.

South side from east

1 to 4. Fixed seats.

5. Three figures (headless) seated. One on left facing inward with outstretched arms; he has second on his lap and is clasped by him. On right a third facing the other two has left arm outstretched holding or offering a bag of money. Supporters, missing.

6. Carving missing.

7 to 11. Fixed seats.

12. (Detached.) A separate stall of black oak. Two mermaids face each other, clasping one mirror. Supporters: Left and Right, stiff leaf. The carved dossier to this stall has a human head flanked by two serpents.

On the south side nearer the Nave are three misericords

1. Two two-legged monsters facing each other aggressively. Supporters: Left and Right, stiff leaf.

2. Cock and hen, the latter pecking from a dish. Supporters: Left and Right, stiff leaf (broken).

3. A standing nude human figure bending at the waist to the left so that the upper part of the body is parallel to the ground and supporting the shelf. Supporters: Left and Right, stiff leaf.

DATE: 14th century. (Ernest F. Smith, *Tewkesbury Official Guide*, 1931, p. 35, and J. Charles Cox, *Gloucestershire*, 1914, p. 203.)

HAMPSHIRE

ALTON St. Laurence *Nine*

In the north chapel are fourteen plain misericords, seven on both the north and south sides.

Those on the north and the first two and a half on the south side are old; the remainder are about a hundred years old.

The chapel is probably that mentioned in a royal licence of the 20 October 1473 to Sir Maurice Berkeley and others to found a chantry of one chaplain to celebrate daily in a chapel lately built by John Chamflour in the parish church.

The seats are all nailed down except one.

DATE: Probably 15th century.

CHRISTCHURCH   The Priory   *Thirty-nine*

In the choir there are fifty-eight stalls. They are in two rows, fifteen in each upper row and eleven in each lower row, and three on each side returned. The whole of the upper row of stalls on the south side and the easternmost stall in the lower row on the same side have lost their misericords.

North side from east
Lower row

1. Winged lion holding a scroll in its paw (the emblem of St. Mark). Supporters missing. DATE: *c.* 1350. (PLATE 23*a*.)

2. Seated angel wearing a crown, holding a scroll (the emblem of St. Matthew). Supporters: Left and Right, two-legged animal with human head. DATE: *c.* 1350. (PLATE 23*b*.)

(These two misericords were found lying in the lumber room of the church and would have been destroyed but were recognized in time.)

3. Large winged cherub, the wings being fastened together. Supporters: Left, bird's head. Right, missing.

4. Rabbit warren; one rabbit running, another emerging from one of the holes.

5. Bat with extended wings. Supporters: Left and Right, fruit.

6. Ape collared and chained to tree-stump.

7. Contortionist in cap with long, pointed ears. On his left a broken object, possibly a snail.

8. Two central dragons and foliage side by side. No supporters. DATE: *c.* 1250.

9. Jester, in hood and laced-up jerkin with split shoulders, holding in his left hand a platter with a piece of bread on it which a goose, swimming in water, is about to seize. On the right some broken object.

10. Salmon lying on rocks.

11. Greyhound, every rib showing, gnawing a bone.

North side from east
Upper row

1. Jester wearing ecclesiastical robes, his hands at his neck-band. (PLATE 23*c*.)

2. Cowled fox or wolf with head lying on a cushion.

3. Bat-faced demon with long claws, nails, and talons with his wings outspread.

4. Crowned king, carrying a sceptre in his right hand and with long, flowing robes, lying on his side supporting the bracket.

5. Small demi-demon with open mouth, long, pointed ears, fat feet, and extended claws, with his head on a cushion.

6. Man lying on his side, hood over his head, with jerkin and bell, legs crossed, right arm stretched out with palm open, left hand on hip.

7. Crouching beast, perhaps boar.

8. Long-haired gymnast seated, legs extended sideways, holding his feet.

9. Gymnast in long drapery with jerkin showing below, tongue out, holding liripipe of hood with right hand and foot with left. (PLATE 23*d*.)

10. Upper half of a woman with voluminous robes, her coif and veil extending behind, crouching, fists clenched against bosom.

11. Jester sitting sideways, left leg extended in front with arm beneath holding thigh, his left foot seized by hound with only its head and shoulders showing.

12. Bat with open mouth and extended wings.

13. Jester in long cloak, with large face and ass's ears, holding in right hand bauble containing a death's head with pointed ears and belled hood, in left hand short, thick staff.

14. Man on knees and elbows, supporting the bracket with his back and holding a begging-bowl, doublet turned up and showing trunk-hose pierced and fastened with a point, legs crossed, tight wrist-bands. (PLATE 24*a*.)

15. Large bearded face, arms extended grasping foliage of supporters.

16. Kneeling man wearing long, loose robe, soles of feet showing beneath, back supporting bracket, holding in right hand large square-headed mallet and in left chisel.

17. Head and shoulders of laughing oldish man with curly hair, wearing slashed doublet with puffed sleeves and holding a ribbon decorated with a pattern which passes behind his back.

18. Grotesque face with ass's ears and gaping mouth (lower jaw broken), wearing draped cloak with slashed sleeves from which protrude long fingers. (The Sub-Prior's stall.)

South side from east

Lower row

1. Three boldly undercut foliate crockets. DATE: *c.* 1250.

2. Upper half of man wearing cap and jerkin with sleeves, right arm extended as if throwing.

3. Eagle with outspread wings holding a rosary in its beak.

4. Embroidered chaplet (broken).

5. Shield charged with a rose (The County of Southampton); mantling with an l-border behind.

6. Man in peasant's dress lying face downwards with axe in left hand (head missing).

7. Vase, full of berries or cones, from which hangs drapery.

8. Upper half of fat child holding a scroll which passes behind his back and has l-pattern.

9. Upper half of a woman in a coif, wings springing from her shoulders.

10. Long-haired man, in pointed cap and flowing robes, lying on his chest and supporting the bracket with his left hand and right foot.

Supporters (except misericords North 1, 2, and 8, and South 1) are diaper work surrounded by conventional foliage. Date of the misericords is 1515, except where dated otherwise above.

The date when the missing ones were destroyed or stolen is not known, but it was before 1834 when the existing number was mentioned.

WINCHESTER   The Cathedral   *Sixty-six*

There are sixty-eight stalls in the choir, thirty-one in the upper row on the north side, thirty-one on the south, and three each in the lower rows; all have carved misericords except two stalls on the south upper row.

North side from west

1. Head of ecclesiastic in a mitre. Supporters: Left and Right, leaves and acorns.

2. Posture-maker in crouching attitude, his hands (large and out of proportion) on his knees. Supporters: Left and Right, oak-leaves and acorns. (PLATE 24*b*.)

3. Head of woman in wimple and gorget, mouth very large, on body of biped monster. Supporters: Left and Right, bird in foliage.

4. Foliage. Supporters: Left and Right, scroll foliage.

5. Posture-maker grimacing. Supporters: Left and Right, leaf.

6. Squatting man playing pipe. Supporters: Left and Right, leaf.

7. Posture-maker turning a somersault (head gone). Supporters: Left, crowned head of a king. Right, woman with curly hair.

8. Human-headed bird. Supporters: Left, mermaid with comb in right hand and mirror in left. Right, merman with fish in left hand.

9. Owl with outspread wings. Supporters: Left and Right, beech-leaf and nut.

10. A mock-bishop in a long-eared cap (right broken off) clasping a pastoral staff. Supporters: Left, man in hood fighting a wolf or dog which bites his

left cheek; he is thrusting his sword into it. Right, old woman with hair in net, spinning; behind is a large cat.

11. Foliated head with teeth. Supporters; Left and Right, foliage.

12. Fool, with protruding tongue and breasts, lying on his side attempting to draw his sword. Supporters: Left, winged double-bodied monster. Right, two long-eared winged dragons, with long tails interlaced, fighting.

13. Grimacing man, with profusion of wavy hair, extending his mouth with his hands. Supporters: Left and Right, foliage.

14. Lion with very long hind legs. Supporters: Left, a small naked boy in foliage. Right, man's head with large mouth and teeth on body of biped in foliage.

15. Grotesque clothed in quilted leather, his head lolling on one side, and large tongue protruding from mouth. Supporters: Left and Right, leaf.

16. Large cat's head. Supporters: Left and Right, leaf.

17. Two men with wrists bound together; one has a large mouth. Supporters: Left and Right, foliage.

18. Posture-maker, his legs crossed over his head. Supporters: Left and Right, foliate mask.

19. Ape bringing a blinking owl forward. Supporters: Left, oak-leaves. Right, oak-leaves and acorns.

20. New seat but old carving supports bracket: A man and woman, who wears a wimple and gorget, back to back with arms linked.

21. Woman in wimple and gorget, seated, hands on knees. Supporters: Left, female tumbler in foliage, head thrown back, foot held by hand. Right, male tumbler very similar.

22. Ram's head with curly horns. Supporters: Left, ape playing harp. Right, dog curled up.

23. Grotesque face. Supporters: Left and Right, foliate mask.

24. Ape holding up two-handled, two-legged pitcher or crock filled with eggs. Supporters: Left and Right, leaf.

25. Two dogs on hind legs, muzzled together. Supporters: Left, pig playing viol, another listening (or it may be a singer being accompanied). Right, sow playing double pipe and suckling her litter; a little pig listens in background.

26. Woman's head in wimple and gorget, the latter drawn over mouth. Supporters: Left and Right, leaf.

27. Diaper work. Supporters: Left and Right, leaf.

28. Cat with mouse in its mouth. Supporters: Left and Right, squirrel in beech-tree eating nuts.

29. Woman's head in wimple and gorget. Supporters: Left, similar to those for No. 26 but smaller. Right, bearded head.

30. Man's head in hood of mail. Supporters: Left and Right, winged dragon.

31. Crouching, seated man, hands clasped round knees. Supporters: Left, foliate mask, tongue protruding. Right, foliate mask.

South side from west

1. Woman's head. Supporters: Left, missing. Right, ivy-leaves.

2. Man supporting bracket with head and shoulders. Supporters: Left and Right, foliage.

3. Dog lying down. Supporters: Left and Right, leaf.

4. Ram with curly horns lying down. Supporters: Left and Right, leaf.

5. Man's head with curly hair. Supporters: Left, woman's head with gorget over mouth. Right, man's head.

6. Grotesque human-headed monster. Supporters: Left and Right, leaf.

7. Man in hood blowing a hunting horn. Supporters: Left and Right, foliate mask.

8. Crouching, seated peasant-woman, supporting bracket with her back. Supporters: Left, woman's head in wimple and gorget. Right, man's head in hood.

9. A hare or rabbit feeding. Supporters: Left and Right, foliage.

10. Hooded man, with wrists bound, lying on his side, supporting bracket. Supporters: Left and Right: leaf.

11. Demon with horns and tail. Supporters: Left, woman's head in wimple and gorget. Right, woman's head with veil fastened by a chaplet on which are small scalloped ornaments.

12. Human-headed winged monster. Supporters: Left and Right, leaf.

13. Lion's mask. Supporters: Left and Right, foliate mask.

14. Tusked boar. Supporters: Left and Right, ivy-leaf and berries.

15. Female head with profusion of hair. Supporters: Left and Right, leaf.

16. Crowned female-headed monster with long serpentine tail; a long-eared bird looks over her left shoulder. Supporters: Left and Right, leaf.

17. Fox coming out of earth. Supporters: Left and Right, cock.

18. Woman's head in wimple and gorget. Supporters: Left and Right, leaf.

19. Wolf or dog with paws on throat of prostrate man, who cries out and tries to hold back the animal by its ear. Supporters: Left, oak-leaves. Right, oak-leaves with acorns.

20 and 21. Missing.

22. Bearded man with profuse hair. Supporters: Left and Right, leaf.

23. Crouching, seated man with head bent forward and hands held to cheeks. Supporters: Left and Right, foliage.

24. Demi-figure of man upside down. Supporters: Left and Right, human-headed bird or harpy hooded in foliage.

25. Woman seated sideways with a parcel of books or papers bound with strap in right hand. Supporters: Left and Right, boy with foliage.

28. Demi-figure of woman upside down. Supporters: Left, woman's head with wimple and gorget drawn over mouth. Right, man's head.

27. Large hooded head of a man. Supporters: Left and Right, foliage.

28. Ape with arm round neck of ape in female dress. Supporters: Left, woman playing double pipe. Right, woman playing viol.

29. Human-headed bird or harpy in hood. Supporters: Left and Right, oak-leaves with acorns on right.

30. Crouching, seated hooded man with hands on knees. Supporters: Left and Right, leaf.

31. Cloven-hoofed beast biting his near hind foot. Supporters: Left and Right, leaf.

North lower row

1. Hooded figure with gauntlets on hands laughing, with right eye closed in a wink. Supporters: Left, woman's head in wimple and gorget. Right, man's head in hood, with wagging tongue (the tongue is movable).

2. Large head with protruding tongue. Supporters: Left and Right, leaf.

3. Man's head. Supporters: Left and Right, leaf.

South lower row

1. Man stretching corners of mouth with hands. Supporters: Left and Right, leaf.

2. Harpy with large talons. Supporters: Left and Right, beech-leaf and nut.

3. Man, in chain armour with hood, carrying short broad-sword and round target. Supporters: Left and Right, human-headed bird.

These misericords are unusual because the centre carvings are smaller and the supporters larger than usual. It is to be noted that there is not a single misericord in this cathedral that has a religious subject.

DATE: *c.* 1305 (F. Bond, *Misericords*, p. 218).

WINCHESTER   The College Chapel   *Eighteen*

North side from west

1. The head and forelegs of a dragon showing its wings. No supporters. (Headmaster's stall.)

2. Seated countryman with hat tied under his chin, wearing laced boots, one arm round a sheep, the other round a ram. Supporters: Left, man wearing a hood, holding a stout staff, and standing on a twisted vine of convolvulus. Right, shepherd dropping his crook and seized by a lion.

3. Falcon standing on mallard. Supporters: Left and Right, foliate ornament.

4. Foliage. Supporters: Left and Right, stiff leaf.

5. Dragon very similar to No. 1. Supporters: Left and Right, foliate ornament.

6. Foliage. Supporters: Left and Right, square foliate ornament.

7. Bust of a man with curly hair and high-buttoned coat. (Probably a portrait.) Supporters: Left and Right, foliate mask.

8. Foliate ornament. Supporters: Left and Right, stiff leaf.

9. Foliate mask. Supporters: Left and Right, leaf.

South from west

1. Fox carrying a goose over his shoulder. Supporters: Left, bird (roughly carved). Right, dog.

2. Beggar, wearing a hood and clogs, on his knees and one hand, the other held out for alms. Supporters: Left, man wearing a cloak and holding a broad-bladed sword. Right, ape wearing a jagged hood and tunic.

3. Man with curly hair and beard. Supporters: Left, lion's mask with protruding tongue. Right, face surrounded with stiff curls.

4. Female-headed winged monster. Over her shoulder curve the head and body of a snake. Supporters: Left and Right, foliate square.

5. Lion's mask with protruding tongue. Supporters: Left and Right, dragon curled in a circle.

6. Foliate head. Supporters: Left and Right, foliate square.

7. Pelican in her piety. Supporters: Left and Right, stiff leaf.

8. Two goats standing on their hind legs facing each other and eating leaves from a tree. Similar representations occur in the Bestiaries. Supporters: Left and Right, double-bodied dragon.

9. Curly-headed man in quilted tunic holding a dagger. Supporters: Left and Right, grinning sprite.

DATE: The chapel was begun by William of Wykeham (1387–93), but finally consecrated in July, 1395 (*V.C.H., Hampshire*, ii. p. 263).

HEREFORDSHIRE

CANON PYON   St. Lawrence   *Nine*

North side back row from east

1. Chained antelope. Supporters: Left and Right, mask.

2. Four roses. Supporters: Left and Right, formalized leaf.

3. Demi-angel with blank shield. Supporters: Left and Right, lozenge-shaped leaf.

4. Fox carrying off goose, watched by another goose. Supporters: Left and Right, rosette.

South side back row from east

1. Pelican in her piety. Supporters: Left and Right, rose.
2. Catherine wheel. Supporters: Left and Right, rose.
3. Dwarf with open mouth, and hands holding sides of his hood. Supporters: Left and Right, leaf.
4. Hawk or eagle in flight. Supporters: Left and Right, leaf.

The front row of stalls on each side is modern but incorporates old material. One old misericord on the south side, two lions fighting.

DATE: 15th century (*R.C.H.M., Herefordshire*, ii, p. 47).

HEREFORD   The Cathedral   *Thirty-nine*

In the presbytery the stalls with their misericords were reset in their present position, having been reduced in number by Sir Giles Scott.

North upper row from west

1. Reclining wodehouse with flat hat.
2. Two half-human monsters fighting.
3. Squatting woman.
4. Lion and lioness.
5. Two grotesque animals.
6. Human head with wings, having flowing hair and beard.
7. Wodehouse fighting lion.
8. Leopard seizing beast by its neck.
9. Modern.
10. Reclining man in hood with liripipe.
11. Draped figure of man looking through his legs.
12. Birds pecking fruit on branch.
13. Wyvern attacking horse.
14. Two monsters; one winged, dog-headed.
15. Winged bust, head wearing conical cap.
16. Two birds and a dog.

The lower north row of stalls is modern but incorporates two old misericords: opposite No. 12 in upper row, nude man facing backwards astride galloping horse, and, opposite No. 16 in upper row, human face, with enormous ears and mouth open, frowning.

South upper row from east

1. Griffin attacking a ram.

2. Two men with cords round their necks running.

3. Two deer and hounds.

4. Two birds, one with man's and one with woman's head (sirens).

5. Centaur stabbing horned monster.

6. Bearded man's head set on twin animal bodies.

7. Modern.

8. Man and woman with cauldron.

9. Man and woman seated; the woman appears to be putting a bandage on the man's ankle.

10. Male harpy.

11. Double-bodied monster.

12. Fox being attacked by two geese.

13. Winged man's head.

14 and 15. Modern.

The lower row is modern but incorporates nine old misericords.

1. Opposite No. 3 above—Foliage.

2. Opposite No. 4 above—Bearded head.

3. Opposite No. 5 above—Centaur.

4. Opposite No. 6 above—Two beasts fighting.

5. Opposite No. 9 above—Two hogs fighting.

6. Opposite No. 10 above—Bat.

7. Opposite No. 11 above—Goat playing lute and cat playing viol.

8. Opposite No. 12 above—Mermaid suckling lion. (PLATE 8a.)

9. Opposite No. 13 above—Hunter spearing boar in thicket.

In the triforium of the north transept are numerous pieces of the stalls not included in Scott's reconstruction. There is also a misericord with a dragon looking at a snail on its tail.

All the misericords have foliage bosses as supporters except two, which have lion's faces.

DATE: Early 14th century (*R.C.H.M., Herefordshire*, i, pp. 113 f.)

HEREFORD   All Saints   *Sixteen*

Two ranges of five stalls on either side of the chancel with misericords as follows:

North side from east

1. Man's face between two leaves. Supporters: Left and Right, monster.

2. Bearded and moustached man's head in hood. The bracket is supported by

the shoulders and the back of the head. Supporters: Left and Right, conventional flower.

3. Double-bodied monster with face of a crowned and bearded man. Supporters: Left and Right, sunflower with a face in the middle.

4. Two ram-headed beasts, back to back. Supporters: Left and Right, conventional flower.

5. Man's head with leaves issuing from mouth. Supporters: Left and Right, roses.

Returned stalls north

1. Two beasts face to face. Supporters: Left and Right, foliate boss.

2. Bearded man with spurs, riding a horse, face to tail. Supporters: Left and Right, foliate boss.

3. Demi-angel. Supporters: Left and Right, triple rose.

South side from east

1. Two reptiles fighting. In appearance they resemble asps. Supporters: Left and Right, foliate boss.

2. Two winged monsters fighting. Supporters: Left and Right, flower with human face in the middle.

3. Bearded man in shirt on hands and knees. Supporters: Left and Right, conventional flower.

4. Two small beasts back to back; head of third above and between them. Supporters: Left and Right, conventional flower.

5. Bearded man's head between his legs, hands, and two leaves. Supporters: Left and Right, flower.

Returned stalls south

1. Two mermen each with a club and one claw foot. Supporters: Left and Right, human head and beast-head in sunflower.

2. Two lion-like beasts face to face. Supporters: Left and Right, foliage.

3. Lion-like beast without forelegs but with an enormous growth of hair under its chin. The brackets are slighly curved in front and curved at the sides. Supporters: Left and Right, lion's head.

DATE: Late 14th century. (*R.C.H.M.*, *Herefordshire*, i, pp. 125 f.).

HEREFORD   St. Peter's   *Fourteen*

In the chancel two ranges each of nine, the two westernmost on each side being modern. Misericords corbelled, finished with carved roses.

DATE: *c.* 1430–50 (*R.C.H.M.*, *Herefordshire*, i, p. 122).

HOLME LACY   St. Cuthbert   *Five*

Block of three from east

1. Recumbent man, lying on his right side, with knees drawn up so that his feet support the bracket. He wears a short quilted tunic and doublet, and high boots.
2. Defaced horned demon, or perhaps a bull's head.
3. Bird, probably a hawk in flight.

Block of two from east

1. Dog with drooping ears.
2. Grotesque head, with curly hair and mouth agape.

All have vine-leaf supporters, most of which are badly decayed.

DATE: Early 16th century (*R.C.H.M., Herefordshire*, i, p. 147)

LEDBURY   St. Michael and All Angels   *Nine*

In the chancel on the north side are six stalls with moulded misericords, carved with foliations. On the south side are three similar.

DATE: Late 15th or early 16th century (*R.C.H.M., Herefordshire*, ii, p. 105).

LEINTWARDINE   St. Mary Magdalene   *Six*

There are on the south side six stalls with misericords.

1. The Resurrection. Supporters: Left, a man (headless) wearing a girdled tunic. Right, a broken carving.
2. Man kneeling at a prayer-desk. Supporters: Left, mutilated crucifix. Right, Virgin and Child.
3. Seated man wearing flat cap and holding sceptre or sword. Supporters: Left, man's head with flowing hair and forked beard. Other supporter missing.
4. The Annunciation. Supporters: Left and Right, censing angel.
5. Two wrestlers. Supporters: Left, mermaid. Right, a shell with mutilated figure.
6. Carving broken off.

DATE: Early 15th century. They are said to have come from Wigmore Abbey (*R.C.H.M., Herefordshire*, iii, p. 108).

MADLEY   St. Mary   *Eleven*

In the chancel are seven stalls on each side, one on the north side and two on the south side having plain fixed seats. The remaining eleven are carved with a plain vaulting, but some have foliage supporters, as detailed below.

North side from east

1. Supporters: Left and Right, acanthus-leaf.
2. Supporters: Left and right, acanthus-leaf.
3. Supporters: Left and Right, vine-leaf.
6. Supporters: Left and Right, acanthus-leaf.
7. Supporters: Left and Right, vine-leaf.

South side from east

2. Supporters: Left and Right, vine-leaf.
3. Supporters: Left, vine-leaf in a volute. Right, a rose.
4. Supporters: Left and Right, vine-leaf.
7. Supporters: Left and Right, rosette.

DATE: Late 15th or early 16th century (*R.C.H.M., Herefordshire*, i, p. 197).

MOCCAS   St. Michael   *Fourteen*

All the misericords consist of a plain vaulting, and there are no supporters; the vaulting is similar to that at Madley (q.v.), close by, and may have been copied from that model, but the bracket shape suggests a later date, late sixteenth or even seventeenth century. There is no documentary evidence of their installation.

HERTFORDSHIRE

ANSTEY   St. George   *Seven*

There are twelve stalls in the chancel, seven of which have misericords, which have been mounted on new boards. These display foliage of late thirteenth-century character, and the stalls are probably *c.* 1300, about which date a major rebuilding of the church took place (*East Herts. Arch. Soc. Trans.*, x, part II (1938), pp. 132–3).

North side from east to west

1. Conventional foliage design, terminating at each side in a double spray of similar foliage.
2. A simple oak-leaf spray. No supporters.
3. Conventional fan-shaped design with a small scroll curled at foot. No supporters. The misericord is narrower than its fellows, and it is suggested that this design may have been cut in the seventeenth century on a formerly plain board.

South side from east to west

1. Bunch of stiff-leaved foliage, extended to each side to form the stalk for a spray of similar foliage.

2. Spray of stiff-leaved foliage, with upright flower. Supporters: Left and Right, head of man in hood, holding an arm aloft. The arms are badly formed, the hands being undersized. The hood is pointed at the back.

3. Grotesque man's head, full face with tongue out and long hair at sides. A narrow board with no supporters.

4. A trefoil-headed arch set upon two columns with moulded caps and bases. Resting on the pents of the arch is a pair of human arms with gloved hands projecting sideways. On each hand is perched a hawk. The birds face each other and are symmetrically drawn with tails having a trefoil termination. A narrow misericord with no supporters.

BISHOP'S STORTFORD   St. Michael   *Eighteen*

North side from east to west

1. Lion's head, full face, with human ears; fringe of hair, and mane.

2. Woman's head and shoulders, full face; she wears a short veil with crimped edge.

3. Dragon with bat's wings and webbed feet, with head turned back.

4. Woman's head, full face, with long veil crimped in front.

5. Man's head, full face, with beard and moustache. He wears a hood.

6. Man's head and shoulders, three-quarter face. He has flowing hair and beard, and wears a turban with drapery. This may be a Saracen's head, as in Lingfield, Surrey.

7. Returned stall. Man's head and shoulders, full face. Clean-shaven and wearing hat with roll brim and crown of soft material falling to the left.

8. Returned stall. Woman's head and shoulders, full face, with hood. A little arm and hand project on either side of the hood.

9. Returned stall. Semi-figure of angel, full face, holding plain shield.

South side from east to west

1. Owl, full face, with outspread wings (PLATE 24c).

2. Man's head and shoulders, full face, with curly hair.

3. Man's head and shoulders, full face, with beard, wearing a low cylindrical crown-shaped hat.

4. Man's head and shoulders, full face, no beard, but with moustache and curly hair.

5. Man's head and shoulders, full face, slight beard, wearing a turban-like twist on head with flowing drapery.

6. Swan on water, with raised wings (PLATE 24d).

7. Returned stall. A large fish set on waves, having a blunt head with teeth, scales, pectoral fin, and a formidable ridge of saw-teeth along its back. This represents a rare subject, the Serra or sawfish, said to have wings, with which it competed with ships in sailing until exhausted (PLATE 25a).

8. Returned stall. A bird perched on a branch, with outspread wings and a long uninscribed scroll round its body. Possibly the eagle of St. John.

9. Returned stall. Demi-figure of a winged angel, full face, in clouds, holding a scroll. Supporters: Left and Right, angel head in clouds.

With the exception of No. 9, returned stall, south side, the supporters in all cases consist of a conventional leaf.

All the stalls have elbows carved with winged angels in clouds or with scrolls, grotesque figures and beasts, or foliage, and elaborate angle carvings.

DATE: Probably 15th century.

STEVENAGE   St. Nicholas with Holy Trinity   *Five*

North to south

1. Blank.

2. Man's head with mouth-foliage extended to form supporters. The carving may be possibly 15th century.

3. Conventional foliage extending right across the board (PLATE 25*b*).

4. Angel with outspread arms and wings, with two leaves below. This extends across the board.

5 and 6. Vine sprays with grapes, extending across the board (PLATE 25*c*).

DATE: Early 14th century, except No. 2.

The origin of these stalls is obscure, but it is thought that they may have come from Little Wymondley Priory (G. C. Druce, 'Stalls and Misericords in Herfordshire Churches', *East Herts. Arch. Soc. Trans.*, x, Part II (1938), pp. 131–40).

HUNTINGDONSHIRE

BRAMPTON   St. Mary Magdalene   *Three*

There are three stalls in the church with carved misericords.

1. Bulbous-shaped shield (once painted with a coat of arms) supported by a knight holding a lance and wearing armour, a peaked helmet (bassinet), and camail (of the time of Edward III), and a lady wearing a hood and wimple who holds the shield with both hands. Foliage behind. Supporters: Left, a man seated with a stool before him on which is an inkstand and open case, writing on a long scroll. Right, a lion.

2. A man mowing and wearing a tight jerkin buttoned down the front with large buttons, flat cap, pointed shoes, and *gypcière*. A woman raking the hay up with a large toothed rake. Supporters: Left, a carver, wearing a belt to which a wallet and knife are hung, carving the little arches of a

wooden screen. Right, a weaver, with a large pair of shears, standing at a table cutting smooth the pile of a piece of stuff, velvet or pile carpet, which is pinned down on each side (PLATE 14c).

3. Man and woman reaping corn with sickles. Behind, a third figure blowing a horn. Supporters: Left, a woman gleaning. Right, a pile of sheaves.

DATE: c. 1350 (J. H. Middleton, *Camb. Ant. Soc. Pub.*, vii. 1888–91, pp. 28–30).

These stalls were originally in the church, but disappeared. In 1888 they were recovered and presented to the Cambridge Archaeological Society's museum but were later returned to the church. They were described by Professor Middleton while they were in the museum at Cambridge.

GODMANCHESTER   St. Mary the Virgin   *Twenty*

North side from east

1. Mask of man with flowing beard, moustache, and hair.
2. Dog wearing a collar of bells and lying on a tasselled cushion.
3. Bird with expanded wings on branch.
4. Shield charged with fleur-de-lis.
5. Hare or rabbit crouching on cabbage or similar vegetable (PLATE 25d).
6. Demons and horned head with tongue protruding.
7. Foliage.
8. Crouching cat.
9. Seated ape (partly broken).
10. Amphisbaena.

South side from east

1. Fox carrying off goose.
2. Crowned angel holding scroll. The emblem of St. Luke.
3. Angel, with wings expanded, hair bound with circlet, holding shield charged with the letters WS intertwined (slightly restored).
4. Crouching lion.
5. Lion mask with protruding tongue.
6. Horse lying down (PLATE 26a).
7. Cat holding mouse in teeth and claws.
8. Eagle holding scroll in its beak. The emblem of St. John.
9. Dappled fawn crouching and scratching nose with hind foot.
10. Shield charged with fleur-de-lis.

The supporters to these carvings are foliate bosses.

DATE: 15th century. The initials WS on one misericord may refer to William Stevens, vicar 1470–81, and the fleur-de-lis probably indicates that the stalls were made for Godmanchester, which incorporates the flower in the borough arms. There is a panel over the west door of the church carved with a fleur-de-lis and the words *Burgus Gumecestre 1623* (*R.C.H.M., Huntingdonshire*, pp. 110–11).

ST. NEOTS   St. Mary   *Four*

In the chancel there are four misericords, three bearing shields, two with a cross flory and one with the letters IHS above a scroll inscribed *Jesu Merci*, and one damaged. Supporters: Left and Right, conventional leaves (PLATE 26b).

DATE: Late 15th or early 16th century (*R.C.H.M., Huntingdonshire*, p. 224).

KENT

ALDINGTON   St. Martin   *Six*

There are three stalls with carved misericords on each side of the choir. Numbers 1 to 5 consist of conventional floral subjects, deeply undercut, with foliate supporters.

The sixth misericord (on the south side) consists of a triple corbel and vaulting, with castles as supporters, enclosed by marginal moulding (PLATE 26c).

DATE: Probably *c.* 1475.

ASHFORD   St. Mary the Virgin   *Sixteen*

North side from east

1. Vine and grapes. Supporters: Left and Right, vine-leaf.
2. Sycamore foliage. Supporters: Left and Right, sycamore-leaf.
3. Juniper and berries. Supporters: Left and Right, leaf of juniper.
4. Cypress foliage. Supporters: Left and Right, cypress-leaf
5. Vine and three clusters of grapes. Supporters: Left and Right, vine-leaf.
6. Twin branch of foliage, possible acanthus. Supporters: Left and Right, similar leaf.
7. Branch of vine foliage. Supporters: Left and Right, vine-leaf.
8. Oak tree and acorns with three pigs feeding at base. Supporters: Left and Right, cluster of oak-leaves and acorns (PLATE 26d).

South side from east

1. Pendant twig bearing two large nine-lobed leaves. Supporters: Left and Right, similar leaf.

2. Foliage of juniper and berries. Supporters: Left and Right, similar leaf.

3. Vine and grapes. Supporters: Left and Right, vine-leaf.

4. Triple group of sycamore leaves. Supporters: Left and Right, similar leaf (PLATE 27a).

5. Vine with five branches. Supporters: Left and Right, vine-leaf.

6. Large branch of sycamore or maple leaves. Supporters: Left and Right, similar leaf.

7. Branch of foliage (damaged), probably sycamore. Supporters: Left and Right, similar leaf.

8. Pelican in her piety. Supporters: Left and Right, pelican in nest (PLATE 27b).

DATE: c. 1475. The church was rebuilt, including stalls, as a collegiate foundation in 1475 by Sir John Fogge (d. 1490) (A. J. Pearman, 'Ashford Church', *Arch. Cantiana*, xxviii (1909), p. 84.

CANTERBURY   Holy Cross   *Four*

There are four misericords in the sanctuary. Two are badly mutilated and the other two are carved with foliage.

DATE: Probably early 15th century.

CLIFFE-AT-HOO   St. Helen   *Two*

In the choir are twelve stalls with carved misericords of which only two are old. Each has a grotesque face below a plain corbel. Supporters: Left and Right, conventional leaf (PLATE 27c).

DATE: Early 14th century, when the chancel was rebuilt. (A. R. Martin, 'The Church at Cliffe-at-Hoo', *Arch. Cantiana*, xli, p. 80).

COBHAM   St. Mary Magdalen   *One*

The present chancel of this church dates from 1362 (*V.C.H., Kent*, ii, p. 231). It was built to replace a smaller chancel, in order to accommodate the needs of the adjoining College (a subsidiary of the Priory of Bermondsey). It originally contained eighteen stalls with misericords, seven stalls and two returned stalls on each side. Only one now remains, the others having been replaced with fixed seats during a restoration in 1862.

The remaining misericord merely contains a single border-line of moulding, and no other decoration or supporters.

DATE: 14th century.

FAVERSHAM   St. Mary of Charity   *Sixteen*

There are sixteen stalls, twelve having the original carvings. These were possibly transferred from the Abbey at Faversham. The remaining four misericords were carved by an unnamed Pole in 1874 (E. Phipson, *Choir Stalls and their Carvings*, 1896, p. 83).

North side from East

1. Wodehouse kneeling, holding tree bough. Supporters: Left and Right, formal leaf.

2. Man's head with curly hair emerging from under a cap. Supporters: Left and Right, formal leaf.

3. Jester in cap with scalloped edge, crouching in a cramped position, and playing a bagpipe. Supporters: Left and Right, conventional flower.

4. Demi-figure of a man, holding a loaf and a full cup (? Elijah). Supporters: Left and Right, formal leaf. (1874).

5. Demi-angel with flaming sword. Supporters: Left and Right, grapes (1874).

6. Ape chained to clog, and holding a urine-flask reversed. Supporters: Left and Right, conventional flower.

7. Triple-faced man's head, having four eyes, three noses, and three mouths arranged to show features full face and to left and right. Supporters: Left and Right, formal leaf.

8. Demi-angel holding a shield, charged with a pair of leopards or lions and a pair of horned sheep. Supporters: Left and Right, rosette.

South side from east

1. A camel crouching, and having a large hair-covered hump. Supporters: Left and Right, bunch of grapes.

2. Fox carrying off a goose on his back, two others he has killed lying at his feet. Supporters: Left and Right, four leaves spread out and four small leaves folded to the centre.

3. A winged, horned demon carrying off a clothed man. Supporters: Left and Right, double rosette. (1874.)

4. A horse on its knees. Supporters: Left and Right, formal leaf. (This may be modern.)

5. A fox standing on a vine-branch gazing at two bunches of grapes. Supporters: Left and Right, conventional flower. (1874.)

6. Wodehouse spearing a griffin, with both hands holding the spear, and protected by a large shield made of framework covered with hides and having large boss. Supporters: Left and Right, conventional flower.

7. A wolf with heavy mane licking its forefoot to make its tread more silent. Supporters: Left and Right, formal leaf. (PLATE 13c).

8. Demi-angel holding a shield charged with a pair of leopards or lions and a pair of horned sheep. Supporters: Left and Right, grotesque face.

DATE: Late 15th century (G. C. Druce, 'Stall Carvings in the Church of St. Mary of Charity, Faversham', *Arch. Cantiana*, l (1939), p. 11).

HERNE   St. Martin   *Six*

There are six original misericords as follows, all on the south side.

1. Head and shoulders of a man holding in front of him a large St. Andrew's cross. Supporters: Left, formalized leaf. Right, rose.
2. A bat with wings outspread. Supporters: Left and Right, flower.
3. A duck preening itself. Supporters: Left and Right, rose.
4. An angel holding a plain shield. Supporters: Left and Right, St. Andrew's cross in a shield.
5. A duck alighting on the water. Supporters: Left and Right, circular ornament beaded on the rim (PLATE 27*d*).
6. The head and shoulders of a crowned angel holding open a large book, which he appears to be reading aloud. Supporters: Left and Right, St. Andrew's cross (PLATE 28*a*.)

The misericords on the north side aremodern.

In the church is a brass which has an inscription, the translation of which is 'This choir was unsightly, now it is seemly. I am the Andrew who adorned it.' This Andrew was Andrew Benstede, who was vicar from 1511 to 1531. The St. Andrew's crosses on Nos. 1, 4, and 6 may indicate his connection with the restoration. Probably 16th century.

MAIDSTONE   All Saints   *Twenty*

The parish church of St. Mary was refounded as the collegiate church of All Saints by William de Courtenay in 1395 under a licence of Richard II. The church was to have a master or warden and as many chaplains as Courtenay should think fit. (E. Phipson, *Choir Stalls and their Carvings*, p. 57.)

North side from west

1. Lion's head with tongue protruding. Supporters: Left and Right, similar small lion's mask.
2. Leaf. Supporters: Left and Right, leaf.
3. Shield charged with the arms of Canterbury. Supporters: Left and Right, the same smaller.
4. Two large oak-leaves entwined. Supporters: Left and Right, leaf.
5. Demi-figure of a cook, wearing a hood and tight jerkin turned back and scalloped and buttoned with large buttons, and holding a flesh-hook and a ladle. Supporters: Left and Right, rosette backed by four leaves forming a square pattern.
6. Demi-figure of a boy wearing a cap. Supporters: Left and Right, leaf.
7. Leaf. Supporters: Left and Right, leaf.
8. Bearded head. Supporters: Left and Right, leaf.

9. Large leaf. Supporters: Left and Right, leaf.

10. Shield charged with the arms of Guido de Mono, the last rector of St. Mary's (1395), *a chevron engrailed between three leaves.* Supporters: Left and Right, the same.

South side from west

The first misericord of the missing return stalls on this side (which should be the Master's stall) was stated by a correspondent in the *Gentleman's Magazine*, vol. 64, to be an ecclesiastic, possibly John Wotton, the first Master.

1. Shield charged with the arms of William de Courtenay, Archbishop of Canterbury (1381–96) impaling Canterbury. Supporters: Left and Right, leaf.

2. Shield charged with the arms of Edward Courtenay, the Archbishop's third brother.

3. Three leaves. Supporters: Left and Right, leaf.

4. Shield charged with the arms of Thomas Courtenay, the second brother. Supporters: Left and Right, smaller shield similarly charged.

5. Sunflower. Supporters: Left and Right, smaller sunflower.

6. Large leaf. Supporters: Left and Right, leaf.

7. Similar to No. 5.

8. Shield charged with the arms of Philip Courtenay, the fifth brother. Supporters: Left and Right, smaller shield similarly charged.

9. Large leaf. Supporters: Left and Right: leaf.

10. Bearded head. Supporters: Left and Right, leaf.

DATE: Early 15th century.

Note: The arms of the Courtenays are those of Godfrey de Bouillon. One of the cadets of the family took part in the First Crusade, married a kinswoman of that famous warrior, and was allowed to bear the same arms, *or, three torteaux, gules.*

MINSTER-IN-THANET   St. Mary   *Eighteen*

North side from west

1. Bird Siren wearing a hennin. Supporters: Left and Right: a snake with female head wearing a hennin, perhaps an allusion to the Virgin-headed Serpent of the Fall of Man.

2. Shield charged with *a fess between three mullets* (Manston). Supporters: Left and Right, leaf.

3. Hart with collar and chain. Supporters: Left and Right, conventional foliage.
(There is a tradition that King Edgar I of Kent gave the mother of Mildred of Kent as much land for her monastery in Thanet as her tame hart could

compass in one run, but the motif is more probably the hart badge of Richard II.)

4. Shield charged as in No. 2 with a crescent for difference. Supporters: Left and Right: uncharged shield.

5. Shield charged *ermine, a chief quarterly.* (Possibly arms of the Peckham family of Yaldham and elsewhere in Kent: see 'The Visitation of Kent in 1663–1668', *Harleian Society,* liv, p. 128.) Supporters: Left and Right, demi-angel with curious head-dress, bearing uncharged shield.

6. Woman wearing a large hennin, between the points of which a demon is seated Supporters: Left and Right, lion's mask with protruding tongue (PLATE 15*a*).

7. Two birds, back to back. Supporters: Left and Right, a dolphin biting its tail.

8. Angel bearing an uncharged shield. Supporters: Left and Right, a double rose.

9. Plain bracket. Supporters: Left and Right, a four-petalled rose.

10. Old woman with distaff in hand, flanked by, left, a cat, right, a dog. Supporters: Left, a grotesque head. Right, fox bearing off a fowl (PLATE 28*b*).

South side from west

1. Demi-angel playing a cithern. Supporters: Left and Right, lion's mask.

2. Man's face with curly hair, eyes looking sideways. Supporters: Left and Right, dragon curled up.

3. Bust of man laughing. Supporters: Left and Right, lion's mask.

4. Bearded man's head, wearing a round cap. Supporters: Left, demi-angel clothed in feathers, around whom is a scroll inscribed 'Johanes'. Right, similar angel and scroll inscribed 'Curteys'. (John Curteys was rector from 1401 to 1419.)

5. Cook stirring an iron pot. He has a basting ladle and a shovel for putting bread into the oven. He appears to be shouting (possibly orders to scullions). Supporters: Left and Right, birds, said to be swan or fowl (PLATE 28*c*).

6. Foliate mask, with oak mouth-foliage. Supporters: Left and Right, bird perched on foliage, with scroll in beak.

7. Angel clothed in feathers, holding a scroll across his breast inscribed *I.H.C.* Supporters: Left and Right, dragon curled up.

8. Head of a man with beard and long hair. Supporters: Left and Right, sensual-looking man's head. F. Bond, *Misericords,* p. 145, says this subject may represent Christ between the two thieves.

DATE: *c.* 1410.

SANDWICH   St. Clement's   *One*

There are fourteen stalls in the choir but only one misericord remains.

> A shield charged with *fess lozengy with five fleur-de-lis springing above.* Supporters: Left and Right, plain shield. The arms are unidentified (PLATE 28*d*).

DATE: 15th century.

THROWLEY   St. Michael and All Angels   *Four*

From the east

1. Winged dragon with second head on its breast pursuing a naked boy. Supporters: Left and Right, grotesque lion, its tail being a continuation of the bracket moulding.
2. Headless figure, perhaps an ape, riding a quadruped with a ring of rough hair round its neck, followed by another headless figure. Supporters: Left and Right, dragon standing on its head, its tail being a continuation of the bracket moulding (PLATE 5*c*).
3. Winged animal with human features facing a man. Supporters, lions.
4. Foliage. Supporters: Left and Right, floral designs.

DATE: *c.* 1520 (Nos. 1 and 2 are copied from marginal ornaments in books printed *c.* 1490–1520). See Bristol.

WESTWELL   St. Mary   *Four*

There are four returned stalls with misericords, backing on to the triple chancel arch. They are plain, though there is a vaulted boss on the underside of each, as if it had been intended to carve them. They are now screwed down.

DATE: Probably 14th century.

WINGHAM   St. Peter   *Ten*

None of the carvings has supporters.

North side

1. Horse's head with spreading ears. An oak-leaf and two acorns emerge from either side of the mouth.
2. Cluster of oak-leaves and acorns.
3. Woman's head in a wimple head-dress. Oak-leaves adorn the sides.
4. Man's grinning head peering from between oak-leaves. He has a pronounced fringe of hair low on his forehead.
5. Inverted triangular cluster of oak-leaves and acorns (PLATE 29*a*).

South side

10. Cluster of three flowers.

11. Elaborate cluster of vine-leaves and grapes. (PLATE 29*b*.)

12. Mule's (?) head, with eyes closed and widely spread pointed ears. An oak-leaf and an acorn emerge from either side of the mouth.

13. Cluster of five oak-leaves arranged in a symmetrical pattern, and sprouting from a common central stem (PLATE 29*c*).

14. Another floral cluster, similar to No. 10.

G. C. Druce, *Jour. Brit. Arch. Assoc.*, N.S., xxxvi (1931), p. 244, says these misericords are early fourteenth-century. A college was founded in 1287 by Archbishop Peckham (Knowles and Hadcokk, *Medieval Religious Houses*, 1953, p. 345). Compare foliage at Stevenage, Herts (PLATE 26*b*).

LANCASHIRE

BLACKBURN   St. Mary   *Eight*

1. Bold wing-like treatment of conventional leaf pattern.

2. Similar, but less bold treatment.

3. Hunting scene. The huntsman, long-haired and kilted, cross-belts over chest and belt round waist, is blowing up his hounds on an ape-hunt. One hound is running from the left and on the right two (somewhat mutilated) are fighting the apes. A male ape has hold of one hound by the muzzle, and the mother with her baby on her back is looking back whilst running away.

4. Fox preaching from a pulpit to geese.

5. Angel with long hair holding a scroll in front of him (probably St. Matthew).

6. Lion (St. Mark).

7. Bull (rather mutilated—St. Luke).

8. In the centre the Tree of Life standing in the Garden of Eden; around the stem of the Tree is coiled the Serpent. The fruit of the Tree is very conspicuous. Supporters: Left, Adam and Eve naked; a bird is apparently whispering to them from another tree. Right, Adam and Eve, slightly clothed, fleeing from the angel with the flaming sword.

These misericords are said to have come from Whalley Abbey, as did those in Whalley itself (q.v.), and are similar in design.

DATE: 15th century (F. H. Crossley, 'Remains of Medieval Stallwork in Lancashire', *Trans. Lancs. & Cheshire Hist. Soc.*, lxx, N.S. 34 (1919), pp. 1–2).

BOLTON-LE-MOORS   St. Peter   *Three*

The fifteenth-century church was demolished in 1866 and a new church built in 1871.

In the chapel on the south side of the chancel are three stalls from the old church with carved misericords.

1. The badge of the Bartons (an acorn between two oak-leaves).

2. The badge of the Stanleys (eagle nurturing child).

3. Angel holding plain shield.

DATE: 15th century.

CARTMEL   The Priory   *Twenty-five*

Cartmel was a priory of Austin canons that was preserved at the Dissolution. In 1618–23 the choir was restored, new screens given, and misericords replaced in new stalls, twenty-six in number, with one blank seat.

North side from east

1. Pair of large formal leaves rising from central stem. Supporters: Left and Right, simple flower within square design of four leaves.

2. Winged and clawed demon or dragon, full face. Supporters: Left, rosette. Right, lion mask.

3. Elaborate group of pendant leaves. Supporters: Left and Right, similar to No. 1.

4. Elephant and castle, the animal leaning against a tree. Supporters: Left, spray of flowers and leaves. Right, lion mask (PLATE 29d).

5. Design of three intertwined acanthus leaves. Supporters: Left, as for No. 1. Right, lion mask.

6. Group of animals, young deer, and three hunting dogs entering a wood. Supporters: Left, crowned monogram 'WW' for Prior William (1441). Right, hedgehog.

7. Large double rose flanked by leaves. Supporters: Left, head of an ox. Right, bunch of fruit and leaves.

8. Large head of man, having curled hair and fringed beard and whiskers, and wearing a soft head-dress ornamented with rosette and fruit. Supporters: Left, simple formal leaf. Right, lion mask.

9. Griffin passant left. Supporters: Left and Right, lion mask.

10. Blank.

11. Grinning lion mask with foliage issuing from mouth. Supporters: Left and Right, leaf design as for No. 1.

12. Acanthus-leaf design similar to No. 5. Supporters: Left, spray of three small leaves. Right, lion mask.

13. Oak tree in which the horn of a unicorn (right) is embedded. Supporters: Left and Right, lozenge-shaped pattern of three and four leaves.

South side from east

1. Intricate design of serrated leaves. Supporters: Left, fruit and leaf group. Right, rose and leaves.

2. Grinning foliate mask. Supporters: Left and Right, circular pattern of four leaves.

3. Two geese eating from a sack or bowl of corn. Supporters: Left and Right, circular pattern of fruit and flowers.

4. Eagle in flight carrying bunch of grapes in beak. Supporters: Left and Right, square pattern of four small leaves.

5. Peacock with tail spread. Supporters: Left, formal leaf pattern. Right, bat hanging head downward (PLATE 30*a*).

6. Dragon passant right, with flapping wings Supporters: Left, four-petalled flower with human face at centre. Right, round pattern of indented leaves.

7. The Flight of Alexander. Supporters: Left, Lombardic initial T. Right, oak-leaf.

8. Double-tailed mermaid with comb and mirror. Supporters: Left, leaf pattern. Right, round flower.

9. Ape-doctor holding a flask, and flanked by fruit and leaves. Supporters: Left, bird with outstretched wings on nest. Right, four leaves and four small fruits.

10. Demi-angel with raised wings, holding shield with unidentified design. Supporters: Left and Right, fruit and leaf pattern.

11. Pelican in her piety. Supporters: Left and Right, lion mask.

12. Crowned head with triple face in foliage. Supporters: Left and Right, formal leaf group.

13. Arabesque design between supporters-monogram 'WW', for Prior William (1441).

DATE: *c.* 1440.

GARSTANG   St. Helens   *Eight*

North side from east

1. Fox.

2. A shield bearing *a chevron between two roses in chief and a fleur-de-lis at base.* Supporters: Left and Right, scroll.

3. Blank.

4. Blank.

5. A shield bearing *a bend sinister charged with a crescent between a flower-bud and a fleur-de-lis.* Supporters: Left and Right, slight ray effect.

6. Elephant and castle facing left.

South side from east

1. Bearded man's face. Supporters: Left and Right, fold work.
2. A shield charged *reversed chevron with rose in chief.* Supporters: Left and Right, scroll.
3. Blank.
4. Blank.
5. Demon's face. Supporters: Left and Right, bat-wings.
6. An acanthus-leaf curling right from slightly to left of centre.

DATE: Probably 15th century. F. H. Crossley, 'Remains of Medieval Stallwork in Lancashire', *Trans. Lancs. & Cheshire Hist. Soc.* lxx, N.S. 34 (1919), p. 13, states that the three heraldic carvings are post-Reformation, and that the arms may be fanciful. The College of Arms has no records of these coats.

HALSALL   St. Cuthbert   *Seven*

South side

1. Two naked men wrestling, each apparently encouraged by a monk. Supporters: Left and Right, flower, delicately carved.
2. An angel, winged and feathered, holding a key in each hand and wearing a cap and breast-plate on the front of which is a plain cross. Supporters: Left and Right, dragon.
3. Head of an old bearded man. Supporters: Left and Right, conventional flower.
4. Eagle flying. Supporters: Left and Right, eaglet.
5. Fox and goose. Supporters: Left and Right, rosette, boldly carved.
6. Angel, winged and robed, holding a book and wearing a similar cap to that in No. 2. Supporters: Left and Right, rosette.

The carving on the north is of two dragons fighting.

DATE: 16th century. F. H. Crossley, 'Remains of Medieval Stallwork in Lancashire', *Trans. Lancs. & Cheshire Hist. Soc.*, lxx, N.S., 34 (1919), p. 9, suggests that the same carver was employed here and at Gresford, Denbighshire (q.v.).

LANCASTER   Priory Church of St. Mary   *Twelve*

There are fourteen stalls in the chancel, seven on each side. They have beautiful canopied work, but almost all of the misericords have been badly mutilated, especially the faces of figures, and two of the carvings on the south side are missing and have been replaced by fixed seats. The seven stalls on each side consist of blocks of five and two.

The Priory was an alien Benedictine one, and was confiscated and suppressed in 1428. The misericords are of the fourteenth century, and the church guide, by L. I. and M. E. M. J. Cowper, states that the stalls were used by the monks of St. Martin in the earlier church which preceded the fifteenth-century rebuilding. There is an alternative opinion that they came from Cockersand Abbey in 1537. F. H. Crossley, *Trans. Lancs. & Cheshire Hist. Soc.*, N.S. 68 (1916), p. 89, dates them at *c*. 1340.

North side from east

1. Bust of figure in flowing robes, full face, with arms raised so that the elbows and head support the bracket. Supporters: Left and Right, formal leaf motif.

2. Pair of lions (mutilated). Supporters: Left, bust of young girl in wimple and round-necked buttoned gown. Right, a wyvern rampant. Both have roundels.

3. Composite monster with a human torso, beast's haunches, and four-clawed feet. The legs are fringed with hair or fur. Supporters: Left and Right: formal leaf motif.

4. Frontal bust of man with flowing curled hair, moustache, and beard. He wears a round-necked tunic, buttoned in front. Supporters: Left and Right, formal leaf motif.

5. The whole design includes the supporters, and appears to represent a ceremony. In the centre two figures, male and female, kneel facing forward, with hands folded within the sleeves of their gowns. To left of them is a panelled structure, possibly a font, with a cowled head at its base, while behind the woman stands another figure, now badly mutilated, which appears to have been holding a goblet or similar object. On the extreme left are two nuns kneeling in prayer, facing the centre, while on the extreme right stand three figures, two female, with a man between them. The women wear gowns, one buttoned in front, the other caped, and face forward, while the man, wearing belted tunic with wallet slung at his side, stands with body turned to right, but facing forward. It might perhaps represent a baptism.

6. On left, a winged figure bearing in left hand a round shield. From the waist down, below a flared tunic, it has feathers and a bird's claws. On right, another figure, in head-dress with side-flaps and a girdled tunic, has beast's haunches and five-toed feet, and holds a large hilted knife dagger-wise. Both faces are mutilated. Supporters: mutilated.

7. Lion or leopard courant right. Its tail is curved forward over its back. Supporters: missing.

South side from east

1. On left, figure of priest or cleric facing right and bearing a casket. He stands within an arcade or shrine, and on his right are two small figures (mutilated). Supporters: missing.

2. Winged and feathered figure, similar to an owl, in flight, and having a human face (mutilated) wearing a caftan. Supporters: Left and Right, formal leaf motif (damaged).

3 and 4. Missing.

5. Badly mutilated. On left, an upright oak leaf, flanked by a broken part of a human figure. On right, a frontal female figure in wimple (face broken) and flared gown with buttoned front and buckled girdle. One arm is raised against large, upright oak-leaf and twig. Supporters: Left, frontal nude angel in squatting position. Right, an athlete in act of running. Both are within roundels.

6. Crowned figure on left, with elaborate crown of oak-leaf design, and full beard and hair. On right, walking towards him, a figure (face mutilated) in caftan, tunic, and hose. Supporters: Left, a curious form of figure with no body, but legs and head, wearing hood and cap, crouching within a roundel. Right, a two-legged creature with human lower limbs and lion's man ande tail (head missing).

7. Full-face lion mask (mutilated) with flowing mane and two bodies facing inward. Supporters: Left and Right, formal leaf motif.

MANCHESTER   The Cathedral   *Thirty*

In the choir are fifteen stalls on each side with carved misericords, three of them on each side being returned.

North side from west

1. Demi-angel with extended wings, bearing a shield charged with the cross of St. George. Supporters: Left and Right, fir-cones.

2. Pelican in her piety. Supporters: Left and Right, chestnut-leaf.

3. Two dragons fighting. Supporters: Left and Right, sunflower.

4. Badly damaged version of Joshua and Caleb carrying grapes from the Promised Land, cf. Ripon and Beverley Minster. Copied from *Biblia Pauperum*. Supporters: Left and Right, vine-leaf.

5. Woman following a man. Between, a pot overturned. Supporters: Left and Right, columbine.

6. Dragon biting its own back. Supporters, Left and Right, leaf.

7. Demi-figure of a child, issuing from a spiral shell, driving his spear into an attacking dragon. Supporters: Left and Right, three sunflowers.

8. Two man playing tric-trac or backgammon on a board lying between them. On either side of them a reclining figure; one plays a musical instrument, the other draws ale from a barrel a good deal broken. Supporters: Left and Right, rose.

9. Fox with a pole over his shoulder, to which is hung a dead hare, is riding a hound through a grove of trees, on the branches of which birds are perched. Supporters: Left and Right, flower.

10. Hound pulling a stag amongst trees. Supporters: Left and Right, sunflower.

11. Huntsman disembowelling a stag; its throat is cut and it lies on its back. Supporters: Left and Right, sunflower.

12. Centre broken. Supporters: Left and Right, fir-cone.

13. Cock and a cockatrice. Supporters: Left and Right, flower.

14. Unicorn couchant among trees. Supporters: Left and Right, back view of a rose.

15. Hunter, from whose belt hangs a bugle, is bound to a pole used as a spit, which is being turned before a fire by a rabbit or hare (head broken off). Four pots stand on the fire, three are covered, the lid of the fourth is being lifted by a hare, showing the head of a hound. Supporters: Left and right, rose, side view. Copied from an engraving by Israel van Meckenen, reproduced by Ottley, *History of Engraving*, ii (1816), p. 661.

South side from west

1. Three woodmen, with wallets and axes over their shoulders, going towards a castle; a fourth is knocking at the gate. A baby is in an eagle's nest and the eagle is perched on the baby. (The Lathom Legend. In this family there was the story of a baby who had been carried off by an eagle but who lived and grew up to inherit the family title.) Supporters: Left and Right, leaf.

2. Eagle flying. Supporters: Left and Right, an eagle's leg erased, with talons (the badge of Sir John Stanley, the natural son of Warden James Stanley, 1485–1506, later Bishop of Ely).

3. Dragon. Supporters: Left and Right, fruit with triple stem.

4. Demi-angel, with wings outspread and wearing a loose surplice and an amice, bearing a shield charged with the arms of the Isle of Man (*three legs, conjoined, armed and spurred*). Supporters: Left and Right, oak-leaf and acorn. A member of the Stanley family was Bishop of Sodor and Man.

5. Elephant (very unrealistic and without a trunk) carrying a double-turreted castle. Supporters: Left and Right, sunflower.

6. Two wodehouses, the left mounted on a camel and the right on a unicorn, fighting. Supporters: Left and Right, fir-cone.

7. Fox, with a goose in his mouth, running away from a farm house; in the doorway is a woman with a child holding her skirt. Supporters: Left, a fox holding a birch on his shoulder, teaches two cubs to read. Right, a fox seated on a stool with an open book in front of him.

8. Pedlar lying asleep while a number of apes rifle his pack. Supporters: Left, ape holding up a bottle. Right, ape nursing a baby or perhaps a baby doll from the pack (PLATE 9*b*).

9. Bear, collared and chained, baited by five dogs; the bear seizes one dog, two hold the bear by the neck and two hold it by the haunches. Supporters: Left and Right, sunflower.

10. Lion couchant regardant with tail about three times longer than normal. Supporters: Left and Right, rose and bud.

11. Lion and dragon fighting. Supporters: Left and Right, lion's mask with protruding tongue. J. S. Purvis (*Archeologia*, 85, p. 119) draws attention to the striking resemblance of this carving to a bracket carving on the Eleanor Percy tomb at Beverley (*c.* 1340).

12. Wodehouse, round whose waist is a wreathed belt, armed with a shield and club, fighting a dragon. Supporters: Left and Right, leaf.

13. Boar on its hind legs plays the bagpipes; four young pigs are dancing. Supporters: Left, a boar plays the harp. Right, a boar with a packsaddle strapped round him.

14. Antelope. Supporters: Left and Right, flowers and fruit.

15. Griffin with wings outspread. Supporters: Left and Right, three flowers.

All the supporters are enclosed in roundels.

DATE: Early 16th century. F. H. Crossley, 'Remains of Medieval Stallwork in Lancashire', *Trans. Lancs. & Cheshire Hist. Soc.* lxx, N.S. 34 (1919), p. 7.

MIDDLETON   St. Leonard   *Eight*

On each side of the chancel are four misericords, very simply carved with leaves.

DATE: Probably 16th century.

PRESCOT   Our Lady   *Eleven*

The stalls are of black oak and have tip-up seats but the carvings have been removed.

DATE: 1636 (F. H. Crossley, 'Remains of Medieval Stallwork in Lancashire', *Trans. Lancs. & Cheshire Hist. Soc.* lxx, N.S. 34, (1919) p. 5).

WHALLEY   St. Mary   *Twenty-two*

The stalls are said to have come from Whalley Abbey Church, but there is no confirmation of this. They are now twenty-two in number, but they were very much altered and mixed up with modern work in 1866.

North side from east

1, 2, and 3. Flowers (modern).

4. Man and two dogs pursuing a fox with a bird in its mouth.

5. St. George and the Dragon.

6. Two eagles tearing intestines of lamb.

7. Satyr and woman, inscribed *Penses molt et p[ar]les pou*, 'think much and speak little'.

8 and 9. Foliage.

10. Three-faced head.

11. Oak with sprays of flowers and mouse on branch.

12. Warrior, with sword and buckler thrown down, kneeling before wife, who is beating him with frying pan.

South side from east

1. Angel (modern).

2. Flying dragon carrying in claws swaddled infant.

3. Shoeing the goose, inscribed *Who so melles hȳ[m]of y al mē[n] dos let hȳ[m]cū[m] heir & shoe ye ghos*, 'whoever meddles in other people's affairs is sure to make a failure of it.'

4. Vine and grapes, with initials 'W. W.' at either side, and inscribed *Semp[er] gaudentes sint ista sede sedentes*, 'joyful be they who sit here.' (Abbot's stall.)

5. Face with mouth-foliage.

6. Angel.

7. King's head with scroll held by griffin.

8. Pelican in her piety.

9. Pomegranates between two sharp-beaked birds.

10. Lion and winged dragon. Supporters: Left and Right, stiff leaf foliage.

From the initials 'W.W.' on the Abbot's stall (South No. 4) the misericords date from the abbacy of William Whalley (1418–38). A. Wolfgang, *Trans. Lancs. & Cheshire Hist. Soc.* lxiii (1911), p. 81, states 1435.

LINCOLNSHIRE

BOSTON   St. Botolph's   *Sixty-two*

North side from east
  Upper Tier

1. Nun's head in a veil.

2. Floral design.

3. Dragons.

4. Ape, wearing hood and sitting with legs crossed, about to pour out of a pitcher into a bucket held by a fox; behind him another fox.

5. Rose-bush bearing flowers and buds.

6. Grotesque head.

7, 8, and 9. Floral designs.

10. Bearded lion with two bodies of birds. Supporters, dragons.

11. St. George and the Dragon.

12. Capture of the Unicorn. Supporters: eagles.

13. Knight fighting dragon and eagle. Supporters: Left and Right, eagle.

14. St. George and the Dragon.

15. Pelican in her piety.

16. Damaged.

17. Man with bellows and woman with ladle and basin sitting by fire over which hangs a cauldron. Behind man is a pitcher and behind woman is a distaff and spindle.

18. Bear playing organ, another bear with a chain round its neck blowing the bellows. Supporters: Left, bear beating drum. Right, bear playing bagpipes.

19. An owl. Supporters: Left, missing. Right, wild man clinging to leafless tree.

Returned Stalls

1. Man lassoing lion and jumping on to its back. Supporters: Left and Right, dragon.

2. Griffin (damaged). Supporter: right, fox eating.

3. Spread eagle (damaged). Supporters: Left, eagle. Right, fox.

Lower Tier

1. Buck seated between two trees. Supporters: Left and Right, bird eating snail.

2. Man cutting undergrowth with an axe. Supporters: Left and Right, two heads under one cap.

3. Lion with two winged bodies. Supporters: Left and Right, hare playing pipes.

4. Hunter sharpening knife on a flint. His hounds are beside him.

5. Griffin.

6. Angel holding a mitre.

7. Man's head with beard in ringlets.

8. Two jesters, each squeezing a cat under his arm and biting its tail.

9. Master seated birching a boy who is trying to protect himself with a book. Three other boys are looking on.

10. Two swans, with wings spread gorged, with one ducal coronet. Supporters: Left and Right, swans swimming.

South side from east
Upper Tier

1. Rose bush similar to North Upper 5. Supporters: Left and Right, spray of roses.

2. Lion with two winged bodies. Supporter: Left missing. Right, dog on leash.

3. Bear-baiting. Supporters: Left and Right, chained bear, that on right licking its paws.

4. Woman, with distaff and spindle, chasing fox carrying a cock. Two hens are left. Supporters: Left and Right, head with protruding tongue.

5. Foliated design.

6. Helmet with large chin-piece, crowned with a wreath and covered with a flowing mantle.

7. Monster.

8. Siren piping to two sailors (PLATE 13a).

9. Two-headed eagle. Supporters: Left, man's head in profile with cap. Right, woman's head in hood.

10. Winged monster.

11. Sir Yvain's horse cut into by the portcullis as he enters the enemy castle.

12. Dragon and a griffin confronted.

13. Lion mauling dragon.

14. Mounted knight in armour leaning back and picking up a horseshoe.

15. Helmet.

16. Two eagles scratching their feet.

17. Stag. Supporters: Left, hound. Right, kneeling camel (PLATE 10d).

Returned Stalls

1. Eagle with outstretched wings.

2. Two antelopes.

3. Angel (damaged) with feathered legs and outstretched wings. Supporters: Left, bishop seated on his throne with his staff in his left hand. Right, the Rector reading his office. (This was originally the Rector's stall.)

Lower Tier

1. Bird perched on tree.

2. Queen being crowned by two bird-like angels. (This may represent Anne of Bohemia, first wife of Richard II. She was granted the manor of Boston for three years, and on her petition the Guild of St. Mary was incorporated.)

3. The pillar to which Christ was bound and then scourged. Supporters: Left and Right, kneeling angels with censers.

4. Man being eaten by wolves; he still holds his sword in his hand.

5. Man, clad in skins and armed with a large club, fighting a lion. His shield lies on the ground behind him. With his left hand he seizes the lion by the mane. Supporters: Left, man, and Right, lion, before the fight.

6. Fox, dressed in cope trimmed with lace and holding a pastoral staff, preaching to two hens on his right. On his left is a fox wearing a ruff and holding an open book. Supporters: Left and Right, hen sitting on nest.

7. Hunter about to shoot a stag with a very large arrow.

8. Hunter, in his left hand a bow and under his arm two very large arrows. With his right hand he is defending himself from his wife, who has seized him by the chin and is threatening him with her distaff.

9. Two winged monsters, their necks encircled with a coronet.

10. Crowned and bearded heads.

The date of these misericords is said to be 1390 (F. Bond, *Misericords*, p. 226). The foundation-stone of the church was laid in 1309, and the nave and chancel built before the end of the fourteenth century (M. R. Lambert and R. Walker, *Boston, Tattershall and Croyland*, 1930, pp. 80–1).

St. Botolph's was not strictly speaking a collegiate church, but, as each of the medieval guilds of that town had a chapel in the church with its own priest, these would meet in the choir of the church to say daily offices and would use the misericords.

LINCOLN   The Minster   *Ninety-two*

North side
  Upper Tier

1. The Ascension of Christ. Kneeling Apostles gaze up at the feet of Christ and the hem of his garment as these disappear into a cloud. Supporters: Left and Right, censing angel on castellated corbel. (This was the Dean's stall.)

2. The Assumption of the Virgin, borne by angels (damaged). Supporters: Left, the angel of the Annunciation. Right, the Virgin Mary. Both hold scrolls.

3. Foliage. Supporters: Left and Right, pair of leaves.

4. Wyvern. Supporters: Left and Right, pair of leaves.

5. Two roses with buds and foliage. Supporters: Left and Right, single rose.

6. Foliate mask among oak-leaves and acorns. Supporters: Left and Right, pair of oak-leaves (PLATE 6b).

7. Conventional foliage springing from a cut branch. Supporters: Left and Right, single leaf.

8. Satyr, with hindquarters of a lion, hiding among oak-leaves. Supporters: Left, man-headed monster with cloven hind feet. Right, lion-headed monster with two lion's feet and a snake's tail.

9. Lion's mask with curled beard and mouth-foliage. Supporters: Left and Right, pair of large oak-leaves.

10. Man ploughing with two horses and two oxen. Man in centre (head lost). Supporters: Left, man harrowing with one horse. Right, seated figure (damaged) with two sacks of corn.

11. Griffin. Supporters: small birds of prey on small sprays of oak-foliage.

12. Lion and dragon fighting in a wood. Supporters: Left, wyvern. Right. Lion.

13. Conventional oak-leaves. Supporters: Left and Right, oak-leaf.

14. Mermaid with mirror and comb. Supporters: Left and Right, lion and large leaf.

15. Lion-mask with mouth-foliage. Supporters: Left and Right, lion-mask.

16. St. John the Evangelist (damaged) in a cauldron of boiling oil over a fire, a man on each side, one with bellows before the Latin Gate at Rome. Supporters: Left, forepart of a winged lion with a reptile's tail. Right, forepart of a griffin with a reptile's tail.

17. Conventional foliage. Supporters: Left and Right, foliate square.

18. Mask of a crowned man with long hair, beard, and moustaches. Supporters: Left and Right, profile head of moustached man with fillet round his head.

19. Vine. Supporters: Left and Right, vine-leaves, tendrils, and grapes.

20. Boy, riding a crane, attacked by two others. Supporters: Left, crane eating from a sack. Right, boy putting a stone into a sling with a dead crane behind him, two sacks, and a receptacle for carrying seed.

21. Conventional foliage. Supporters: Left and Right, foliate square.

22. Demon, with protruding tongue, holding a scroll in its claws. Supporters: Left and Right, wyvern.

23. Conventional oak-leaves. Supporters: Left and Right, foliage.

24. Sir Yvain mounted; his horse is trapped by the fall of a portcullis and only its hindquarters can be seen. Supporters: Left and Right, head of man-at-arms.

25. Bust of a figure wearing a fillet ornamented with flowers alternately large and small. Supporters: Left and Right, conventional leaf.

Returned Stalls

1. Lion sleeping under foliage. Supporters: Left and Right, lion curled up in the centre of a foliate square.

2. Wodehouse shaking down acorns. Supporters: Left and Right, pigs feeding under trees.

3. Foliage. Supporters: Left and Right, foliate square.

4. Wyvern. Supporters: Left and Right, wyvern.

5. Head of bearded man with short hair which curls over the fillet crossing his brow.
(Stalls 2, 3, 4, and 5 are those of four archdeacons.)

6. A knight attacked by dragons. Supporters: Left and Right, lion-mask with protruding tongue.
(This was the seat of the Precentor.)

Lower Tier

1. Lion with two bodies. Supporters: Left and Right, single lion.

2. Conventional foliage. Supporters: Left and Right, foliage.

3. Two cranes with foliage. Supporters: Left, lady with falcon on wrist. Right, two cranes fighting.

(The eight next stalls forming the middle block of the lower tier are un-carved.)

4. Lion-mask with mouth-foliage. Supporters: Left and Right, single leaf.

5. Oak-leaves. Supporters: Left and Right, oak-leaves and acorns.

6. Foliage and fruit. Supporters: Left and Right, single leaf.

7. The same.

8. Vine bearing grapes growing out of a whelk-shell. Supporters: Left and Right, vine-leaf.

9. Five roses. Supporters: Left and Right, spray of roses.

10. Pelican in her piety. Supporters: Left, bird preening its wings. Right, bird pecking the throat of its fledgling.

11. Mask of a bearded devil with long hair and mouth-foliage. Supporters: Left and Right, foliage.

12. Dragons fighting. Supporters: Left and Right, foliage.

Returned Stalls

1. Lion stamping among foliage. Supporters: Left and Right, rose.

2. Foliage. Supporters: Left and Right, single leaf.

3. Dead monkey carried on a bier by two others. Supporters: Left and Right, large single leaf.

4. Naked child arising from whelk shell to attack a dragon. Supporters: Left and Right, similar figures in shell.

(This subject also appears in misericord carvings in Chester Cathedral, Nant-wich, and Manchester Cathedral.)

South side
  Upper Tier

1. Man in armour said to be fighting a griffin, though there is not much appearance of actual fighting in the carving. Supporters: Left and Right, griffin.

2. Monster, half man, half lion, having a shield with a lion's head carved on it and bearing a lance with a pennon. Supporters: Left and Right, wyvern.

3. Wodehouse fighting a lion. Supporters: Left and Right, lion's mask with protruding tongue.

4. Lion and dragon fighting. Supporters: Left and Right, human-headed animal with forequarters draped in cloak.

5. Eagle in flight holding a ball. Supporters: Left and Right, pair of leaves.

6. King upon canopied throne, from the sides of which spring tree-roots and foliage. Supporters: Left and Right, figure standing in scroll with winged seeds of maple.

7. Foliate mask with leaves springing from the eyebrows to form a crown. Supporters: Left and Right, foliate square.

8. Long-haired beasts, back to back, climbing trees. Heads of birds in centre above. Supporters: Left and Right, monster like basilisk but with hoofs and hairy tail.

9. Bird-siren, crowned, with bat's wings, wading in water. Supporters: Left and Right, leaves.

10. Two lions counter rampant. Supporters, destroyed.

11. Foliage and acorns. Supporters: Left and Right, foliage.

12. Wodehouse riding a lion holding it by a chain. Supporters: Left and Right, foliate square.

13. Three rose-blooms. Supporters: Left and Right, single flower.

14. Man-headed winged monsters wearing pointed caps terminated by animals' heads. Supporters: Left and Right, monster with crane's body, lion's feet, and snake's tail which is coiled round its neck.

15. Two peacocks, their bodies crossing diagonally with a tree behind. A striking pattern. Supporters: Left and Right, two cranes drinking from a fountain.

16. Ape mounted on a unicorn and wearing a collar and chain and holding a mace faces another ape mounted on a lion and brandishing a staff. Supporters: Left and Right, pet dog on foliage.

17. Head and forepaws of a lion with mouth-foliage. Supporters: Left and Right, foliate square.

18. Seated woman (headless) holding the horse of a knight sleeping with his head in her lap. Supporters: Left, helmet with griffin's head as crest. Right, squire drawing sword (PLATE 4b).

19. Vine-leaves, tendrils, and grapes (damaged). Supporters: Left and Right, square leaf.

20. Lion climbing amongst foliage; small dragon lying at the foot of the tree. Supporters: Left and Right, foliate square.

21. Woman in flowing robe holding a man by the beard and preparing to strike with a sword (Judith and Holofernes). Supporters: Left and Right, foliate square.

22. Wodehouse fighting with griffin. Supporters: Left and Right, wodehouse.

23. Nativity and adoration of the Magi. The Virgin lies in bed holding the Child (both headless), another damaged figure stands behind. One king

kneels, another holds a gift, and the third points to the star. An ox and an ass in foreground. Supporters: Left, angel playing a portable organ. Right, angel (damaged).

24. Crowned head, the shoulders indicated as though seen from above. Supporters: Left and Right, head of moustached man with beard twisted into spiral curls, wearing flat fillet, decked with flowers round his head.

25. The Flight of Alexander. Supporters: fleur-de-lis.

Returned Stalls

1. Tristram and Iseult meeting under a tree in which King Mark has hidden. Supporters: Left, squire, headless, holding a sword. Right, waiting-woman with pet dog (PLATE 7*a*).

2. Capture of the unicorn. Supporters: Left, angel with harp. Right, a man-lion, headless, holding a shield.

3. Coronation of the Virgin (both figures headless). On each side a censing angel. Supporters: Left, angel with harp. Right, angel with a musical instrument.

4. Seated lion facing to the front. Wodehouse behind. Supporters: Left and Right, foliate square.

5. Knight in plate armour falling from his horse. Supporters: Left and Right, dragon. (The stall of the Sub-Dean.) (PLATE 7*d*.)

6. The Resurrection. Christ steps over the sleeping guard. Censing angels on each side. Supporters: Left, St. Mary Magdalene with a jar of spices. Right, Christ as the gardener, holding an iron-shod wooden spade. (PLATE 16*a*.)

Lower Tier

1. Lion and dragon fighting. Supporters: Left and Right, foliate square.

(The next nine seats are uncarved.)

2. St. George fighting the dragon. Supporters: Left and Right, lion.

3. Wyverns fighting. Supporters: Left and Right, dragon.

4. Eagle fighting dragon. Supporters: Left and Right, small birds of prey amongst foliage.

5. Lion and dragon fighting among oak-leaves. Supporters: Left and Right, dragon among foliage.

6. Web-footed lion-man. Supporters: Left and Right, lion.

7. Samson, wearing a cote-hardie (a short tunic covering the fork of the legs and fitting closely to the body and arms) and a hood with a liripipe, forcing open the jaws of a lion. Supporters: Left and Right, lion (PLATE 6*c*).

8. Two wyverns with their necks intertwined. Supporters: Left and Right, wyvern.

9. Monster with hind legs of a lion, bat-wings, a human head wearing hood with liripipe. Supporters: Left and Right, foliate square.

10. Centaur, with hind legs of a lion but with cloven hooves on front legs, holding a shield. Supporters: Left and Right, wyvern.

Returned Stalls

1. Foliage. Supporters: Left and Right, foliage.
2. Triple-arched canopy. Supporters, niches (now empty).
3. Wyvern. Supporters: Left and Right, small wyvern.
4. Demi-angel in feathered tights holding a crown. Supporters: Left and Right, square leaf with a face in the centre.

DATE: Late 14th century (M. D. Anderson, *Choir Stalls of Lincoln Minster*, 1951).

STAMFORD   Browne's Hospital   *Six*

In the chapel there are six returned stalls with carved misericords.

From the north

1. Bearded man with rayed halo, arms stretched out to height of head, left hand holding a disc, right hand missing. A bird's wing covers part of the naked torso. On the right there is also a body naked from waist, covered by a wing. Supporters: Left and Right, vine-leaf.
2. Birds with large beaks crossing one another; feet are like hedgehogs. Supporters: Left and Right, leaf.
3. Two birds, back to back, on a nest. Supporters: Left and Right, bird as if impaled, both wings half-outspread, head facing outward, with beak resting on the outside wing.
4. Two monsters with lion-shaped bodies and claw-like feet with four toes facing outwards. Supporters: Left and Right, monster rampant with head facing outwards.
5. Eagle with outspread wings on nest. Supporters: Left and Right, leaf.
6. Human face surrounded by a framework of elaborately carved leaves. Supporters: Left and Right, leaf.

DATE: c. 1480 (*J. C. Cox, Bench-ends in English Churches*, 1916 p. 118).

TATTERSHALL   Holy Trinity College Chapel   *Two*

In the north transept are two stalls with carved misericords. About 1754 the stained-glass windows in the choir were sold and it was left unglazed for fifty years with the result that the other stalls perished.

1. A crowned and bearded king (possibly Henry VI). Supporters: Left and Right, treasury purse (a symbol to denote Ralph Cromwell's office as Treasurer to that king).
2. Winged monster with bird's feet and very long snake-like tail. In front of it is a prone man (head missing). Supporters: Left and Right, dog's face.

DATE: Early 15th century. The college was founded by Ralph, Lord Cromwell, and the licence issued in 1439 (*V.C.H., Lincolnshire*, ii, p. 237).

LONDON

STEPNEY   The Royal Foundation of St. Katharine, Butcher
                                                          Row   *Thirteen*

In the modern chapel are fourteen stalls, thirteen with carved misericords. These misericords are in perfect condition owing to the fact that the hospital, then St. Katharine's by the Tower, was under the patronage of successive Queens of England. It was founded in 1148 by Queen Matilda, the wife of Stephen, and enlarged by Eleanor, widow of Henry III, in 1273. In 1350 Queen Philippa (d. 1369), wife of Edward III, founded a chantry there. In 1518 Henry VIII founded a fraternity there. In 1827, when St. Katharine's Dock was built, the hospital was transferred to the east side of Regent's Park, and in 1952 was installed in its present position on the site of St. John's Vicarage, Stepney.

Three stalls on each side are returned, and the corner-pieces are said to be faithful portraits of Edward III and Philippa, the latter closely resembling her effigy in Westminster Abbey, which was from a portrait by Liege in 1369.

1. Bust of bearded man wearing striped cap and cloak clasped at neck, with trailing drapery, knotted at back. Supporters: Left and Right, winged monster with long tail (PLATE 30*b*).

2. Grotesque head surrounded by foliage. Supporters: Left and Right, stiff leaf.

3. Man's head with long, thick moustache and forked beard. He wears a flat round cap. Supporters: Left and Right, leaf.

4. Man's head, with flowing hair and full, forked beard. Supporters: Left and Right, rose.

5. Angel playing bagpipe. Supporters: Left and Right, lion-mask (PLATE 30*c*).

6. Lion leaping on amphisbaena. Supporters: Left and Right, snake-monster. (PLATE 30*d*.)

7. Wyvern, with outstretched wings. Supporters: Left and Right, stiff leaf.

8. Pelican in her piety, with three chicks. Supporters: Left and Right, swan, with crown encircling its neck (PLATE 12*c*).

9. Woman riding man-headed beast (perhaps head of Aristotle). Supporters: Left and Right, grotesque face with protruding tongue, in square-foliage design.

10. Large leaf design. Supporters: Left and Right, stiff leaf.

11. Hawk pouncing on duck. Supporters: Left and Right, stiff leaf.

12. Elephant and castle, surmounted by crowned head and surrounded by foliage. Supporters: Left and Right, beast with man's head, one bearded, the other hooded. (PLATE 31*a*.)

13. Winged devil eavesdropping over two busts of women. Supporters: Left,

recording demon holding parchment. Right, centaur-like figure, with club and shield. (PLATE 15c.)

DATE: 1377. *R.C.H.M.*, *London*, ii, p. 89, suggests late fourteenth century.

SOUTH KENSINGTON Victoria and Albert Museum *Thirty-one*

1. Crouching man with feet curled up beneath him, elbows raised to level of his head. Supporters: Left and Right, acanthus-leaf.
Said to have come from Wells Cathedral. Date about 1330.

2. Foliage in high relief. Supporters: Left and Right, leaf. The seat is six-sided with slightly projecting point in front, and is bordered with a sunken moulding carved at intervals with quatrefoil rosettes. Said to have come from Lincoln Cathedral. Date about 1370.

3. Reclining nude man, bearded, leaning his head on his left hand, supporting the bracket. Said to have come from East Anglia. Possibly 14th century.

4. Two men in short tunics, threshing wheat with two flails. Supporters: Left and Right, blemya.

5. Man loading a farm cart with sheaves, which are passed to him on a fork by a woman. The horse turns his head to watch them. Supporters: Left and Right, grotesque bird, with head set on man's shoulders, the lower part covered by drapery.

6. Man piling sheaves in stook. A woman brings two more to him. Supporters: Left and Right, grotesque dwarf, cloaked and hooded.

7. Eagle, with wings extended, holding a scroll. Supporters: Left and Right, grotesque bird, the lower part covered by drapery.

Nos. 4, 5, 6, and 7, were thought to have come from St. Nicholas, King's Lynn, together with the six following, via the old Architectural Museum, Tufton Street, Westminster, in 1921, but a close scrutiny suggests that although they may have come from East Anglia they are not by the same hand as those from Lynn.)

8. Lion gorged and chained. Supporters: Left, a merchant's mark in initial W. Right, a tun, flowers, and leaves in an initial N.

9. Ecclesiastic praying at an altar on which is a book; behind is a sedile. Supporters: Left, an eagle in a letter N. Right, a floriated letter, possibly W.

10. Carver at work, with dog at his feet; two apprentices at work at a bench behind him, and one before him. Supporters: Left, an initial U and a saw. Right, an initial V and a gouge (PLATE 14b).

11. Stag hunted by hounds; at the side is a rabbit in its burrow. Supporters: · Left, a hunter's horn in a letter V. Right, a merchant's mark in a letter U.

12. Eagle grasping a rabbit. Two young rabbits look out of their burrows. Supporters: Left and Right, a five-petalled flower.

13. Fat lion, couchant regardant. Supporters: Left and right, a rose. From St. Nicholas, King's Lynn. 15th century.

In addition to the misericords already listed, of which the origin is known, there is a set of eighteen, probably of sixteenth-century date, the origin of which is unknown. They came into the possession of the Museum in 1910. It is possible that they may be Continental, as no comparable design surviving in this country comes to mind. The seat is plain, with a single rounded moulding, and there are no supporters. The order of the numbering has no significance, as most of the carvings are in store at Osterley House and at Bethnal Green Museum.

1. Two storks or cranes standing back to back, with their necks arched so that their heads touch over their backs.

2. Woman's head, in a flat head-dress with scarf drapery (PLATE 31b).

3. Man's head, with well defined features and protruding ears, wearing a biretta-like cap.

4. Woman's head, with parted lips, showing irregular teeth. She wears a close-fitting cap, that covers the ears.

5. Two amphisbaenae, standing back to back on a machicolated base.

6. Man in crouching position, with hands holding his head, as if the whole supports the bracket. He is wearing a long coat and boots.

7. Two parrots, with wings outspread, standing side by side on a T-shaped perch (PLATE 31c).

8. Two men dancing, with raised knees. They wear long-skirted coats. (PLATE 31d).

9. Owl with outspread wings.

10. Wyvern standing upright with outspread wings. One leg is raised and his neck turned, as if dancing.

11. Man's head, with bat's wings for ears, and having his mouth agape.

12. Two cockerels, facing each other with raised wings, as if fighting.

13. Small, plump dog, in profile.

14. Eagle, with raised wings, on a pedestal.

15. Basilisk, with raised wings, and its tail sweeping upwards between its legs.

16. Two bat-like creatures intertwined, with raised wings, possibly meant for wyverns.

17. Head of woman, wearing elaborate head-dress with flowing veil. The collar of her gown is pointed.

18. Two dancers facing each other, each having one arm raised and the other outstretched, with the hand resting on his companion's shoulder. They wear skirted coats, girdles with wallets hanging from them, and ankle boots with openings in the front of the anklets.

WESTMINSTER The Abbey, Henry VII's Chapel *Forty*

North side from east
Upper Range
First bay
All modern

Second Bay

1 and 2. Foliage.

3. Mermaid with comb in right hand and mirror in left; background of rocks and coral. Supporters: Left and Right, conventional flower and foliage.

4. Monster with beard, club in left hand, attacking dragon, apparently with several heads that are now broken off. Supporters: Left and Right, foliage and flower.

5. The Judgement of Solomon. King seated under canopied throne, two mothers at sides, dead child in front, three councillors beside throne, and on left a soldier about to cut the child in half. Supporters: Left, a small house, two women holding live baby, dead baby in front. Right, small house, woman exchanging dead baby for live one.

Third Bay

1. Forest scene; man, possibly Balaam, and ass (broken off). Supporters: Left, windmill with beast on steps. Right, winnowing-fan.

2. Forest scene; three monkeys, middle one seated in a cooking pot, right one assisting, left one seated with rose in hand (all heads broken off). Supporters: Left, man riding a goat (both heads gone). Right, man riding a unicorn.

3. Two monsters, right like a dog, left with scales and long tail, both chained to stump on which sits a falcon. Supporters: Left, goose riding fox. Right, fox riding goose (both damaged).

4. Large winged dragon. Supporters: Left, wingless dragon. Right, reptile looking at a serpent.

5. Seated man playing fiddle, and a woman with an unidentifiable object, possibly a musical instrument, in mouth. Her left hand and the main part of the object are missing. Both figures are nude. Supporters: Left and Right, water-flower.

Fourth Bay

1. Man and woman in early sixteenth-century dress, seated, man's arm round woman's waist, left hand in bag. Supporters: Left, wingless dragon. Right, sow playing pipe.

2. Devil carrying away monk. Supporters: Left, woman holding up hands in horror. Right, devil playing drum.

Returned Stall

Group of men in vineyard, one seated on barrel and one pushing him off with foot. Supporters: Left and Right, bunch of grapes.

Lower Range
First and Second Bays
All modern.
Third Bay

1, 2, and 3. Foliage springing from moulding. Supporters: Left and Right, conventional foliage boss.

4. Royal Arms with crown, and dragon on left, the other supporter lost. Supporters: Left, rose. Right, pomegranate.

5. Grotesque face and foliage. Supporters: Left and Right, conventional foliage boss.

6. Elaborate figure group: (*a*) on left David standing beside headless body of Goliath, (*b*) group of uncertain significance, possibly the return of David with the spoils of Goliath. Supporters: Left, David fighting Goliath; man and woman in castle at back. Right, Goliath reaching over walls of a castle.

7. Two wild men fighting with clubs, one with a heavy hat or cap. Supporters: Left and Right, boss of acanthus-leaves.

South Side from east
Upper Range
First Bay
All modern.
Second Bay

1. Grotesque face and foliage (a 'green man'). Supporters: Left and Right, conventional fruit and foliage boss.

2. Two winged dragons fighting. Supporters: Left and Right, conventional flower.

3. Three children, one in middle stripped and kneeling, one on left holding him down, one on right with birch. Supporters: Left and Right, conventional foliage.

4. Lion couchant. Supporters: Left and Right, arum.

5. Conventional foliage. Late 13th century (PLATE 32*a*).

Third Bay

1. Naked and bearded wild man fighting with bear. Supporters: Left and Right, conventional flower.

2. Man with club fighting two dragons (one with wings and head lost). Supporters: Left, man with three cranes. Right, Samson astride a lion, forcing its jaws open.

3. Foliage springing from moulding. Supporters: Left and Right, conventional flower.

4. Large winged dragon. Supporters: Left, wingless dragon. Right, beast looking at serpent.

5. Samson fighting lion, forcing jaws open. Supporters: Left, lion killing lamb. Right, lion licking itself.

Fourth Bay

1. Man and woman seated facing each other. There is some mutilation, but the woman appears to be holding the man's extended foot. Supporters: Left and Right, conventional flower.

2. Devil seizing tonsured clerk; bag of money on right. Supporters: Left, monkey playing drum. Right, two cocks fighting.

Returned Stall

Wild man with woman and four children, all nude; vines in background. Supporters: Left and Right, conventional flower.

Lower Range

First and Second Bays

All modern.

Third Bay

1. Monkey feeding female with young. Supporters: Left, chained bear playing bagpipes. Right, monkey drinking from flask.

2. Two monsters, one with wings. Supporters: Left and Right, nuts and foliage.

3. Two boys cock-fighting. Supporters: Left, boy with 'whirligig' and shield. Right, boy on hobby-horse.

4. Two wild men, one with shield and one with arrow. Supporters: Left and Right, conventional flower.

5. Seated man and woman in rustic surrounding amid foliage, apparently in conversation. Supporters: Left, naked child. Right, boy with bird.

6. Man with ball of yarn and winding frame (Hercules spinning), being beaten by woman with birch. Supporters: Left and Right, conventional flower.

7. Woman with distaff beating prone man. Supporters: Left, jester with eared cap. Right, man making a gesture with fingers.

All the stalls are sixteenth century except that on the south side, upper range, second bay, No. 5. The Revd. J. S. Purvis, 'Use of Continental Woodcuts and Prints by the "Ripon School" of Woodcarvers', *Archaeologia* lxxxv, identifies the following as derived from prints by Dürer and van Meckenen:

North side:
Upper row, fourth bay, No. 1 (Dürer).

South side:
Upper row, third bay, No. 5 (Dürer, *c.* 1496–8);
fourth bay, No. 1 (Dürer, *c.* 1495).
Lower row, third bay, No. 1 (van Meckenen); No. 5 (Dürer, *c.* 1496); No. 6 (van Meckenen); No. 7 (van Meckenen).

NORFOLK

ATTLEBOROUGH   St. Mary   *Two*

There are two stalls with misericords in the south aisle, one on each side near the screen.

1. Lion-mask with protruding tongue. Supporters: Left and Right, oak-leaf.
2. Head with full, curled beard and hair. Supporters: Left and Right, flower.

DATE: 15th century. A college of chantry priests was founded in 1405. (*V.C.H., Norfolk*, ii., p. 454).

AYLSHAM   St. Michael   *Four*

Four misericords have been detached from their stalls and built into the reredos.

1. Bearded man, with club and shield, fighting a dog-headed nude man armed with club and with shield slung on his back.
2. Man with club fighting griffin.
3. Man with sword raised in left hand, grasps with right hand the snout of an open-mouthed dragon.
4. Man's face with protruding tongue, wearing turban or loose cap.

All supporters: Left and Right, dragon.

DATE: *c.* 1470 (A. B. Whittingham draws my attention to several strong resemblances to later misericords (after 1472) in Norwich Cathedral, and to paintings on Aylsham screen given by J. Fannys (d. 1460)).

BINHAM   St. Mary   *Two*

There are two misericords of identical design, one on each side of the chancel. They show bearded heads with full, curled hair. Supporters: Left and Right, stiff leaf.

DATE: Probably 15th century.

BLAKENEY   St. Nicholas   *Six*

There were originally twenty-two stalls with misericords. Only six remain. The others have been added but make no pretence to being copies of the originals.

North side from east

1. Shield with the Knowles arms, *on a chevron, three roses, in chief a crescent charged with a mullet.*

2. Shield with the Wylton arms, *on a chevron, three crosses crosslet fitchée.*

3. A flying dragon.

4. Foliage.

North returned stall: Shield charged with the arms of Dalling, *two chevrons.*

South returned stall: Shield with the arms of Bardolf, *three cinquefoils.*

DATE: 14th century. In the reign of Edward III Thomas de Estley and Sir Edmund Bacon held one fee in the town of Lord Bardolf, who held it of the Bishop of Norwich (F. Blomefield, *History of Norfolk*, ix, Norwich, 1806, p. 362).

CASTLE ACRE   St. James   *Three*

From north

1. Angel holding plain shield. Supporters: Left and Right, stiff leaf.

2. Lion-mask. Supporters: Left and Right, stiff leaf.

3. Eagle with raised wings and head facing to rear. Supporters: Left and Right, rosette in lozenge-shaped leaf pattern.

DATE: Early 15th century, when the church was rebuilt (H. Monro Cautley, *Norfolk Churches*, Adlard, Ipswich, 1949, p. 185).

CASTON   The Holy Cross   *Two*

There are two misericords both of the face of a cherub surrounded by leaves. DATE: *c.* 1425, judging by cusped stops to mouldings and beaded knecking-roll mouldings to poppy-heads (information by letter from A. B. Whittingham).

CAWSTON   St. Agnes   *Three*

1. Two women seated facing each other. Supporters: Left and Right, foliage.

2. Man's head, probably a portrait, with long hair. Supporters: Left and Right, animal-masks.

3. Stag's head surrounded by foliage. Supporters: Left and Right, hound's head, looking inward, showing its teeth.

DATE: 15th century (E. Phipson, *Choir Stalls and their Carvings*, 1896, p. 121; *Country Life*, xviii (1905), p. 812).

CLEY   St. Margaret   *Six*

In the chancel of this church are six old oak stalls with misericords. They are all carved with the initials J. G., a merchant's mark, and the arms of the Grocers' Company, *a chevron between nine cloves, three, three, and three.* They probably date from the first half of the fifteenth century and are stated to have been at the base of the old screen, so forming returned stalls. Their measurements confirm this. The arms of the Grocers' Company were not granted until 1532, but the carving may well have been added by J. G. when they were repaired. J. G. may be the initials of John Greneway, a member of a family connected with Cley and Wiveton. The merchant's mark on the misericords is similar to that in Wiveton church. All are of floral subjects (B. Cozens-Hardy, *History of St. Margaret's, Cley*, 1928).

EAST HARLING   St. Peter and St. Paul   *Six*

There are six stalls with misericords in the chancel, four on the south side and two on the north side.

North side from west

1. Shield *parted per pale*: dexter *quarterly, 1st and 4th, on a bend cotised a crescent and three pairs of wings* (arms of Wingfield of Letheringham), *2nd and 3rd parted quarterly* (arms not identified); sinister *quarterly, 1st and 4th a unicorn salient* (arms of Harling of Suffolk), *2nd and 3rd semé de lys* (arms of Harlinge); over all an inescutcheon charged, *on chevron indented three escallops* (arms of Chamberlain). Supporters: Left, arms of Chamberlain. Right, shield charged *barry* (arms not identified).

2. Shield charged *quarterly, 1st and 4th, a fess between three lion-heads erased two and one* (arms of Lovell), *2nd and 3rd, on a bend cotised three pairs of wings* (arms of Wingfield). Supporters: Left, arms of Wingfield. Right, a *unicorn salient* (arms of Harling).

3. Shield *parted per pale*: dexter *quarterly, 1st, a chevron between three escallops with a label for difference* (arms of Wingfield), *2nd and 3rd, a saltire engrailed* (arms of Harling), *4th a chevron between three escallops*; sinister *quarterly, 1st and 4th, a unicorn salient, 2nd and 3rd, semé de lys*. Supporters: Left, shield charged *semé de lys*. Right, shield charged *a saltire engrailed*.

4. Shield *parted per pale*: dexter *three lions passant gardant with a label for difference* (arms unidentified); sinister *quarterly, 1st and 4th, a wolf salient* (arms of Lovell), *2nd and 3rd, chequy of fifteen* (arms of Warren). Supporters: Left, shield charged *a cross engrailed* (arms of Yngoldthorpe). Right, shield charged *six escallops, three, two, and one* (arms of Boynton, or Bonyton, of Suffolk). (PLATE 32*b*.)

North side from east

Both are later copies.

1. As for No. 1 South.

2. As for No. 3 South.

Sir William Chamberlain (d. 1462) and Sir Robert Wingfield (d. 1480) were the first and second husbands of Anne Harling. Sir William Chamberlain instituted the rebuilding of the church, which was continued by his successor.

EAST LEXHAM   St. Andrew   *Three*

This church has one stall; its misericord is of an angel. A box has been fitted beneath, and on the front of this is fixed another misericord, a winged dragon. Above the back of the seat is a third fine misericord, a man's head with curling hair and beard. All supporters: Left and Right, leaf. J. C. Cox, *County Churches, Norfolk*, Allen & Unwin, London, 1911, i, p. 62, says the carvings came from the stalls at Castle Acre Priory.

DATE: 15th century.

GRIMSTON   St. Botolph   *Six*

In the chancel are six stalls with misericords; one, the Rector's stall, has a fine head, probably a portrait. The other five have smaller crowned heads. All are well preserved.

DATE: 15th century (H. M. Cautley, *Norfolk Churches*, p. 202).

KING'S LYNN   St. Margaret   *Sixteen*

North side from west

1. Head wearing ermine-trimmed cap. Supporters: Left and Right, flower.
2. Head wearing cap and hood. Supporters: Left and Right, leaf.
3. Man's head. Supporters: Left and Right, foliage.
4. Foliage. Supporters: Left and Right, flower.
5. Shield charged *six escallop shells* (arms of Scales). Supporters: Left and Right, five-petalled flower.
6. Head of old man, with arms and hands supporting the bracket. Supporters: Left and Right, flower.
7. Foliage. Supporters: Left and Right, large formal leaf.
8. Head of man with curly hair and beard, his hands on each side of his head supporting the bracket. Supporters: Left and Right, acanthus-leaf.

South side from west

1. Head of Henry Despencer, Bishop of Norwich (1370–1407). Supporters: Left, shield charged *diapered, three mitres* (arms of the See of Norwich). Right, shield *parted quarterly, 1st, 2nd, 3rd, 4th, diapered, 1st and 4th, a bend, 2nd and 3rd, fretty* (arms of Despencer). From each shield depends a six-petalled flower.
2. Head of Edward the Black Prince. Supporters: Left, shield charged *three ostrich feathers*. Right, shield charged *diapered, six water bougets* (arms not recorded; Papworth gives no coats bearing as many as six).

3. Spray of flowers. Supporters: Left and Right, flower.

4. Foliage. Supporters: Left and Right, flower.

5. Head wearing cap bent sideways; the right hand, together with the head, supports the bracket; the left hand is bent downwards. Supporters: Left and Right, leaf.

6. Face with foliage springing from mouth. Supporters: Left and Right, leaf.

7. Foliage. Supporters: Left and Right, leaf.

8. Head of Edward III. Supporters: Left and Right, foliage.

The portrait heads are said to have been identified from monumental effigies.

DATE: 1370–7.

LITCHAM   All Saints   *Two*

From east

1. Crowned man's head, much defaced, with forked beard and curled hair. Supporters: Left and Right, large rosette in roundel.

2. Animal's head, much defaced, with short horns between the ears, possibly a goat. Supporters: Left and Right, formal stiff leaf.

DATE: Early 15th century. The screen dates from *c.* 1430 (J. C. Cox, *County Churches, Norfolk*, i, p. 62).

NORTH ELMHAM   St. Mary the Virgin   *One*

There are three old stalls in a block to the north of the west door. Although they all have hinged seats, the outer misericords are missing. The subject of the centre seat is missing, but the supporters are: Left and Right, stiff leaf.

DATE: Early 15th century.

NORWICH   St. Gregory   *Four*

There are four stalls with misericords on the south side of the sanctuary.

From east

1. Demi-angel in quilted doublet and square-necked tunic with arms raised and hands before him.

2. Bearded man in skirted tunic squatting with hands on knees. He has pointed shoes.

3. Winged lion passant, right regardant, standing on a long scroll, which rises to encircle his tail (emblem of St. Mark). (PLATE 3*a*.)

4. Seated angel in long flowing robes, holding large scroll (emblem of St. Luke). The right hand supporter is missing.

All supporters are forms of acanthus-leaves, and the edges of the brackets are ornamented with lozenge motif.

DATE: 15th century (J. C. Cox, *County Churches, Norfolk*, ii, pp. 169–70).

NORWICH St. Mary-at-Coslany *Six*

North side from east

1. Uncharged shield.
2. Uncharged shield.
3. Mitred head. Supporters: Left and Right, a hart courant, facing inward (head missing).

South side from east

1. Woman's head in wimple and gorget, at base of plain vaulting.
2. Small head with curled hair, at base of plain vaulting.
3. As No. 2, but head wears a flat cap.

All supporters are formal leaf in roundels, except where stated.

DATE: 15th century. The church was entirely rebuilt in 1477 (J. C. Cox, *County Churches, Norfolk*, ii, p. 176).

NORWICH St. Peter Mancroft *Two*

South side

Triple vaulting based on castellated corbels. Supporters: Left and Right, volute encircling design of grapes and vine-leaves.

North side

Similar to the other, but supporters: Left and Right, leaves and fruit.

DATE: 15th century (F. Blomefield, *History of the County of Norfolk*, iv, Part II, Norwich, 1806, p. 182).

NORWICH St. Stephen *Six*

There are six stalls with misericords, two on each side of the chancel and two on the south side of the sanctuary near the high altar.

North side of Chancel from east

1. Unicorn and tree. Supporters: Left, grotesque lion-mask. Right, foliate mask.
2. Entwined serpent or asp. Supporters: Left and Right, formal acanthus-leaf.

South side of Chancel from east

1. Small, grotesque head at foot of plain vaulting. Supporters: Left and Right, large, upright acanthus-leaf.

2. Mitred head at foot of plain vaulting. Supporters: Left and Right, large, upright acanthus-leaf.

In Sanctuary from east

1. Main subject broken off. Supporters: Left and Right, acanthus-leaf.

2. Headless griffin. Supporters: Left and Right, stiff leaf.

DATE: 16th century (H. Monro Cautley, *Norfolk Churches*, p. 230).

NORWICH   St. Margaret   *Two*

There are two fifteenth-century stalls with misericords. They were brought from St. Swithin's Church, which is now used as a furniture store. They are identical, having an uncharged shield, with supporters, Left and Right, being a large rosette encircled by a stalk entwined in cable form.

DATE: 15th century. J. C. Cox, *County Churches, Norfolk*, ii, p. 183, says there were at the time of writing (1911) six stalls at St. Swithin's.

NORWICH   The Cathedral   *Sixty-One*

The original number of stalls was seventy (as can be ascertained by the numerals incised on the back of the misericords), for the Prior, the Sub-Prior, and sixty monks, the Sacrist Precentor, the Bishop Chancellor, and four Archdeacons, but eight have been destroyed. Originally they formed one continuous row at the raised level. Their canopies blocked off the transepts, which were only opened out for the first time in 1851 for congregational use.

South side from west

1. Dean's stall (formerly the Bishop's?). The misericord has been lost.

2. Lion and dragon bite each other. Supporters: Left and Right, oak-leaf.

3. Bush of Lancaster roses (on modern board). Supporters: Left and right, rose.

4. Sir William Clere of Ormesby (d. 1384), in armour and cloak, holds a label and his wife, Denise Wichingham, reads her prayer-book (both headless); over his shoulder is W. Supporters: Left, shield charged with Clere arms, *on a fess three eagles*. Right, shield charged with Wichingham arms, *ermine, on a chief three crosses patee*.

5. Dragon. Supporters: Left and Right, lion's face with tongue out.

6. Seated monk reading a book. R C, above, stands for Richard Courtenay. Supporters: Left, as Bishop of Norwich (1413–15) he tends his sheep. Right, as Chancellor of Oxford (1411) he feeds his scholars.

7. Two wodehouses fight with clubs. Supporters: Left and Right, leaf.

8. St. George, mounted and in armour, spears dragon (spear broken); both beasts small in scale. Supporters, coats of arms. Left, Sir Thomas Hoo, *quarterly with a label impales two lions passant ermine* (for Eleanor Felton, his first wife, d. 1400). Right, St. Omer of Brundall, *a fess between six cross crosslets*.

9. Lion and collared bear fight. Supporters: Left, collared monkey. Right, squirrel eating nut.

10. John Clere, robed, with gloves and dagger at his girdle, and his mother, Denise Wichingham, praying with hands clasped round rosary at her belt. Supporters: Left, Wichingham arms. Right, Clere arms (See South 8).

11. Wodehouse with club; two chained lions paw his knees; a scroll 'War Foli: wat' ('Beware of folly, man'). Supporters: Left, wodehouse clutching ear of dog that bites his hand. Right, two lambs.

12. Young King Henry V. Supporters: Left and Right, leaf.

13. Eagle claws dove and pecks lamb. Supporters: Left and Right, death-mask in profile, wreathed.

14. Wyvern. Supporters: Left and Right, small wyvern.

15. Seated angel holds scroll (emblem of St. Matthew). Supporters: Left and Right, herald angel.

16. Bare-legged wrestlers at the ready; fashionable seconds have tall hats and puffed or slit sleeves. Supporters: Left, boar and acorns. Right, man crowned on neck.

17. Two bare-legged men in leather helmets spear a lion who mauls a man wearing drawers below tunic. Supporters: Left and Right, wyvern.

18. Ape in hood squeezes howling dog that is birched by chained ape; another dog looks on grinning. Supporters: Left and Right, chained ape blows pipes.

19. Missing.

20. Missing.

21. Angel holding girdle. Supporters: Left and Right, leaf.

22. Bishop's head, mitre worn sideways. Supporters: Left and Right, dove on cloud.

23. Man's face sprouting foliage. Supporters: Left and Right, leaf.

24. Owl in a vine mobbed by small birds. Supporters: Left and Right, eagle pecking dove (PLATE 12a).

25. Man in jerkin spears griffin which claws a lamb. Supporters: Left and Right, lion-mask with tongue out.

26. Winged lion with scroll (emblem of St. Mark). Supporters: Left and Right, formal flower.

27. Winged ox with scroll. Supporters: Left and Right, angel's head.

28. Schoolmaster thrashes boy; four others read books. Supporters: Left and Right, schoolboy writing a scroll.

29. Ox boldly carved (square flowers on edge of seat). Supporters: Left and Right, leaf.

30. Fox running away with a cock; dog chasing him; woman with distaff; pig eating broth. Supporters: Left and Right, back view of rose.

31. Man with club holds lion by chain (broken). Supporters: Left and Right, lion, with tufted mane, curled up.

32. Lion (mane is of wavy early thirteenth-century type); square flowers along seat edge. Supporters: Left and Right, leaf.

33 to 35. Destroyed by 1630 for Bishop's throne and Chancellor's seat.

36. Hooded pilgrim rising out of a shell, holds dagger and packsaddle. Supporters: Left and Right, wingless wyvern.

On North side from west

1. Vice-Dean's stall. Seat lost.

2. Seat missing.

3. Virgin crowned by two angels and child holding dove. Supporters: Left, arms of William de Ufford, Earl of Suffolk (d. 1382), *sable a cross engrailed or, with bendlet sinister.* Right, arms of John Lestrange (d. 1375), *gules two lions argent, semé de molets.* Both married Isabella Beauchamp of Warwick.

4. Sir Robert de Illey of Plumstead (d. 1398), helmet laid aside, bearing his armorial shield charged, *ermine two chevronels sable*; his hair is fluffed out round his head. Supporters: Left, arms of Sir Thomas Hoo of Brunvald (d. 1420). Right, arms of Sir Robert de Ufford of Wrentham, *sable a cross engrailed or, a bendlet impales Felton* (see South 8). Both married Eleanor Felton.

5. Bearded huntsman blowing horn, with bow (broken) and arrows, stags, and dogs. Supporters: Left, stag. Right, two stags.

6. Naked man bitten by lion and two dragons. Supporters: Left and Right, vine-leaves and grapes.

7. Sir William Wingfield of Letheringham (d. 1378) and his wife Margaret hand in hand and small dogs. Supporters, their arms: Left, Wingfield, *on a bend three pairs of wings.* Right, Boville, *quarterly.*

8. Angel with harp, crown, and viols (head lost).

9. Mermaid suckling lion; mirror on a couch. Supporters: Left and Right, dolphin swallowing its young (PLATE 8c).

10. Hawk. Supporters: Left, face rayed by hair. Right, the same crowned.

11. St. Michael slays seven-headed dragon. Supporters: Left and Right, leaf.

12. Pelican in her piety Supporters: Left and Right, pelican (heads lost).

13. Samson astride lion, rending its jaws. Supporters: Left, crane. Right, owl with mouse in beak.

14. Ape riding leering beast, backwards, holding its tail and beating it. Supporters: Left and Right, ape apparently with toothache, holding birch.

15. Cow-headed leopard. Supporters, lost.

16. Man (Anger), lurching on a restive boar, grits his teeth and draws his sword. Supporters: Left and Right, leaves and berries.

17. Owl mobbed by little birds. Supporters: Left and Right, crested bird.

18. Man (Greed), with his cap falling off, wearing pointed boots and riding a sow, holds a tankard in each hand. Supporters: Left and Right, beaked merman.

19. Angular corbel on small head with hair on each side. Supporters: Left and Right, leaf.

20. Over-dressed man (Vanity) holding stick with three dogs. Supporters: Left and Right, leaf.

21. Antelope showing its two horns. Supporters: Left and Right, leaf.

22. Devil as wyvern. Supporters: Left and Right, face, with almost-Victorian side-whiskers, but with shaved crown, upper lip, and chin.

23. Man (Lechery), dressed in net and tall hat, riding a hart gripping its horn with one hand, holding a hare in the other. Supporters: Left and Right, blemya (i.e. man with face on the chest) with dagger.

24. Shaggy calf with four-toed forefeet (bracket and supporters lost).

25. Wyvern whispers into lion's ear. (The Tempter.) Supporters: Left and Right, wild rose.

26. Pomegranates sprouting from corners of mouth of scowling mask. Supporters: Left and Right, curled leaf.

27. Satan as a wyvern. Supporters: Left only, leaf.

28. Castle with domed tower, trees in court, portcullis raised, and gate ajar. Supporters: Left and Right, leaf.

29. Ape, hopping on one foot (Lust), raised in barrow, birching two apes pushing it. Supporters: Left and Right, man-headed wyvern.

30. Rich-turbanned, two-faced man (Deceit) soothes his smiling dupe but puts his tongue out at a snarling underling.

31. Two dogs lean grinning over ape; two more dogs grinning. Supporters: Left and Right, pomegranate.

32, 33, 34, and 35. Destroyed.

36. Wodehouse with club in an oak sits on chained lion. Supporters: Left and Right, eagle pecking wing or claw. (This is a separate stall on the north of the High Altar.)

The now accepted dates of the misericords are about 1420 for the western stalls, about 1480 for those below the tower and just west of it, and about 1515 for a few at the east.

The 1420 misericords are South 2 to 12, North 3 to 11, North 13, and North 36. The 1480 ones, South 13 to 18, South 21 to 28, South 30, 31, 36, and North 12, North 14 to 18, and North 20 to 31. The remainder are those of 1515. A. B. Whittingham, *Friends of Norwich Cathedral Report*, 1948.

NORTH WALSHAM   St. Nicholas   *Two*

There are two stalls with misericords standing at the west end of the church behind the font.

1. Crowned king's head, with triple-forked beard. Supporters: Left and Right, large rosette in circular pattern of leaves.

2. Wodehouse, or wild man, in tree, holding a large club over his left shoulder with both hands. Supporters: Left, wyvern. Right, missing.

DATE: 15th century. The church was destroyed in the Peasant Rising of 1381, so it is safe to assume that rebuilding took place soon after that date, and the ledge pattern is consistent with this.

RANWORTH   St. Helen   *Four*

There are six stalls, three on each side of the chancel, all returned. They have four misericords, two on each side in the seats nearest the aisle. The stalls are thought to have been rescued from St. Benet's Priory, which stood on the marshes to the north-east.

1. Vaulted corbel, with, at foot, small grotesque head with pointed ears. Supporters: Left, four-petalled flower. Right, same reversed.

2. Plain vaulting on corbel. At head of vaulting, a tracery pattern. Supporters: Left, grotesque human face with protruding tongue. Right, small rosette in circlet of leaves.

3. At foot of plain vaulting, a small, fat human face with banded flat cap. A tracery pattern at head of vaulting. Supporters: Left, geometrical design of interlaced loops. Right, geometrical design of two interlaced triangles within a roundel; at centre of this a small rose.

4. Head and body of crouching man, with right hand on waist and left hand on knee, legs broken away except for right foot. He wears a belted tunic and round cap with upturned edge. Supporters: Left, rosette. Right, tracery pattern in roundel.

DATE: 15th century.

SALHOUSE   All Saints   *One*

1. A large, full-faced, bearded and moustached head with flowing hair. Supporters: Left and Right, stiff leaf.

DATE: mid 15th century (information from A. B. Whittingham).

SALLE   St. Peter and St. Paul   *Twenty-Six*

North side from east

1. Large, upright lily-flower. Supporters: Left and Right, similar large bloom from end of the bracket.

2. Single large rose. Supporters: Left and Right, similar larger rose.

3. Turbaned head of a man with long hair. He seems of Moorish type, and the top of a V-cut scalloped robe can just be seen. Supporters: Left and Right, rose in lozenge form, surrounded by a circlet of petals.

4. Heraldic spray of three hawthorn-flowers arranged in circular form. Supporters: Left and Right, similar.

5. Grotesque, grinning head with prominent teeth and radiating locks of hair and mane, perhaps a lion. Supporters: Left and Right, large double rose.

6. Turbaned Moorish head with long, flowing hair and forked beard. Supporters: Left and Right, formal sycamore-leaf.

7. Bunch of three strawberries enfolded in leaves. Supporters: Left and Right, large strawberry-leaf.

8. Leopard-mask with large human ears. Supporters: Left and Right, large rose.

9. Double sunflower or marguerite. Supporters: Left and Right, large similar flower.

10. Male head with open mouth and long hair, and wearing a scalloped or frilled flat cap. Supporters: Left and Right, formal vine-leaf.

11. Half-open sunflower, upright. Supporters: Left and Right, similar, pendant.

12. Grinning lion-mask with large ears. Supporters: Left and Right, large vine-leaf on curved stem.

13. Open pomegranate fruit. Supporters: Left and Right, large similar fruit.

South side from east

1. Large heraldic lily, upright. Supporters: Left and Right, large similar flower, pendant.

2. Large fruit or seed-pod fully open, pendant, with upturned petals, possibly honeysuckle. Supporters: Left and Right, formal conventional leaf on upturned stem.

3. Large double rose, pendant and fully open. Supporters: Left and Right, branched stem ending in three small roses (PLATE 32c).

4. Two small strawberries encased in foliage. Supporters: Left and Right, larger similar design.

5. Large sunflower. Supporters: Left and Right, large similar fruit.

6. Double rose, fully open. Supporters: Left and Right, larger similar rose.

7. Double rose, fully open. Supporters; Left and Right, larger similar rose.

8. Large, intricately cut rose-bloom depending from bunch of leaves. Supporters: Left and Right, larger similar pattern.

9. Open pomegranate fruit, similar to North 13. Supporters: Left and Right, larger similar fruit.

10. Spray of three small water-lilies, backed by open leaf. Supporters: Left and Right, similar pattern (PLATE 32d).

11. Large male head with flowing, elaborately curled hair, beard, and moustache, and furrowed brow. Supporters: Left and Right, large acanthus-leaf.

12. Pair of dolphins facing each other, leaping from waves. Supporters: Left and Right, double rose of simple five-lobed form.

13. Clean-shaven male head wearing elaborate upturned cap in shape of serrated leaves. Supporters: Left and Right, large sunflower (PLATE 33a).

In all cases the central motif forms the base of simple vaulting.

DATE: 15th century, the church throughout being of this period. On an arm rest on the south side is a woman's head with hair in side-cauls of mid fifteenth-century style.

STIFFKEY   St. Mary   *Two*

The outer two stalls have misericords of identical design. The centrepiece consists of a vaulting of five ribs springing from a corbel with small scalloped ornament. Supporters: Left and Right, formal type of lotus or lily, encircled by the stem.

DATE: 15th century, probably *c.* 1450–80 (information from A. B. Whittingham).

THOMPSON   St. Martin   *Four*

The College was founded in 1349 by Sir Thomas and Sir John Shardelow (*V.C.H., Norfolk*, ii, p. 461).

North side from east

1. Missing.

2. Mitred head with curled side-locks of hair. Supporters: Left and Right, simple three-lobed leaf.

3. Missing.

4. Man's head with curled hair framing the face. Supporters, missing.

5. Missing.

South side from east

1 and 2. Missing.

3. Arms of Shardelow family, *on a chevron a mullet, the whole between three crosses crosslet fitchy.* Supporters: Left and Right, similar to main subject.

4. Missing.

5. As for No. 3, but supporters missing.
6. Missing.

DATE: Late 14th or early 15th century.

TILNEY   All Saints   *Eighteen*

One has a man's head. The remainder have carved corbels in various designs, mostly of foliage. The supporters are leaves.

DATE: *c.* 1420 (J. C. Cox, *County Churches, Norfolk*, ii, p. 158).

TRUNCH   St. Botolph   *Six*

North side

1. Demi-angel (head mutilated) bearing shield charged with a *St. George's cross*.
2. Demi-angel bearing shield charged with a *cross saltire*.
3. Demi-angel bearing shield charged with a *St. George's cross*.

South side

1. Head with curled beard and full moustache, wearing flat cap with side-flaps.
2. Leopard- or tiger-mask with teeth bared. The two rows of teeth are well defined.
3. Head, bearded and moustached, with flowing curled hair under flat, ridged cap.

All supporters, formal leaf.

DATE: 1502, contemporary with the rood-screen (J. C. Cox, *County Churches, Norfolk*, i, p. 184).

WALPOLE   St. Peter   *Four*

In the chancel of this church remain only four misericords, which rest on stone supports.

North side from east

1. Large head in a circle (badly damaged).
2. Eagle. Supporters: Left and Right, leaf.
3. Pelican in her piety. Supporters: Left and Right, leaf.
4. Missing.

South side from east

1. Bird. Supporters: Left and Right, leaf.

The remaining misericords are missing.

DATE: *c.* 1420 (J. C. Cox, *County Churches, Norfolk*, ii, p. 160).

WEST LYNN St. Peter *Two*

North side

Three figures, mutilated, in long robes. Only the lower parts of the robes and the heads of flanking figures remain. Supporters: Left, the letter M in a roundel. Right, the letter L in a roundel.

South side

Two clerical figures in centre (mutilated), between trees; on the left an angel in prayer, and on the right what appears to be the head of an ox. Supporters: Left, the letter A in a roundel. Right, the letter D in a roundel.

DATE: Late 15th century. A. B. Whittingham by letter suggests 1500, and states that the letters A.D.M.L. on the supporters may have this interpretation. He also suggests that the details are consistent with this assumption, especially the shoulder-terminal of grouped rounds in plan, and the type of lettering.

NORTHAMPTONSHIRE

BENEFIELD St. Mary *Four*

North side from east

1. Floral design. Supporters: Left and Right, rosette.
2. Returned stall. A plain corbel with three small, round knobs at the base.

South side from east

1. Rayed lion's head. Supporters: Left and Right, lion's head.
2. Returned stall. Similar to North 2.

The two returned stalls appear to be modern.

DATE: 15th century. They are said to have come from Fotheringay which was founded in 1411 (H. K. Bonney, *Fotheringay*, 1821, p. 69).

GAYTON St. Mary *Six*

North side from west

1. Woman, in a long, flowing robe fastened at the waist with a rose brooch, standing holding out arms on either side, under which are four small nude figures, two on each side, clinging to her hem. Clouds round woman's head. (The Blessed Virgin protecting souls.) Supporters: Left and Right, flowers and foliage.
2. Fight between a lion and a dragon, over a small animal which may be the lion's cub. Supporters: Left, human-headed quadruped holding a fish in its claws. Right, dragon curled up.

3. Large figure of a devil clothed in feathers and with cloven hooves, a shield on his right arm, astride two prone human figures. They are holding a rosary and they both wear flat caps. (The Devil eavesdropping on chatterers. See Enville, Staffs., and New College, Oxford.) Supporters: Left, an ape. Right, man in short tunic kneeling before a mutilated object, behind him a cushion, at his left side a hammer (PLATE 16b).

South side from west

1. Three figures in long robes seated before an arcaded building. (Possibly the Three Women at the Sepulchre.) Over the central figure is a mutilated object which may have been the Angel. Supporters: Left and Right, crown ending in a scallop shell from which issues foliage.

2. Figure seated on a throne, four small figures on each side. (Probably the Last Judgement.) Supporters: Left and Right, sunflower and leaves.

3. The Entry into Jerusalem. Child shouting 'Hosannah' on the battlements. Supporters: Left and Right, grapes and leaves.

Numbers 2 and 3 are apparently fourteenth century, very similar to those in St. Katharine's Hospital, London. The other four are dated fifteenth-century.

Arthur Gardner pointed out to Lady Trenchard Cox that the supporters of North 1, and all the south misericords, are obviously later than the central carvings, and suggested that these might even be foreign work (having subjects rare in England) set into new seats in the 17th century. The misericords are said to have come from Dunston Abbey, and when the Gifford family sold Dunston in the 17th century a member of the family was Rector of Gayton, and may have retained the misericords for his church.

GREAT DODDINGTON   St. Nicholas   *Four*

In the chancel are four stalls, two on each side. These were formerly returned, but are now against the north and south walls.

South side from west

1. Carver seated at a bench with his tools, at work on a rose. Supporters: Left and Right, large rosette encircled by the stem. Compare Wellingborough (PLATE 14a).

2. Vine-leaves and grapes issuing from the mouth of a small head. Supporters: Left and Right, stiff leaf. (PLATE 33b.)

North side from west

1. A rose surrounded by leaves. Supporters: Left and Right, formal leaf (PLATE 33c).

2. Spray of formalized oak-leaves. Supporters: Left and Right, rosette in lozenge pattern of leaves.

DATE: Late 15th century. In 1415 Henry V allowed the nuns of Delapré Abbey to appropriate the church in exchange for the advowson of Fotheringay, and mass-priests were installed (Revd. R. H. Cromwell, *History of Great Doddington*, p. 33.)

GREAT OAKLEY   St. Michael   *Four*

There are four fine stalls with misericords set against the south wall of the chancel. Report has it that they were removed from the near-by Cistercian Abbey of Pipewell at the Dissolution, but the shape of the bracket suggests that the work is of later date than the Dissolution. One misericord (No. 3) bears part of the arms of the Brooke family, who have lived in Oakley Hall, in the grounds of which the church stands, since the days of Edward IV. The arms of Pipewell were *three crescents impaling a crozier in pale.*

From west to east

1. Father Time with his scythe and hour glass.
2. Grotesque head, with flowing hair in the form of leaf patterns.
3. Demi-angel holding shield charged *on a fess, three escallops.* On his forehead is a fillet surmounted by a cross.
4. Pelican in her piety, with one chick, the whole surrounded by elaborate leaf scrolls.

DATE: Very late 16th or early 17th century.

HEMINGTON   St. Peter and St. Paul   *Ten*

These stalls are believed to have been brought from Fotheringay (H. K. Bonney, *Fotheringay*, p. 67).

North side

1. Dragon. Supporters: Left and Right, small dragon-head.
2. Crown. Supporters: Left, broken off. Right, crown with leaves issuing.
3. Hawk in fetterlock (badge of the House of York). Supporters: Left and Right, perches.
4. Cellarer with flagon. Supporters: Left, a flagon. Right, two casks or tuns (PLATE 33*d*).
5. Mermaid. Supporters: Left and Right, fish.

South side

1. Owl. Supporters: Left and Right, twig with acorn, and with small bird perching thereon.
2. Tailed beast with human head in monk's hood. Supporters: Left and Right, hooded faces.
3. Tumbler, standing on his head and hands. Supporters: Left and Right, turbaned head (PLATE 34*a*).
4. Two boars saltire-wise. Supporters: Left and Right, oak-twig with acorn.

5. Helm and mantling, from which foliage radiates to form the supporters.
DATE: 15th century.

HIGHAM FERRERS   St. Mary   *Twenty*

North side from east

1. Mythological animal with a tail and outspread bat-like wings.
2. Bird with outspread wings and a halo. Supporters: Left and Right, bust of angel with wings outspread.
3. Head of old bearded man with prominent teeth. Supporters: Left and Right, oak-leaf and acorns.
4. Contorted bird. Supporters: Left, plover. Right, snipe or woodcock.
5. Man's head with a small forked beard and moustaches which extend along the cheeks. Supporters: Left and Right, leaf.
6. A sudarium or Veronica's handkerchief (the legend is that when Christ was on his way to Calvary a woman wiped the sweat from his face with a napkin, which thereupon took the impress of his features). Supporters: Left, woman's head with elaborate head-dress. Right, man's head wearing a chaperon.
7. Two dragons back to back, apparently eating snakes. Supporters: Left, man's head with forked beard and long hair. Right, similar head with cap.
8. Foliage. Supporters: Left and Right, leaves.
9. Lion with formal tree behind. Supporters: Left and Right, rosette in leaves.
10. Chichele arms held by an angel. Supporters: Left and Right, rose.

South side from east

1. Lion. Supporters: Left and Right, rosette.
2. Foliage. Supporters: Left and Right, very formal Renaissance-like drop-pendant.
3. Man's head. Supporters: Left and Right, the same.
4. Woman's face with no hair showing. Supporters: Left and Right, the same.
5. Angel. Supporters: Left, eaten away by woodworm. Right, hanging foliage with shield showing primatial cross and pallium.
6. Crowned male head. Supporters: Left, woman's head in a cap with hair in a caul. Right, woman's head in a wimple.
7. Animal with human face, wings, dwarf body, and backward-turned feet. Supporters: Left, man's head. Right, woman's head.
8. Pelican in her piety (head missing). Supporters: Left and Right, pendant of formal foliage.

9. Foliate mask. Supporters: Left and Right, pendant of formal foliage.

10. Portrait of the Archbishop. Supporters: Left and Right, clerk in skull-cap.

DATE: Early 15th century.

Archbishop Chichele, who was a native of Higham Ferrers, founded a chantry college there in 1422, the year after he became Archbishop of Canterbury. The college consisted of eight canons, four clerks, and six 'singing men', whose duty it was to pray for Henry V, his Queen, and the Archbishop during their lives and after their deaths (*V.C.H., Northants*, ii, p. 177).

HOLDENBY   All Saints   *Eight*

There are eight stalls with misericords, four on each side of the chancel. They are of fourteenth-century date, and all except three have been severely damaged.

North side from east

1. Head and bust of a putto or cherub, with raised wings. He has strongly defined curls, and wears a cape with a leaf-edged scalloped pattern. Supporters: Left and Right, long S-shaped volute ending in a simple leaf (PLATE 34*b*).

2. Central carving missing, though there remain traces of small flower-buds and a suggestion that a winged creature may have been portrayed. Supporters: Left and Right, long S-shaped volute looped, and ending in a four-petalled leaf of oak-pattern.

3. Central carving missing, except for traces at sides of flowers with long stamens. Supporters: Left and Right, volute ending in a whorl-pattern of leaves in the centre of which appears a small four-petalled flower.

4. A corbel-shaped intricate pattern of leaves with flower-heads to right and left, and at base a small opened flower. Supporters: Left and Right, long S-shaped volute ending in large fruit.

South side from east

1. Dragon passant (headless) with raised wings and tail, which supports the bracket. Supporters: Left and Right, long S-shaped volute similar to those of North 1.

2. Large, winged creature (headless) facing the front, and having wings raised as if in flight; possibly an eagle. Supporters, as for No. 1.

3. Central carving missing. Supporters, as for No. 1.

4. Bust of an ape-faced creature with long ears and wearing a skull-cap and cape-shaped tunic buttoned at the front. He has raised wings, carries on his

shoulder a small ape, and holds before him a drum, which he beats with a stick. Supporters: Left and Right, long S-shaped volute ending in a large flower with a pomegranate-like centre.

IRTHLINGBOROUGH   St. Peter   *Five*

There are four stalls on each side of the chancel. Four have plain moulded corbel misericords, and the first on the north side from the east has a demi-angel crowned, with outspread wings, holding an uncharged shield. The remaining carvings have been destroyed.

DATE: Late 14th century. A college was founded *c.* 1373 by John Pyel (d. 1388) (N. Pevsner, *Northamptonshire*, p. 258).

ISHAM   St. Peter   *One*

There is one stall, returned, on the south side of the chancel, forming part of a double bench. It has a misericord dating from the 14th or early 15th century.

The central carving is of a small female head, with long curled hair, parted in the centre and framing the features. It is very delicately carved. The supporters are formal stiff-leaved designs.

Cox and Harvey (*English Church Furniture*, p. 260) mention two stalls with misericords, as also does Arthur Mee (*Northamptonshire*, p. 177), but the writer found no trace of a second misericord (September 1962).

PASSENHAM   St. Guthlac   *Twelve*

The misericords in this church were in an advanced state of decay, having been removed from their stalls, and in some instances broken up, but were fortunately recovered in their entirety, and have recently been painstakingly reassembled, together with their matching canopies, although, in the case of the south side, not placed in their original order. Wall-paintings of apostles, contemporary and identical with the stall canopies, were being uncovered when the writer visited the church in September 1962.

North side from east

1. Grotesque human head.
2. Arms of the founder, Sir Robert Banastre, supported by winged cherubs, (headless) holding torches (*cross patonce impaling ermine, on two bars six mullets*).
3. Recumbent bull.
4. Head of a satyr.
5. Recumbent goat.
6. Head of cherub.

South side from east

1. Wyvern. Supporters: Left and Right, grapes and vine-leaves.
2. Grotesque head, flanked by goats' heads. Supporters: Left and Right, cornucopia.
3. Agnus Dei.
4. Grotesque human head, resembling North 4, except that the ears are smaller and feline.
5. Headless lion passant.
6. Head of cherub, similar to North 6.

Except where stated, supporters are fruit and leaves.

DATE: 1628

PETERBOROUGH   The Cathedral   *Three*

In the south aisle are three carved misericords which were removed from the original stalls in the choir.

1. Pigeon. Supporters: Left and Right, foliage.
2. Fox seizing a goose by the neck and running away. Supporters: Left and Right, cock with spurs.
3. Bearded head. Supporters: Left and Right, shield uncharged, *parted per pale*.

DATE: 14th century (Canon R. E. Sibthorp, *Short Guide to Peterborough Cathedral*, 1943, p. 6).

ROTHWELL   Holy Trinity   *Seven*

North to south

1. Saracen's head with a cap turned up back and front, with a rose in the centre. Supporters: Left and Right, formal leaf.
2. Angel holding an uncharged shield. Supporters: Left and Right, formal leaf.
3. Saracen's head with long hair and beard; the eyes have neither lids nor pupils. Supporters: Left and Right, formal leaf.
4. Winged lion of St. Mark courant, and holding a scroll in his mouth and paws. Supporters: Left and Right, formal leaf.
5. Angel with quilted garment and outspread wings, holding some kind of weapon with a broad blade. Supporters: Left and Right, formal leaf.
6. Blank.
7. Saracen's head wearing a turban. Supporters: Left and Right, small animal resembling wyvern passant gardant, except that the right-hand one has a turbaned head instead of a tail.

8. Head of a lady wearing a head-dress. Supporters: Left and Right, formal leaf.

Emma Phipson (*Choir Stalls and their Carvings*, 1896, p. 43) refers to four saracens' heads, but appears to have misinterpreted No. 5.

DATE: Probably late 15th century. This appears to be confirmed by the head-dress of V-roll with draped veil in No. 8.

STANFORD-ON-AVON   Holy Trinity with St. James
the Greater   *One*

In the chancel is one misericord of a conventional floral design.

DATE: Probably 14th century (*Archaeological Journal*, cxii (1955), pp. 192 f.).

TANSOR   St. Mary   *Seven*

North side from east

1. Four ostrich feathers in a vertical position and above them four similar placed horizontally. Supporters: Left, fetterlock. Right, rosette. These are Yorkist badges.

2. Floral design. Supporters: Left and Right, rosette.

3. The head and bust of an angel with wings outspread, holding horizontally a musical instrument (perhaps a viol) in both hands. Supporters: Left and Right, open knot.

4. Angel seated with wings outspread, holding a similar but larger instrument to that in No. 3 in the same position. Supporters: Left and Right, man's head wearing hat and showing formal curls.

South side from east

1. Woman's head in wide horned head-dress. Supporters: Left, man's head wearing a cap. Right, woman's head and neck.

2. Eagle with head turned to the right and wings outspread. Supporters: Left, fetterlock. Right, rosette. All Yorkist badges.

3. Similar eagle with head turned to the left. Supporters: Left and Right, fetterlocks.

DATE: 15th century. Said to have come from Fotheringay (H. K. Bonney, *Fotheringay*, 1821, p. 67).

WELLINGBOROUGH   All Saints   *Six*

North side from west

1. Fox running away with a goose. A branch of a tree on the right. Supporters: Left and Right, ball of foliage.

2. Mermaid, her tail to the left and her arms upheld. In her right hand she holds a comb, in her left a mirror. The sea is represented on the right side. Supporters: Left and Right, fish.

3. Woodcarver at work wearing a hood, a jerkin with sleeves puffed out at the shoulders, hose, and pointed boots, and carving the boss of a rose on a piece of wood resting on his knees. On either side, mallet, chisels, and gouges. Supporters: Left and Right, foliage (PLATE 13*d*).

South side from west

1. Man and a woman standing on either side of a table. The man is wearing a jerkin loosely laced in front, hose, and boots. He scratches his head with his left hand (his right hand is broken off). The woman holds a jug in one hand and a cup in the other. Behind them is foliage. Supporters: Left and Right, rose.

2. Eagle perched on a branch, wings extended. Supporters: Left and Right, small eagle.

3. Two lions advancing from either side, heads close together. Behind each lion is a smaller one. Supporters: Left and Right, small lion passant gardant.

The date of the stalls and misericords can be fixed by the shield carved on the elbow of the stall on the north side. This shield bears a fleur-de-lis, the arms of White. John White held the benefice from 1361 to 1392. The living belonged to Crowland Abbey and its tenants.

NORTHUMBERLAND

HEXHAM   The Abbey   *Thirty-eight*

Six are of modern design, but the remainder are of *c.* 1425.

North side from east

1. Wyvern. Supporters: Left and Right, acanthus-leaf.

2. Bat-like creature, full face, with human head and flowing hair, possibly representing vampire or sphinx. Supporters: Left and Right, triple-lobed leaf.

3. Similar to No. 2 above, but with head broken off, and pendant three-toed feet. Supporters: Left and Right, acanthus-leaf.

4. Bearded and whiskered face, with long flowing hair, having central curled lock or knot. Supporters: Left and Right, vine-leaf.

5. Grotesque two-legged creature, having a bearded human head crowned with a soft conical cap and hooded, a feathered body, and feathered legs with two-toed feet. A short, erect tail appears also to be feathered. Supporters: Left and Right, large three-lobed leaf (PLATE 34*c*).

6. Lion- or leopard-mask with protruding tongue. Supporters: Left and Right, rosette.

7. Similar to No. 6 above.

8. Smiling foliate mask. Supporters: Left and Right, formal leaf (PLATE 34*d*).

9. Foliate mask (green man), having branches issuing from nose, an unusual variant. Teeth are indicated by a zigzag incision. Supporters: Left and Right, formal leaf.

10. Leopard-mask with protruding tongue. Supporters: Left and Right, leaf upturned.

11. Similar to No. 10 above, but the supporters are acanthus-leaves.

12. Foliate mask, similar to No. 8 above, but unsmiling. Supporters: Left and Right, upturned leaf.

13. Triple leaves, probably holly, with two clusters of fruit. Supporters: Left and Right, similar leaves.

14. Demi-angel (headless) holding shield charged with *a cross saltire*, the whole within a shield-shaped surround. (St. Andrew is the patron saint of the church.) Supporters: Left and Right, rose.

15. Shield uncharged. Supporters: Left and Right, leaf. (Modern.)

16. Double five-petalled rose. Supporters, Left and Right, leaf.

17. Shield uncharged. Supporters: Left and Right, leaf. (Modern.)

18. As for No. 17 above. (Modern.)

19. Shield uncharged with decoration of oak-leaves and acorns at sides. Supporters: Left and Right, leaves. (Modern.)

South side from east

1. Group of four roses with interspersed leaves. Supporters: Left and Right, formal leaf.

2. Demi-figure of man, with flowing hair and flat cap or tiara, preaching from a pulpit in the shape of a castellated corbel, having a four-petalled flower at its base. He holds a large key in his left hand and a sceptre in his right. (St. Peter.) Supporters: Left and Right, upturned leaf.

3. Lozenge-shaped conventional leaf pattern, of the same leaf forming the foliate masks at North 7 and 12. Supporters: Left and Right, upturned leaf.

4. Shield charged with a latin cross, having a central ridge down both vertical and horizontal shafts. Supporters: Left and Right, leaf.

5. Large five-petalled rose. Supporters: Left and Right, leaf.

6. Clean-shaven head with flowing hair, and bust wearing a jerkin buttoned down the front, and having a wide serrated collar. The sleeves are scalloped and the hands are clasped in front, but not in prayer. Supporters: Left and Right, rosette.

7. Large, double five-petalled rose. Supporters: Left and Right, leaf.

8. Head of green man, with mouth-foliage. Supporters: Left and Right, leaf.

9. Head of bearded man, having flowing hair and many-forked beard. Supporters: Left and Right, vine-leaf.

10. Similar to No. 7 above.
11. Bearded man's face with flowing hair and curled lock or knot in centre of forehead. Similar to North 4, but very finely and delicately carved. Supporters: Left and Right, upturned leaf.
12. Eagle in flight. Body faces right but head turned back. Supporters: Left and Right, upturned leaf.
13. Four grotesque heads of heraldic-leopard type, in radial pattern. Supporters: Left and Right, upturned leaf.
14. Foliate mask with protruding tongue. Supporters: Left and Right, leaf.
15. Lion- or leopard-mask. Supporters: Left and Right, leaf.
16. Large five-petalled rose. Supporters: Left and Right, leaf.
17. Shield uncharged. Supporters: Left and Right, leaf. (Modern.)
18. Double five-petalled rose. Supporters: Left and Right, leaf.
19. Shield charged with arms of Canon Savage. (Modern.) Supporters: Left and Right, leaf. (Canon Savage (1908–13) was responsible for restoration.)

NOTTINGHAMSHIRE

NEWARK   St. Mary Magdalen   *Twenty-six*

North side from east

1. Face with satyr's ears; from the corners of the open mouth are stalks with leaves attached. Supporters: Left and Right, rose.
2. Centre carving removed. Supporters: Left and Right, rose.
3. Dragon. Supporters: Left and Right, fruit.
4. Demi-angel. Supporters: Left and Right, fruit.
5. Owl. Supporters: Left and Right, leaf.
6. Hawk. Supporters: Left and Right, rose.
7. Bird holding fruit in its beak. Supporters: Left and Right, fruit.
8. Demi-angel holding book to breast. Supporters: Left and Right, leaf.
9. Face, with mouth open and teeth clenched. Supporters: Left and Right fruit.
10. Flowers and fruit. Supporters: Left and Right, fruit.
11. Man and eagle fighting. Supporters: Left and Right, animal with wings, dog's head and tail, and only forefeet.
12. Pigs fighting. Supporters: Left and Right, leaf.
13. Demi-angel holding book to breast. Supporters: Left and Right, leaf.

South side from east

1. Floral corbel. Supporters: Left and Right, lizard curled in a circle and biting its tail.

2. Two swans facing each other, eating fruit. Supporters: Left and Right, rose.

3. Face with a lot of hair and very full beard. Supporters: Left and Right, leaf.

4. Figure with fingers placed together under chin (face damaged). Supporters: Left and Right, fruit.

5. Two bears (?) facing each other. Supporters: Left and Right, rose.

6. Vine with bunches of fruit. Supporters: Left and Right, rose.

7. Satyr with protruding tongue. Supporters: Left and Right, leaf.

8. Bird with outspread wings. Supporters: Left and Right, fruit.

9. Animal (? deer) eating fruit from tree. Supporters: Left and Right, rose.

10. Dragon, below which is a man's head. Supporters: Left and Right, flower.

11. Demi-angel, with outspread wings, holding open book to breast. Supporters: Left and Right, fruit.

12. Swan preening herself. Supporters: Left and Right, leaf.

13. Bird with outspread wings. Supporters: Left and Right, leaves.

DATE: *c.* 1524 (C. Brown, *History of Newark* (1904), pp. 283–4). J. B. Morrell, *Woodwork in York*, 1949, p. 155, says Thomas Drawswerd, 'Carvour', Lord Mayor of York, 1514, carved these stalls.

NORTH COLLINGHAM   All Saints   *Seven*

Above the chancel arch are seven heraldic misericords.

DATE: 15th century. They were removed from the stalls when they were damaged in the nineteenth century.

Extract from E. G. Wake, *The History of Collingham and its Neighbours* (1869):

The remnants of the old rood screen are contemporary with the above. Some panels which yet survive (though away from the church) bear traces of gilt with blue and scarlet pigment. Upon them the rose is often represented, and occasionally the shamrock and thistle. Other portions of the same over the chancel arch are seven shields, *which in the first instance served to decorate the under part of so many misereres*, or half-seats used by the priests in the chancel. On the middle one appears a Latin cross having to its left a sword and spear, and on its right side the figure of a dragon in the attitude of falling. A tableau is thus formed symbolising the power of the Cross in the overthrow of Satan. Two of the shields bear carvings of grotesque animals, in accordance with a common method of ornamentation applied to the misere. One of these, a chimaera-like creature, between an eagle and a horse, holds a label or scroll in one claw, from which issues a poppy capsule. The other one, half dog and half horse, has the shoeing of the fore-foot delineated in a manner truly beautiful. Indeed the whole work well repays an ascent of four and twenty feet for its close inspection. On the shield to the north are *Three water-bougets* (Roos) *impaling a fesse between two bars gemelles* (Badlesmere). The one beside it has *on a chevron, between three annulets, as many crescents* (Erisby, *impaling four fusils in fesse* (Daubney). The shield most to the south bears *a cross patee, shafted and pennoned, rising from a triangle* (indicative of the Holy Trinity) *with a mullet in the dexter chief.* This is probably the device of an ecclesiastic, and not strictly speaking an heraldic bearing. The remaining shield has *Quarterly 1st, a chevron between three mullets; 2nd, a saltire ermine* (Neville of Rolleston); *3rd, on a bend sinister three crescents; 4th, on a bend sinister three escallops.* The bar sinister is sometimes used incorrectly. If such be the case here, Nos. 3 and 4 probably distinguish Cressy of Markham and Basset, instead of Waston and Parott, as they now seem to do. The absence of colour, and of its equivalent marks, prevents our speaking with certainty about this shield.

NOTTINGHAM   St. Stephen, Sneinton   *Eight*

1. Unicorn with shaggy coat, and holding its head turned facing rearward.
2. Fox riding a hound with long, raised tail (PLATE 35*a*).
3. Chained ape seated upon a stool to which the chain is anchored. He holds in his outstretched hands a flagon, and above him are the spreading branches of a tree.
4. Large male head with moustache and radial curly hair and beard, possibly representing the Sun.
5. Lion passant gardant to right.
6. Horse or mule trotting.
7. Jack-in-the-Green. Supporters: Left and Right, formal elaborate flower-pattern in lozenge form.
8. Bi-corporate lion, holding a lamb in its jaws.

The supporters in all cases except No. 7 are a formal vine-leaf pendant.

These stalls were formerly in the parish church of St. Mary, Nottingham.

DATE: Late 15th or early 16th century.

SCREVETON   St. Wilfred   *One*

On the north side of the chancel is a stall with a carved misericord of a man with bare feet, facing right. He is sitting in an armchair in front of a fire, and in his right hand he is holding a flail with which he appears to be fanning the fire. Behind him is a cooking pot on a pedestal.

DATE: 15th century. (Illustrated in Cox and Harvey, *English Church Furniture*, 1907, p. 258.)

On the south side there is a stall with a carved misericord of St. Wilfred, but this is modern.

SOUTHWELL   The Minster   *Six*

South to north

1. Woman riding a horse, with her hands in its mouth. Supporters: Left and Right, oak-leaf.
2. Seated man with a stalk of oak-leaves issuing from each side of his mouth.
3. Man and woman standing holding one another's shoulders. Supporters: Left, oak-leaf motif. Right, the same, with heraldic rose and fruit.

4. Man's head on insect's or bird's body, with his right hand clutching an oak-leaf. Supporters: Left and Right, oak-leaf.

5. Woman kneeling to the left, her body twisted to the front, and her head inclining to right in graceful posture. Supporters: Left and Right, leaf.

6. Young girl sitting on a stool. Supporters: Left and Right, oak-leaf.

DATE: 14th century.

THURGARTON   The Priory Church of St. Peter   *Four*

South side from east

1. Man, with hands outstretched, sitting on a scroll which extends beyond him on each side and is then wound up. Supporters: Left and Right, leaf.

2. Man's face with moustache and beard and wearing a cap. Supporters: Left, woman's face. Right, man's face.

3. Foliage. Supporters: Left and Right, leaf.

On a shelf of a window behind the stalls is a misericord of two wrestlers, one having a brutal face. Supporters: Left, leaves. Right, missing. This misericord is by a different hand from the other three.

DATE: Probably 15th century.

WYSALL   Holy Trinity   *Four*

From south

1. Leaves. Supporters: Left and Right, leaves.

2. Face with oak-branches issuing from mouth. Supporters: Left and Right, Tudor rose.

3. Similar to No. 2. Supporters: Left and Right, leaf.

4. Similar to No. 1 but badly damaged.

DATE: 15th century. (Illustrated in Cox and Harvey, *English Church Furniture*, p. 258.)

OXFORDSHIRE

BAMPTON IN THE BUSH   St. Mary   *Four*

North side

1. Wyvern or salamander, having three toes on each foot. It has a background of corn or grass. Supporters: Left and Right, oak-leaf.

2. Grotesque head, with protruding tongue and wide-spreading whiskers. Supporters: Left and Right, bugle horn suspended from scallop-shell, the arms of Hobbes.

3. A crude unicorn with cloven hooves, also said by some to be a bull (M. D. Anderson (*Animal Carvings*, 1938, p. 80) or a lion (C. E. Keyser, *Jnal. Brit. Arch. Assoc.*, N.S. 22 (1916), p. 8). (PLATE 35*b*.)

4. Spray of oak-leaves spread fanwise to form the supporters.

The initials TH on a stall-end and on the edge of the bracket of No. 2 probably refer to Thomas Hobbes or Howis, Dean of Exeter, 1508–9. The arms of the See of Exeter are carved on stalls elsewhere in the chancel. There is in the area a manor called Bampton Deanery which was granted together with the church to the Cathedral of Exeter by Leofric, and the living is still in the gift of the See (C. E. Keyser, op. cit., p. 8).

KIDLINGTON St. Mary the Virgin *Five*

There are five stalls on the north side of the chancel, with simple misericords that have plain vaulting with flowers at the base and as supporters. One has been nailed down (PLATE 36*a*).

DATE: Early 13th century (Howard and Crossley, *English Church Woodwork*, 1927, p. 149).

OXFORD All Souls College Chapel *Forty-two*

North side

1. Foliage.
2. Lion passant.
3. Queen's head.
4. Oriel window.
5. Man's head and neck surrounded by a collar of scalloped cloth. He wears a flat cap with plumes. Supporters: Left and Right, oak-leaves.
6. Man with salade, round shield, and sword. Supporters: Left and Right, blank heraldic shield depending from extension of the moulding passed through attachments on the shields and twisted.
7. Woman's head.
8. Owl with raised wings, facing left. Supporters: Left and Right, oak-leaves with acorn in centre.
9. Crouching lion.
10. Ancient bearded man, with legs raised over his shoulders. He wears a plumed hat. Supporters: Left and Right, oak-leaves in lozenge formation.
11. Woman's head with curls under round cap, and collar of rosettes.
12. Man's head.
13. Demi-angel with crown.
14. Eagle.

15. Double-headed eagle.

16. Leopard's head.

17. Eagle.

18. Pedlar putting on shoe.

19. Man, seated on a stool, gesticulating with arms and legs. Supporters: Left and Right, smaller figure, dancing. Figure on right has stick and tabor.

20. Mermaid. Supporters: Left and Right, lozenge-shaped rosettes.

21. Man playing bagpipes. Supporters: Left and Right, lozenge-shaped flower.

On south side

1. Goat with bearded man's face. Supporters: Left and Right, four roses on one stalk.

2. King's head.

3. Nun's head. Supporters: Left and Right, nun's head.

4. Monster's head.

5. Two sheep, back to back, sitting up and leaning their sides against a three-sided corbel. Supporters: Left and Right, bunch of leaves and acorns.

6. Winged dragon against a corbel. Supporters: Left and Right, rose.

7. Stag against a corbel. Supporters: leaf inverted.

8. Rose.

9. Winged dragon. Supporters: Left and Right, bishop's mitre.

10. Feathers in a scroll. Supporters: Left and Right, rose.

11. Hart and scroll.

12. Woman filling a jug from a bucket.

13. Mounted man.

14. Griffin. Supporters: Left and Right, bird with outspread wings.

15. Grotesque face, mouth on one side, large ears, bearded. Supporters: Left and Right, group of six leaves, pendant.

16. Man's head.

17. Demi-angel with shields.

18. Bishop's head. Supporters: Left and Right, oak-leaf.

19. Crowned swan. Supporters: Left and Right, oak-leaf.

20. Two goats.

21. Falcon and fetterlock. Supporters: Left and Right, fetterlock.

The supporters (unless otherwise described) are conventional leaves.

DATE: 1442, in which year Archbishop Chichele consecrated the College.

OXFORD Christch Church Cathedral *Four*

In the Latin Chapel at the west end are stalls, four of which have misericords. All are alike, the centrepieces consisting of plain corbels, and the supporters being of meagre foliage ornament.

DATE: Early 16th century. *Ecclesiologist*, vii (1867), p. 55, asserts that they were part of the stalls erected in the choir by Cardinal Wolsey.

OXFORD Lincoln College Chapel *Thirty-four*

All the misericords are alike, the brackets being corbels carved with a simple foliage design. There are no supporters.

DATE: 17th century. The chapel was consecrated in 1631.

OXFORD Magdalen College Chapel *Twenty-nine*

In the south bay of the antechapel are twenty-nine stalls with carved misericords.

North side

1. Grotesque mask.
2. Winged monster.
3. Grotesque mask.
4. Fox and geese.
5. Grotesque mask.
6. Swan.
7. Grotesque mask.
8. Tumbler.

West side

1. Birds fighting.
2. Winged monster.
3. Horse.
4. Grotesque mask.
5. The same.
6. Owl and mouse. Supporters: Left and Right, small bird.
7. Shield of the arms of the College.

South side

1. Bust of bearded man with cap.
2. Beast's head.
3. Winged monster lying curled up on its back.

4. Rose-bush.

5. Pelican in her piety.

6. Grotesque mask.

7. Eagle and prey.

8. Hare.

9. Seated ape.

10. Grotesque mask.

11. The same.

12. Horse curled up on its back.

13. Winged monster.

14. Seated ape.

All have foliage supporters of single leaves or flowers, except one with dog's heads, or where otherwise stated.

The stalls with misericords in the antechapel must almost certainly date from the last quarter of the fifteenth century, when the chapel was built. As far as is known they have always been in the chapel, though probably originally in the choir, not the antechapel. The three stalls detached from the wall returned to the College quite recently as a gift from an Old Member. From the College arms it is clear that they belong to Magdalen, and stylistically everything points to their being part of the original scheme.

OXFORD   New College Chapel   *Sixty-two*

North side from east

1. Eagle with scroll. Supporters: Left, eagle seizing a hare by the ears. Right, eagle with scroll.

2. Lion's mask. Supporters: Left and Right, scallop-shell.

3. Bearded man's head with vine-leaves. Supporters: Left and Right, vine-leaf.

4. Crowned male head. Supporters: Left and Right, harp.

5. Ram's head. Supporters: Left and Right, foliate square.

6. Man's head with foliage. Supporters: Left and Right, foliate square.

7. Shield of Beauchamp of Warwick, *a fess between six cross crosslets.* Supporters: Left and Right, shields of Calverley, *a fess between three calves, two and one,* and Curzon, *diapered, on a bend three popinjays.*

8. Hydra representing the Seven Deadly Sins. Supporters: Left, an exorcism. Right, a bearded man, nude except for drawers, scourging himself. (PLATE 15*b*.)

9. Foliage. Supporters: Left and Right, foliage.

10. Corbel with double rose. Supporters: Left and Right, rose.

11. Castle gate with portcullis. Supporters: Left, man's head in peaked helmet to which a camail is riveted. Right, the same, but the camail is laced. See similarities in Sir Yvain carvings at Lincoln and Chester.

12. Monster in foliage. Supporters: Left and Right, foliate square with face.

13. Mask and foliage. Supporters: Left and Right, leaf.

14. Foliage. Supporters: Left and Right, leaf.

15. Jack and the Beanstalk; the giant grasping animals and a bird. Supporters: Left, Jack's mother. Right, Jack in foliage.

16. Foliage. Supporters: Left and Right, foliage.

17. Winged monsters. Supporters: Left and Right, crowned head.

18. Rose-tree. Supporters: Left and Right, garland of roses.

19. Winged beast. Supporters: Left and Right, foliate mask.

20. Stag-hunt. Supporters: Left and Right, leaves and mask.

21. Male mask with wings. Supporters: Left and Right, foliate mask.

22. Seated man in hood. Supporters: Left and Right, oak-leaf.

23. Foliage. Supporters: Left and Right, leaf.

24. Two parrots facing each other. Supporters: Left and right, oak-leaf.

23. Bearded mask. Supporters: Left and Right, foliage.

26. Foliage mask. Supporters: Left and Right, foliage.

27. Triple-faced man. Supporters: Left and Right, grotesque monster.

Returned stalls from the north

1. Fiend seizing man by the skirt of his tunic. Supporters: Left and Right, square-foliated ornament.

2. Woman with distaff, with a large cat looking over her shoulder. Supporters: Left and Right, monster.

3. Three men standing close to each other in a triangle; the two at the side defending themselves with daggers against (supporters) men with daggers.

4. Lion crowned, with tongue out and two bodies.

South side from east

1. Peacock in his pride. Supporters: Left and Right, peacock.

2. Centaur in hood playing a pipe and beating a tabor. Supporters: Left, centaur blowing a horn. Right, centaur playing a pipe.

3. Foliate mask. Supporters, modern.

4. Foliage. Supporters: Left and Right, leaves.

5. Harpy with raised wings forming a collar. Supporters: Left and right, rose.

6. Bearded mask. Supporters: Left and Right, griffin.

7. Female centaur holding an axe. Supporters: Left and Right, hedgehog.

8. Man at desk lecturing; two small figures behind him hold staves; a small figure below him holds a book (penitent confessing); two other figures in background. Supporters: Left, man carrying books. Right, man wearing liripipe hood, reading.

9. Foliage. Supporters: Left and Right, foliage.

10. Head corbel. Supporters: Left and Right, leaves and mask.

11. Foliage. Supporters: Left and Right, foliage.

12. Bearded head. Supporters: Left and Right, foliage.

13. Foliage. Supporters: Left and Right, foliage.

14. Gateway with portcullis trapping Sir Yvain's horse. Supporters: Left and Right, castle gateway, watchman's head just visible, flag-post with flag blazoned.

15. Ape in a cowl issuing from a whelk-shell surrounded by foliage. Supporters: Left, ape seated on a lily. Right, ape in a hooded cape.

16. Bearded man in a cloak. Supporters: Left and Right, oak-leaves.

17. Swan with partially extended wings. Supporters: Left and Right, grotesque bird.

18. Dragon. Supporters: Left and Right, flower.

19. Large bearded head. Supporters: Left and Right, foliage.

20. Oriel window. Supporters: Left and Right, latticed window.

21. Imp holding money-bags. Supporters: Left and Right, foliage.

22. Pair of tumblers with a head beneath. Supporters: Left and Right, flower.

23. Rose-bush. Supporters: Left and Right, rose.

24. Foliage. Supporters: Left and Right, foliage.

25. Foliage. Supporters: Left and Right, lion-mask.

26. Foliage. Supporters: Left and Right, monster.

27. Two women seated in a pew; standing behind them is a demon with bat's wings, eavesdropping. Supporters: Left, woman kneeling, a pair of crutches under her arms, telling her beads. Right, tonsured monk bending forward asleep.

Returned stalls from south

1. Woman's head with large, quilted hat. Supporters: Left and Right, leaf.

2. Holly branches. Supporters: Left and Right, fleur-de-lis.

3. Winged monster. Supporters: Left and Right, leaf.

4. Walled city (? Oxford) with church. Supporters: Left, bishop, seated on the bridge, exhorting five priests. Right, the heads of five clerics in foliage;

one wears a cardinal's hat, another has a crozier. The main subject could be the 'garden enclosed' symbol of the B.V.M.

DATE: Late 14th century. The Charter was issued in 1379 (G. H. Cook, *English Collegiate Churches*, p. 178). Various types of male and female head-dress, etc., portrayed in the carvings are of styles in vogue in 1380–1400).

SWINBROOK   St. Mary   *Five*

North side

1. Seated woman with hands on knees, wearing a flat hat or cap. Supporters: Left and Right, leaf.

South side from east

1. Floral design. Supporters, damaged.

2. Bare-headed man, holding a rod horizontally, with arms extended but bent at the elbows. No supporters.

3. Similar carving, but the man's head is in profile, turned to the left.

4. Grotesque animal-head. The supporters are missing.

DATE: *c.* 1450 (E. Phipson, *Choir Stalls* (1896), p. 121).

SHROPSHIRE

HOLDGATE   Holy Trinity   *One*

On a window-sill is a carved misericord, two griffins fighting. Supporters: griffins, that on the right asleep.

DATE: Late 15th century. Origin unknown.

LUDLOW   St. Lawrence   *Twenty-eight*

North side from east

1. Grinning, bridled female head (a scold), with winged hat and (hennin) veil. Supporters: Left, man running. Right, similar man carrying a shield.

2. Monster with female face with hennin, having wings, bird's feet, and short, thick tail. Supporters: Left and Right, cockatrice with two feet, large ears and teeth, and winged tail.

3. One devil playing bagpipes, facing another devil (head missing) who is holding by the legs a naked woman, whose body hangs down his back. She is holding a measure in her left hand. (The cheating ale-wife being taken to hell.) Supporters: Left, demon carrying a large, open scroll. Right, female figure emerging from a hell-mouth, into which another is plunging head foremost. (PLATE 15*d*).

4. Mermaid holding a mirror. Supporters: Left and Right, dolphin with mouth open, showing a fine set of teeth.

5. Three figures in long cloaks; the one on the left is apparently falling, the one facing him has a foot slightly lifted, and the other holds him by the back. Supporters: Left, a pot on a fire. Right, floral design.

6. Antelope collared and chained. Supporters: Left and Right, foliate mask.

7. Mitred head and shoulders. Supporters: Left and Right, mitre.

8. Prince of Wales feathers. Supporters: Left and Right, the same, smaller.

9. Mitred fox preaching to geese Supporters: Left, woman and man in caps. Right, floral design.

10. Hart couchant, about to rise. Supporters: Left and Right, dog.

11. Crowned, bearded man. Supporters: Left and Right, foliage.

12. Winged angel with a trumpet (damaged). Supporters: Left and Right, foliage.

13. Falcon and fetterlock. Supporters: Left and Right, fetterlock.

14. Uncarved returned stall.

15. Foliage. Supporters: Left and Right, rose.

16. Uncarved.

South side from east

1. Figure in a pleated cloak, with hammer and bellows at foot. Barrel level with the head, smaller bellows below. Supporters: Left, seated figure. Right, floral design, out of which issues a hand holding the handle of a tall pot in which is a rod with a ball at the end, and other implements.

2. Floral design. Supporters: Left and Right, leaf.

3. Seated figure, with a contorted face, and with head and shoulders leaning against a cushion with a band hinged at each end passing in front of his shoulders. He is holding the top of his right boot with both hands. Supporters: Left and Right, leaf.

4. Head and bust of a woman with coif. Supporters: Left and Right, bust of woman with hennin.

5. Owl. Supporters: Left and Right, eagle.

6. Duck. Supporters: Left and Right, foliage.

7. Man, seated on a chair, dressed in a cloak with his head muffled, warming his hands at a fire. Supporters: Left, a cooking-pot with lid and three legs, standing over a piece of wood laid for a fire. Right, two flitches.

8. Man on left (headless and damaged) in short pleated skirt; two others wrestling, one of whom has grabbed the other round the waist; and two others to the right also wrestling. Supporters: Left, a horse (damaged). Right, formal patterns.

9. Centre badly damaged. Supporters: Left and Right, leaf.

10. Griffin in profile seated. Supporters: two-beaked birds.

11. Man in profile, with legs wide apart, filling a large jug from a smaller barrel. His head is lying on his hands and his eyes are closed. Supporters: Left and Right, leaves.

12. Two figures (headless and damaged)kneeling on one knee and holding a barrel between them. Supporters: Left and Right, a jug and barrel and a cup.

13. Seated man in tall cap, holding a wide scroll across his knees. Supporters: Left, man's face. Right, woman's face.

14. Uncarved.

15. Deeply-cut conventional rose with fetterlock. Supporters: Left, a large, twisted rope. Right, blank.

16. Uncarved.

DATE: North 3, 5, and 7 and South 8, 9, 12, and 13, 1389. These can be identified by the carver's mark in the form of a small twig. The remainder, 1435. (Thomas Wright's *Guide to Ludlow*, 1901, p. 35.)

The church was served by a college of priests. The church guide states: 'In 1447 members of the Palmers' Guild bought 100 planks from Bristol for the purpose of renewing the stalls. The priests were paid by various bequests.'

TONG   St. Mary with St. Bartholomew   *Fifteen*

1. An embattled castle. (This may represent Tong Castle.) Supporters: Left and Right, single multifoil leaf with curved tendril.

2. Five-pointed leaves from central stem. Supporters: Left and Right, three trefoil leaves.

3. Cluster of leaves with stem. Supporters: Left and Right, simple similar leaves.

4. Bacchus or Comus mask entwined in grapes and vine-leaves. Supporters: Left and Right, grotesque mask. (Abbot's stall.)

5. Angel in armour holding shield or book. Supporters: Left and Right, single rose.

6. Vine-leaves. Supporters: Left and Right, single vine-leaf.

7. Vine-leaves in deep relief. Supporters: Left and Right, single leaf.

8. The Annunciation showing the Lily Crucifix. Supporters: Left and Right, pelican in her piety. (Master's stall.) (PLATE 1c.)

9. Grotesque face amongst vine-leaves and grapes. Supporters: Left and Right, vine-tendril ending in lovers' knot. (Cellarer's stall.)

10. Griffin. Supporters: Left and Right, griffin.

11. Cluster of fern-leaves. Supporters: Left and Right, vine-leaf.

12. Armoured angel with shield. Supporters: Left and Right, single rose.

13. Undecorated.

14. Petals. Supporters: Left and Right, double flower.

15. Similar to No. 14. Supporters: Left and Right, vine-leaf.

16. Almost undecorated except for very small leaves at base. Supporters: Left and Right, single rose.

DATE: *c.* 1410. The church became collegiate in 1410 (Knowles and Hadcock, *Medieval Religious Houses*, p. 314).

SOMERSET

WELLS   The Cathedral   *Sixty-four*

Sixty-four misericords remain, fifty of which belonged to the prebendal stalls of the upper row. They were removed from this, their proper position, at the restoration (1848–54) and sixty are in the lower row and the other four in the library.

South side

  First row

1. Goat (broken).

2. Griffin fighting a lion.

3. Man, in hood and drawers, riding on a bare-backed horse with his face to the rear.

4. Hawk preying on a rabbit.

5. Mermaid (unfinished).

6. Two popinjays on a fruit tree.

7. Ape carrying a basket of fruit on his back (broken).

8. Monster with two bodies.

9. Dog-headed griffin.

10. Two goats butting each other (unfinished).

11. Monkey holding owl (unfinished).

12. Two dragons interlocked and biting each other's tail.

13. Ewe suckling lamb (unfinished).

14. Wyvern and horse fighting.

South side

  Second row

15. Mermaid suckling lion.

16. Man holding cup and sitting on the ground, disputing with another man holding a pouch.

17. Cat preying on mouse (unfinished).
18. Monster with bat's wings.
19. Griffin eating a lamb.
20. Puppy biting cat.
21. Man supporting the seat of the misericord.
22. Dog.
23. Cat playing fiddle.
24. Man, seated on the ground, thrusting a dagger through the head of a dragon with feathered wings.
25. Bishop in amice, chasuble, and mitre (unfinished).
26. Peacock in his pride.
27. Fox preaching to four geese, one of which has fallen asleep (broken).
28. Cock crowing.

North side

First row

29. Lion sleeping.
30. Dragon with expanded wings, asleep.
31. Man, with his left eye closed, squatting on the ground with his hands on his knees.
32. Fox running with a goose in its mouth.
33. Man's head with ass's ears.
34. Two monsters with male and female human heads caressing (unfinished).
35. Man on his back, supporting the seat with his right hand and foot.
36. Lion with the ears of an ass.
37. Hawk scratching its head.
38. Sleeping cat.
39. Woman, with dishevelled and agonized expression, crouching on the ground with right hand on shoulder and left extended.
40. Dragon, with hairy belly, biting its back.
41. Two ducks.
42. Two dragons fighting (unfinished).
43. Bat's head (unfinished).

North side

Second row

44. Man's head, with bushy hair and beard, with lion's leg growing out of each side.

45. Man, in tunic and hood, lying on his side and clasping his hands.

46. Man, wearing girdled tunic and holding head downwards, supporting the seat with his back and left hand.

47. Lady's head, with hair in a curl on each side, wearing an ornate fillet.

48. Gentle-looking lion.

49. Bat with wings expanded.

50. Angel's head with amice around neck and expanded wings.

51. Lion.

52. Two doves or parrots about to drink from a ewer standing in a basin (unfinished).

53. Squirrel with collar trying to escape from monkey who holds him by a cord.

54. Wood-pigeon feeding.

55. Man rising and whipping a lion.

56. Boar and cat with cloven feet walking away from each other.

57. Eagle with expanded wings (unfinished).

58. Head and shoulders of a man who supports seat with his hands.

59. Rabbit.

60. Two-legged beast looking at its tail, which is formed of three oak-leaves on one stem.

61. Man, in hood and loose tunic, kneeling and thrusting spear down throat of dragon.

62. Boy, with long wavy hair and wearing gown, lying on his side and drawing a thorn out of his foot. (17th-century work.)

63. Pelican in her piety. (PLATE 12b.)

64. The Flight of Alexander. Perhaps the most beautiful representation of the subject in England. (PLATE 1b.)

Twelve of the misericords are unfinished; this is most unusual. All have supporters consisting of bosses of naturalistic foliage, including specimens of oak, maple, vine, rose, marshmallow, ivy, beech, and other plants and trees.

DATE: c. 1330–40.

WESTON-IN-GORDANO   St. Peter and St. Paul   *Five*

There are eight stalls in the choir of this church, five with carved misericords.

1. Four-petalled square conventional flower. Supporters: Left and Right, the same.

2. Four-petalled flower at the end of a corbel. Supporters: Left and Right, pillar with ornamental base.

3. Face with the mouldings of the bracket carried round into the corners of the mouth.

4. Face with tongue protruding, hands extending from the sides of the face grasping pillar-like supporters with ornamental base similar to the supporters of No. 2.

5. Wyvern having head which looks both forward and backward. The forward face has a barbed tongue. Supporters as for No. 2.

The eight choir stalls are not an exact fit, and it is possible that they were brought to the church from the neighbouring priory of Portbury by James Perceval after the priory's dissolution in 1536. Perceval was adding a chapel of St. Mary Magdalene to the church at that time.

Bond says, p. 223, that the village carpenter was obviously employed in doing the carving.

DATE: Probably early 14th century.

WORLE   St. Martin   *Five*

On the south side of the church are five stalls with carved misericords. They were brought to the church from Woodspring Priory, from which the parish was provided with priests (W. S. Brassington, *Somerset Arch. and N.H. Soc., Bath Branch Proc.*, 1925, p. 55).

1. Two heads under one cowl.

2. Dragon standing over prostrate human figure.

3. Floral design.

4. Two bunches of grapes. Probably of Eucharistic significance.

5. The letter P and the monogram R S. P probably stands for Prior, and R S for Richard Spring, who held the offices of Prior of Woodspring and Vicar of Worle, 1499–1516. (F. Bond, *Misericords*, p. 215, and N. Pevsner, *North Somerset and Bristol*, p. 346.)

All have vine-leaf supporters.

DATE: 16th century.

STAFFORDSHIRE

CLIFTON CAMPVILLE   St. Andrew   *Seven*

South side from east

1. A vigorously carved man's head with chin-beard.

2. Naturalistic foliage of the vine variety, the veins are shown.

3. A man's head in a hood.

4. Foliage of the ivy type.

North side from east

1. A grinning mask, comprising a human face, pig's ears, and a dog's mouth from which protrudes a large tongue. A beard, or more probably a muff, surrounds the neck.
2. Naturalistic foliage of the hawthorn tree.
3. Woman's head in a wimple (this appears to be in the style of the widow's weeds of about Edward I's reign).

The moulded brackets are circular. No supporters.

DATE: Early 14th century (S. A. Jeavons, 'Medieval Stallwork in S. Staffs.', *Birmingham Arch. Trans.*, lxvii–lxviii (1947–8), pp. 42 ff. and 48).

COLTON   B.V.M.   *Three*

Three misericords were installed here about 1850. They were picked up in a mason's yard at Tenby.

1. A crude flying wyvern with a curved tail which ends in a serpent's head. The bracket curves inward and then outward and ends in leaves.
2. Two seated wyverns back to back.
3. Janus, the double-headed god.

DATE: The latter part of the 15th century (S. A. Jeavons, 'Medieval Stallwork', p. 52). In view of the place of origin of the carvings, viz. Tenby, it is interesting to note examples of the Janus head in St. David's Cathedral.

ECCLESHALL   Holy Trinity   *Three*

There are three misericord carvings in the chancel. The stalls to which they were attached have disappeared.

1. Seated male figure, in a robe extending to the feet, holding on his lap a flat object. Face and left hand imperfect. Possibly a scribe or a leather-worker.
2. Winged, hairy or scaly creature resembling the 'Lincoln Imp', seated on a man-faced creature; above are the remains of a human torso.
3. Man wearing a hooded cape on shoulders, a leather belt with scrip or purse hanging from it, and cross-bands and garters round legs. He is riding head to tail on a goat. Fore and hind off-legs are missing.

Supporters of all three misericords, stylized foliage.

DATE: Late 14th or early 15th century. The bracket has a straight front.

ENVILLE   St. Mary   *Four*

North side from west

1. Gate house of a castle. The portcullis has descended and caught a knight on horseback. One of the knight's legs and the rear of the horse can be seen. Two soldiers' heads peer through the upper side-windows of the gatehouse

and a woman's head is looking out of another window. (This is from the romance of Sir Yvain and is a more realistic portrayal than that in Lincoln Cathedral or St. Botolph's, Boston.) Supporters: Left and Right, castle tower with arch under which stands a mailed knight. (PLATE 7c.)

2. Woman holding a rosary and a man holding a missal seated together in a pew. The devil stands behind with wings outspread and eavesdrops. Compare Gayton, Northants. and New College, Oxford. Supporters: Left and Right, grotesque monster.

South side

1. Two dogs attacking a muzzled bear; a man sits in a tree behind watching. Supporters: Left, man seated on the ground holding a pole to which the chain of the bear is attached. Right, a woman carrying her baby on her back slung in a shawl.

2. Angel, covered with feathers and with wings outspread, sitting cross-legged under a battlemented canopy playing a stringed instrument. Supporters: Left, a small angel playing harp. Right (damaged by wood beetle), angel playing a guitar.

DATE: Late 15th century (S. A. Jeavons, 'Medieval Stallwork', p. 50).

FAIRWELL (or FAREWELL)   St. Bartholomew   *Ten*

There are five misericords on each side of the church, two of which are at the eastern end of the chancel. Of these two, that on the south side has a central foliage motif; both the supporters consist of the letters E R with a rose above and below them. In that on the north side, a corbel divides two sprays of roses; the supporters are, Left, the letter E, Right, the letter R. The remaining eight misericords show a plain vaulting and corbel (Jeavons, 'Medieval Stallwork' p. 52).

The carvings appear to be of mid sixteenth-century date, and on this assumption the supporters of the two in the chancel might refer to either Edward VI or Elizabeth, but no documentary evidence of their origin exists. The former nunnery was dissolved by Wolsey in 1528, and the church then became the parish church. *Staffordshire Historical Collections*, 1st Series, VI, part 2, p. 93 records: '1528. 20th November. First payment of a chaplain of Farewell, 8 marks per annum. The Bishop renounces nomination of a priest to Farewell in favour of Dean and Chapter [of Lichfield].'

PENKRIDGE   St. Michael and all Angels   *Six*

Two have identical spade-like leaves. The remaining four have similar central bosses with the four leaves so arranged that a circular ridge and a small central knob form a wheel-like pattern. All supporters have conventional foliage.

DATE: Late 15th century (S. A. Jeavons, 'Medieval Stallwork', pp. 51-2).

TETTENHALL   St. Michael

In February 1950 this church was almost totally destroyed by fire, and nine stalls with misericords were lost. They were fully described by S. A. Jeavons in 'Medieval Stallwork', p. 51. They were presumably contemporary with those at Penkridge, as there were striking similarities in certain foliage subjects in both churches.

WALSALL   St. Matthew   *Seventeen*

There is a tradition which is unsupported that they came from the Abbey of Halesowen.

South side from west

1. Modern leaf and berries.
2. Tree foliage with the leaves pointing towards the branch; a bird's head peers through the foliage on the right side. Supporters curl round and take the form of a diamond-shaped leaf with curly edges.
3. A mask with protruding tongue. Supporters, similar to those for No. 2 but the edges are not curly.
4. A lion-mask with a fringe of hair on the forehead. Supporters: Left and Right, diamond-shaped leaf that almost takes the form of a cross, as four egg-shaped bodies are cut in it.
5. Another variant of a lion-mask with peculiar ears. Supporters: Left and Right, a circle of leaves.
6. A crouching horse-like beast with its head turned over its shoulder. Supporters: a variant of supporters of No. 4.
7. Bearded creature, half-beast, half-man, shooting with a bow and arrow. Supporters: Left, round, grinning mask with the curious ears of No. 5. Right, circular, a bird with outspread wings, attacking a snake.
8. (Damaged) centaur shooting an arrow at its right supporter. Supporters: Left, radiating ring of leaves. Right, in a roundel, a hybrid monster upside down, with four legs and the head and wings of an eagle.
9. Oak-leaf and acorns. Supporters: Left and Right, ring of oak-leaves.

North side from west

1. Modern or completely restored angel. Supporters: Left and Right, diamond-shaped leaf.
2. Man, fully dressed in quilted tunic and hose, lying on his right side with knees bent. His cowled head rests on a pillow, and his left arm, in elaborate puffed sleeve, lies across his body to clasp on his right what appears to be a stout pole or possibly a roll of cloth. The fingers of his right hand clasp the object on a level with his head. Supporters: Left and Right, large, open five-petalled flower. S. A. Jeavons, 'Medieval Stallwork', p. 49, states: 'The figure is not lying upon a cushion, but carrying a sack, of which the ears and sewn-up mouth are visible. Probably a miller carrying grain.'

3. Pelican in her piety. Supporters: Left and Right, ring of foliage.

4. Winged angel holding heraldic shield. Supporters: Left and Right, trefoil leaf in lozenge form.

5. Large leaf with curled edges. Supporters, as for No. 4.

6. Man, wearing cloak and hood with feather in it, playing a wind instrument and seated on a dragon which has a long tail.

7. Double-headed eagle with outspread wings. Supporters: Left and Right, diamond-shaped leaf with volute-like edges.

8. Clean-shaven man in belted tunic holding a club in his right hand and a bunch of three flowers in his left. Supporters, as for No. 4.

9. Running beast with lion's feet and horse's tail. Supporters: Left and Right, diamond-shaped leaf.

DATE: Mid-15th century (S. A. Jeavons, 'Medieval Stallwork', pp. 48 and 49).

SUFFOLK

BILDESTON   St. Mary Magdalen   *Ten*

North side from east

1. Bearded man with face mutilated. Supporters: Left and Right, vine-leaf.

2. Pelican facing front, with head mutilated. She stands on a nest containing six chicks. Supporters: Left and Right, vine-leaf.

3. Similar to No. 1.

4. Cowled head, mutilated. Supporters: Left and Right, vine-leaf.

5. Turbaned head, mutilated. Supporters: Left and Right, vine-leaf.

South side from east

1. Crowned skull, mutilated. Supporters: Left, vine-leaf. Right, missing.

2. Demi-angel, mutilated, wearing buttoned tunic with frilled sleeves. Supporters: Left and Right, vine-leaf.

3. Similar to North 4.

4. Bearded, grotesque head with protruding tongue. Supporters: Left and Right, vine-leaf.

5. Seat screwed down, but carving appears to be similar to No. 4, but badly mutilated. Supporters: Left and Right, vine-leaf.

DATE: Probably late 15th century.

BRUNDISH   St. Lawrence   *One*

There is one stall with a simply carved misericord, not now in position but at the back of the church behind the vestry screen.

The main carving consists of a plain vaulting ending in a corbel base, which has been mutilated. Supporters: Left and Right, lozenge-shaped pattern of acanthus-leaves.

DATE: 15th century.

BURY ST. EDMUNDS   Moyse's Hall Museum   *One*

Displayed on a wall of the Museum is a 14th-century misericord of unknown origin, which was received in the late nineteenth century from an unrecorded donor. The three sections have been remounted on a board, but the carved woodwork connecting centrepiece and supporters is missing. The seat-ledge, which is damaged, had triple moulding and the front is five-pointed. The roundels encircling the supporters have a small leaf at the top terminal, and they closely resemble the fourteenth-century examples at Norton and Occold, (q.v.). Centre carving; A fox in cowled robe stands in a hexagonal pulpit, realistically carved with quatrefoil ornament, preaching to fowls on the right, including two geese and a cock perched on a bough. Behind him on the left another fox is carrying off a bird amid dense trees or bushes. Supporters: Left, a hunting scene within a roundel; a hunter blows his horn, while on each side of him a hound leaps forward. Right, the quarry, a stag, crouches in undergrowth. (PLATE 35c.)

COCKFIELD   St. Peter   *Four*

All except the returned stalls have lost their misericords, and the seats are screwed down. The returned stalls have the centre carvings mutilated and are in bad condition. The supporters are described below, left and right being identical in each case.

North to south

1. Large five-petalled leaf with curled tips.

2. Large rosette.

3. Large rose.

4. Large double rose.

An examination of the centre carvings suggests that they may have been heads.

DATE: Probably 15th century.

CODDENHAM   St. Mary the Virgin   *Two*

On the south side of the chancel are two stalls each with a misericord, having a similar design of a vaulted corbel with a machicolated top and moulded base. Supporters: Left and Right, a double rose.

DATE: Probably early 15th century.

On the north side are two similar stalls with misericords that appear to be later copies. There is no information available regarding the date of these.

DENHAM (near Eye)   St. John the Baptist   *Six*

The church was apparently the chapel of a small religious house, probably a cell of Norwich, but may have been connected with Hoxne, nearby. An adjacent farm is still called 'The College'.

North side from east

1. Plain vault with mutilated base. Supporters: Left and Right, group of large, pendant three-lobed leaves.
2. Plain vault based on circular scroll of acanthus-leaves. Supporters: Left and Right, similar to centre base.
3. Centre mutilated, but probably similar to No. 2. Supporters: Left and Right, group of large pendant three-lobed leaves.

South side from east

1. Plain vault with mutilated base. Supporters, similar to those for North 1.
2. Similar to No. 1.
3. Similar to No. 1.

DATE: Probably early 15th century.

DENSTON   St. Nicholas   *Four*

From the south the first three are of acanthus-leaves and fruit, and the northernmost is of a crane holding a stone in its claw. The crane was supposed to hold a stone in its claw when standing sentinel to the sleeping flock, and if the bird was overcome by drowsiness the dropping stone would arouse it. All supporters: a rose within a roundel. (PLATE 11a.)

DATE: Probably late 15th century.

FORNHAM   St. Martin   *Two*

There are two very fine misericords incorporated in the modern woodwork of the lectern and reading desk.

1. The martyrdom of St. Thomas of Canterbury.
2. St. Martin dividing his cloak and giving half to a beggar.

DATE: Probably 15th century. The seat-ledges have straight fronts.

FRAMSDEN   St. Mary   *Six*

There are six stalls in a line against the north wall of the sanctuary.

North side from east

1. Below a corbel supporting the bracket is an animal in profile, its head broken off, pointing to the right. There is drapery around the neck and forepart. The hindquarters are those of an animal with a long tail and cloven hooves. Supporters: Left and Right, a body with a short tail with the hind legs of a horse but the feet of a cock. There is no head to the body but instead a hand which grasps the continuation of the plain moulding of the bracket.

2. Seated monk in drapery beside the model of a church; on each side of him are dragons. Supporters: Left and Right, simple floral design.

3. Plain seat.

4. Angel with wings outspread, face badly damaged, holding a shield, defaced. Supporters: Left and Right, trefoil leaf.

5. Two draped figures, heads broken off, the left kneeling, the right seated. Supporters: Left and Right, wyvern, walking outwards with head raised.

6. Similar to No. 1, except that the central figure faces left. It could be identified as a lion.

DATE: Probably 15th century. The shelves of Nos. 1, 5, and 6 are of earlier date than No. 4. The bracket of No. 2 is broken off. Pevsner says they are early 14th century, but this is unconfirmed (Pevsner, *Suffolk*, Penguin, 1961, p. 201).

LAVENHAM   St. Peter and St. Paul   *Five*

North side

1. A dead man's head, his ears being pulled by an ibis on one side and a spoonbill on the other. No supporters. The ibis was said to feed on carrion. (PLATE 11c.)

2. Man wearing a hood, in a crouching position. Supporters: Left and Right, leaf.

3. Composite creatures; one, half woman, half beast (perhaps a dragon) playing a viol, and another, half man with the hindquarters and tail of a beast, mimicking her by playing a pair of bellows with a crutch. No supporters.

4. Pelican in her piety. Supporters: Left and Right, leaf.

South side, nearest entrance to chancel

A man holding a pig under his right arm and clutching its right hindleg; with his left hand he is pinching the pig's tail.

DATE: Late 15th century. The church was built with the help of the Earl of Oxford and Thomas Spring (H. Munro Cautley, *Suffolk Churches*, p. 286).

NORTON   St. Andrew   *Eight*

North side from east

1. Woman carding wool. (PLATE 36*b*.)
2. Pelican in her piety. Beneath her is a scroll bearing the text: *In omni opere memento finis.*
3. Martyrdom of St. Andrew. (PLATE 36*c*.)

South side from east

1. Lion devouring wodehouse.
2. Two animals, mutilated, under a tree; probably pigs eating acorns.
3. Two hounds; head of one is missing.

Block of two on south side

1. Monk reading, seated at a desk on which he rests his elbow, his hand supporting his head.
2. Martyrdom of St. Edmund, one of whose legs has been broken off. Supporters: Left and Right, archer taking aim at the main figure. (PLATE 2*c*.)

Supporters in all cases except the Martyrdom of St. Edmund consist of a lozenge pattern of vine-leaf in a roundel.

DATE: Late 14th century (H. Monro Cautley, *Suffolk Churches*, p. 299).

OCCOLD   St. Michael   *One*

In the sanctuary on the north side is a stall with a carved misericord.

The carving is of a crowned female figure shown to the waist, wearing a low square-necked dress. The palms of her hands are held together, the fingers pointing upward in an attitude of prayer. On each side is the head and torso of a winged cherub. The central figure appears to be on a cloud, which suggests that this could represent the Assumption of Our Lady.

Supporters: Left, enclosed in a circle, a bearded man's head and shoulders; he has flowing hair. Right, in a circle, crudely carved head and shoulders of an angel, who is holding a three-stringed musical instrument in her left hand and a bow in his right. (PLATE 36*d*.)

DATE: Probably 14th century. Supporters resemble those at Norton and Bury St. Edmunds Museum.

OULTON   St. Michael   *One*

There is one misericord, a curious one, in this church. The seat is no longer hinged, but is fixed by iron brackets in the chair used by the Bishop on diocesan visits.

The misericord consists of vaulting ending in a short tail like that of a pig. There are no supporters. When the Bishop sits in the chair he is said to 'sit on the devil's tail'.

The misericord was presented to the church about the year 1946, and its origin is not known. The ledge is of simple oval shape and seems to be of early date.

SOUTHWOLD   St. Edmund   *Fourteen*

The centre carvings are all alike and consist of a four-sided corbel with a carved base of triple moulding.

The supporters are contained within a circular moulding, pendant from the bracket-ends.

North side from east.

1. Left and Right, a hound lying on his back, curled up so that his feet and body fit into a circular extension of the moulding.
2. Left, a dragon curled up as above. Right, supporter missing.
3. Supporters missing.
4. Left and Right, conventional foliage pattern.
5. The same.
6. Left and Right, conventional entwined design.
7. The same.

South side from east

1. Left and Right, simple flower and leaf.
2. Left and Right, one large formal leaf.
3. Left and Right, two formal leaves.
4. Left and Right, one large leaf.
5. Left and Right, smaller leaf.
6. The same.
7. Left and Right, pattern of three simple flowers, the stems of which point to west, south, and east to form a radial design.

DATE: 15th century. The church was rebuilt 1470–90 after destruction by fire (T. H. Bryant, *County Churches, Suffolk*, 1912, i, p. 60).

STOKE BY NAYLAND   St. Mary the Virgin   *Four*

There are seven stalls in the church, but three of their misericords have disappeared.

North side of Sanctuary

1. Plain vault, having at the base a saracen's head, turbaned, with forked beard. Supporters: Left and Right, vine-leaf.

In the Chancel
North side

1. Large, elaborate design of oak-leaves and acorns. Supporters: Left and Right, rose.

South side

1. Woman's head in coif and drapery. Supporters: Left and Right, elaborate circular pattern of small leaves and flowers.

Block of four stalls in North aisle, from east

1. Head of an animal, possibly a deer, or alternatively a demon with large ears. Supporters: Left and Right, vine-leaf.

2, 3, and 4. Carvings missing.

DATE: Late 14th century (H. Monro Cautley, *Suffolk Churches*, p. 319).

STOWLANGTOFT   St. George   *Six*

North to south

1. Bird of prey killing hare. Supporters: Left and Right, cowled, full-bearded head in a roundel.

2. Winged ox of St. Luke. Supporters: Left and Right, lion-mask.

3. Winged lion of St. Mark, holding scroll in mouth. Supporters: Left and Right, dove in flight.

4. Eagle of St. John with scroll in beak. Supporters: Left and Right, demi-angel holding book (heads missing).

5. Winged angel of St. Matthew with fillet head-dress, holding book. Supporters: Left and Right, male head with hair in form of radial rays.

6. Griffin with tongue protruding. Supporters: Left and Right, large rosette.

DATE: T. H. Bryant, *County Churches, Suffolk*, 1912, i, p. 137, says 'late 14th century.'

SUDBURY   St. Peter   *Two*

North side

Corbel, having at the base a pomegranate and leaves. Supporters: Left and Right, formal leaf in roundel form.

South side

Four-sided corbel, with sides corresponding to the four sides of the bracket. At base a scroll bearing an indecipherable inscription. Supporters: Left and Right, uncharged shield, within a rosette, and hanging by a ring from the bracket extension.

DATE: Mid-15th century.

SUDBURY   St. Gregory   *Eighteen*

This collegiate church was founded by Simon of Sudbury, Bishop of London 1361–75. The licence to found the church was confirmed in 1381 (*V.C.H., Suffolk*, ii, p. 150). There are nineteen stalls remaining, ten on the south side and nine on the north side.

North side from east

1. Uncharged shield. Supporters: Left and Right, five-petalled flower.
2. Head of a demon with large ears. Supporters: Left and Right, vine-leaf.
3. Cockerel in flight, with head turned to right. Supporters: Left and Right, group of small flowers.
4. Clean-shaven man's face, delicately carved, in ornamented cowl. Supporters: Left and Right, large rosette.
5. Head of an ox. Supporters: Left and Right, large daisy or marguerite.
6. Central carving missing. Supporters: Left and Right, vine-leaf.
7. Face of a man in elaborate cap. Supporters: Left and Right, large rosette.
8. Long, narrow female face, with eyes closed and lips parted, surmounted by head-dress of drapery. Supporters: Left and Right, bunch of acanthus-leaves.
9. Uncharged shield. Supporters: Left and Right, large five-petalled flower.

South side from east

1. Bird, probably a dove, in flight. Supporters, missing.
2. Carving resembling a twisted fold of cloth. Supporters: Left and Right, formal leaf.
3. Woman's face surrounded by coif. Supporters: Left and Right, large rose.
4. Ram's head (jaw broken). Supporters: Left and Right, vine-leaf.
5. Grimacing lion-mask, showing teeth. Supporters: Left and Right, rosette.
6. Plain seat.
7. Head of winged animal, possibly a wyvern, lying on its side, showing one limb and claw. Supporters: Left and Right, vine-leaf.
8. Head of bat-winged animal, with pig-like snout and front paws. Supporters: Left and Right, formal leaf.
9. Head and shoulders of a man with curled beard. Supporters: Left and Right, large rosette.
10. Talbot dog's head, showing its flopping ears and front paws. (A talbot dog formed part of the arms of Simon of Sudbury.) Supporters: Left and Right, triple flower.

DATE: *c.* 1362 (F. Bond, *Misericords*, p. 217).

UFFORD   The Assumption   *Three*

North side

1. Shield bearing *a cross engrailed* (arms of de Ufford). Supporters: Left and Right, folded acanthus-leaf.

South side

1. Clean-shaven, turbaned head. Supporters: Left and Right, acanthus-leaf in lozenge form.
2. Grotesque head with horns and large ears. Supporters: Left and Right, vine-leaf.

DATE: Probably 14th century.

WETHERINGSETT   All Saints   *Two*

On the north side of the sanctuary are two stalls with misericords, the centres consisting of three-sided corbels, carved at the head with double machico-lated moulding, and at the base with fruit and flower. The supporters are conventional triple flowers in every case.

DATE: Early 15th century.

WINGFIELD   St. Andrew   *Fifteen*

All the misericords are alike, the central carving being a four-sided vaulted corbel with machicolated head and moulded base. The supporters are conventional designs of a vine-leaf in a roundel, except those for South 2, which are a finely-carved acanthus-leaf, and South 7, which are a rosette. The central carving is missing from South 5.

DATE: 1362 is suggested, but the bracket design appears to be later than this, possibly early 15th century. The church became collegiate in 1362 (Knowles and Hadcock, *Medieval Religious Houses*, p. 345).

SURREY

BEDDINGTON   St. Mary the Virgin   *Nine*

In the chancel are twenty stalls with misericords, ten on each side, but only nine misericords are old, of late 14th-century date. By his will, which was proved in 1390, Sir Nicholas de Carew directed that four fit chaplains should 'pray for his soul and all Christian souls' in the church at Beddington.

From north-east to south-east

7. A shield *lozengy* (arms not known), flanked by inverted scallops surmounted by foliage. Supporters: Left, a shield, *fourteen roundlets figured on bordure, within, a leopard regardant salient* (arms not known, but possibly Oxenbridge). Right, a shield *parted per pale, on a chief three roundlets* (arms not known).
8. On a shield *a cross moline* (probably the arms of Uvedale, or Copley), the whole flanked by oak-leaves. Supporters: Left and Right, vine-leaf in lozenge pattern.

11. A shield uncharged, flanked by oak-leaves. Supporters: Left and Right, oak-leaf.

13. A clean-shaven face, wearing a mitre richly decorated with flowers and flanked by rays. Supporters: Left and Right, vine-leaf. (PLATE 37*a*.)

14. As for No. 11.

15. A woman's head, wearing richly decorated head-dress and caul. Supporters: Left and Right, vine-leaf. (PLATE 37*b*.)

18. An elaborate pattern of acanthus-leaves. Supporters: Left and Right, acanthus-leaf.

19. As for No. 11.

20. As for No. 11.

LINGFIELD   St. Peter and St. Paul   *Eight*

North side

1. Missing.

2. Angel holding a shield charged with *three cinquefoils*. Supporters: Left and Right, similar cinquefoils (arms of Bardolf).

3. Head with flowing hair and beard. Supporters: Left and Right, star-shaped foliage.

South side from east

1. Large rosette on a branch. Supporters: Left and Right, rose-leaf.

2. Missing.

3. Similar to North 3. Supporters: Left and Right, foliage.

4. Missing.

5. Woman's head wearing wimple. Supporters: Left and Right, foliage. (PLATE 37*c*.)

6. Uncharged shield surrounded by foliage. Supporters: Left and Right, foliage.

7. Bishop's head mitred. Supporters: Left and Right, mitre. (PLATE 37*d*.)

8. Angel holding shield charged with *three estoiles on a chevron*. Supporters: Left and Right, similar estoile (arms of Cobham).

DATE: 15th century. Sir Reginald, third Lord Cobham of Stoborough (Sterborough), founded a college of secular priests in 1431, and the church was rebuilt about that time (J. W. Flower, 'Notices of the family of Cobham of Sterborough Castle, Lingfield, Surrey', *Surrey Archeological Collections*, ii, 1864, p. 149).

SUSSEX

ARUNDEL   FitzAlan Chapel, the Castle   *Four*

In the north section of the FitzAlan Chapel, i.e. the original chapel, there are twelve stalls, six on each side, but only four in all have original misericords, the remainder being good reproductions.

North side

1. Large heraldic rose. Supporters: Left and Right, stiff leaf.
5. Clean-shaven man's head, with flowing curled hair. He has prominent eyes and a twisted lip. Supporters: Left and Right, formal leaf, with scroll decoration.

South side

8. Square-shaped formal flower, with four petals and four leaves. Supporters: Left and Right, formal oak-leaf.
12. Square-shaped pattern of oak-leaves. Supporters: Left and Right, fleur-de-lis.

In the main chapel, which was formerly the choir of the collegiate church, there are ranged in rows facing the altar thirty-two new stalls richly carved with modern misericords.

DATE of original misericords: late 14th century. The collegiate church was rebuilt, 1380–1400 (G. H. Cook, *English Collegiate Churches*, p. 121).

BROADWATER   St. Mary   *Six*

1. Rose, fully open, with four leaves. Supporters: Left and Right, similar rose.
2. Oblong pattern of two elaborate leaves. Supporters: Left and Right, diamond-shaped serrated leaf.
3. Similar to No. 2, but leaf design varied.
4. Two small leaf patterns springing from a common stem, and forming base of corbel. Supporters, as for No. 2.
5. Elaborate pattern of curving leaves. Supporters: Left and Right, similar design of leaves in a circular format.
6. Fully-open blossom of four petals, backed by two small leaves. Supporters: Left and Right, leaf pattern, resembling fleur-de-lis.

N.B.: No. 5 appears to be of different date from the other five, probably later. The seat bracket has a heavy quadruple moulding.

DATE: Probably 15th century.

CHICHESTER   The Cathedral   *Thirty-eight*

With the exception of North 8, which is probably 15th century, they all date from *c.* 1330.

From east end on north side

1. Jester, nude except for a hood, dancing with an ape-like beast. Supporters: Left and Right, hooded faces upside down.

2. Unidentifiable branch of foliage. Supporters: Left and Right, leaf from the main branch.

3. Bust with human head and arms, with the elbows of his very long arms supporting the bracket; he grasps his tail with his left hand. Supporters: Left and Right, grotesque face with protruding tongue and large ears (PLATE 38*a*.)

4. Slip of a branch with two large oak-leaves. Supporters: Left, bald head, Right, head with long hair and a skull-cap.

5. Two cowled heads placed back to back; on the left that of a young clean-shaven man, on the right that of a bearded man. From beneath their cowls issues a flat-headed monster with a serpent's body. Supporters: Left, head with long hair. Right, head wearing a close-fitting cap.

6. Two demons with serpentine bodies and folded membranous wings, having between them a crouching beast with long hind legs, suspended by its tail from the bracket. Supporters: Left and Right, a three-lobed toothed leaf.

7. Dancing woman or posture-maker being kissed by a man holding a viol in his left hand. Supporters: Left and Right, grotesque dog-like head, upside-down, with sweeping tongue. (PLATE 38*b*.)

8. Bold lion's mask. Supporters: Left and Right, lion's head in profile, with jaws open to reveal teeth and tongue. N.B.: Probably 15th century.

9. Bat-like creature with webbed hindfeet, possibly representing a wyvern. Supporters: Left and Right, formal vine- or maple-leaf.

10. Elaborate carving of an old man's head, crowned, with his long hair being licked by two amphisbaenae, one on each side. Supporters: Left, grotesque human head with protruding tongue. Right, lion-mask with protruding tongue. The main subject could be a variant of the Flight of Alexander. (PLATE 38*c*.)

11. Four-toed beast with long ears and a mane, facing to the right and eating foliage, which looks like acanthus. Supporters: Left and Right, boss of stylized foliage.

12. Cowled and draped human with the hindquarters of a beast with cloven hooves. Above the rump of the figure is a large stylized vine-leaf. Supporters: Left, young man's head in a soft, round, bonnet-like cap. Right, woman's head in a wimple.

13. Large vine-leaves and small bunch of grapes. Supporters: Left and Right, small lizard-like reptile.

14. Two feathered, claw-footed beasts with bulls' heads, similar to those in No. 10 above. They are seated facing each other, with one forelimb each supporting the bracket. Supporters: Left and Right, leopard-mask.

15. Two hounds killing a hare; above them and between them is a bat-like creature with outspread wings. Supporters: Left and Right, vine-leaf.

16. Composition of vine-leaves and grapes. Supporters: Left and Right, inverted hound's head.

17. Inverted triangular bunch of acanthus-leaves. Supporters: Left and Right, inverted dog's head with protruding tongue.

18. Two hairless apes looking backwards and supporting the bracket with their forefeet. They sit with their hind feet intertwined. Supporters: Left and Right, flat head of dog-like monster, flanked by one paw on the outer side.

19. Clean-shaven, nude figure with long hair thrusts a broad sword through the mouth of a beast with an ape-like face and short tail. Its feet have three large claws, and it has a noose around its neck. Supporters: Left and Right, inverted grotesque head.

Southern range

20. Wyvern-like creature, whose tail has an amphisbaena head instead of a barb. Its head is turned backwards. Supporters: Left and Right, inverted head of dog, that on the left with small ears, that on the right with long, drooping ears.

21. Two cowled heads back to back, an old man on the left, a young one on the right. A hand grasps the old man's beard, which is parted in the centre; he has a roll of hair along the top of his forehead. Supporters: Left and Right, clean-shaven head with long, curled hair, that on the left smiling, that on the right scowling, eyes closed.

22. Formal oak-leaves and acorns. Supporters: Left, man's head with long hair. Right, woman's head in a wimple.

23. Harper with an English harp and a piper seated facing each other in high-backed chairs. Supporters: Left, woman's head in a wimple. Right, man's head with long hair. (PLATE 38d.)

24. Finely carved mermaid, in a cap and holding a mirror. Supporters: Left and Right, inverted head of long-eared dog. (PLATE 39a.)

25. Similar theme to Nos. 5 and 21. The old man, on the left, strokes his beard with his left hand; the young man, scowling, has a foot touching his head. The subject rather resembles a wrestling match, but below these figures is a creature with horse's or ass's body with mane and saddle and protruding tongue. Supporters: Left and Right, serpentine coils with flat head, having protruding tongue.

26. Similar theme to No. 19. A draped figure is grappling with a lion, down whose throat it has thrust a broad sword so that it emerges at the back of the neck. It is not certain if the figure is female, but if so it is unusual for the feet to be shown. Formal leaves flank the group. Supporters: Left, female head in wimple. Right, female head in frilled hood.

27. Another variant of Nos. 5 and 21, but more resembling a cloven-hoofed monster, half man, half beast, with a pointed beard, centrally parted and caressed by the right hand. The rear part is a face ugly with grimacing. Supporters: Left and Right, animal head with mouth open showing teeth.

28. A monster with cloven hooves on its hind feet, claws on its front feet, and long, drooping ears. It is devouring a serpentine creature. The tail of the larger beast appears to be holding a third creature with a bull's head and a fish-like body. Supporters: Left, draped head. Right, head with long hair.

29. Composite creature with hooded face, human torso, beast's haunches, and four claws instead of a hoof. It tramples on an unidentified object which looks like the hind leg of a beast; the creature has human hands and is beating a tabor. Probably a satyr. Beneath its uplifted curly tail is a clean-shaven human face. Supporters: Left and Right, formal vine-leaf.

30. Two dragons or asps have their necks crossed and turned to face each other; one has the other's tongue in its mouth. They stand on the flowing hair of a small human head on the ground between them. Their tails are curled and terminate in the mouths of the supporters. Supporters: Left and Right, grotesque heads in horizontal position, wearing cap.

31. Large composition of acanthus-leaves. Supporters: Left and Right, lion-mask.

32. Vine and grapes, similar to No. 16. Supporters: Left and Right, large vine-leaf.

33. Two asps curled, with their heads horizontal and facing each other, supporting the bracket. Supporters: Left and Right, clean-shaven head with long, curled hair.

34. Two monsters, with long, curled ram's horns, sit supporting the bracket with heads and upraised arms. Between them, pointing upwards, is a creature with a bird's body and outspread wings, but having a flat head and bared teeth. Supporters: Left and Right, female head in wimple.

35. Griffin facing left and supporting the bracket with wings and tail. Supporters: Left, face in torment. Right, bearded grotesque.

36. Two lions sejant sharing a common head from whose ears issue serpentine bodies terminating in grotesque heads which are horizontal and form the supporters.

37. Old man, bearded and moustached, performs a contortive feat. He holds his shins with his hands, and is dressed in knee-breeches and a short-sleeved jacket. Supporters: Left and Right, grotesque dogs' heads with protruding tongue and outstretched forepaws.

38. Fox sits playing a harp; his feet rest on a goose gazing up. Opposite is an ape, mutilated, so that it is uncertain if he was playing an instrument or dancing to the fox's music. Supporters: Left and Right, formal maple foliage.

CHICHESTER St. Mary's Hospital *Thirteen*

North side from east

1. Plain seat.
2. Group of leaves and fruit, probably hawthorn.
3. Seated web-footed and winged monster with fox's head. Supporters: Left, man's head with long, curled hair and fringe. Right, a woman's head in a wimple.
4. Plain seat.
5. Jack-in-the-green. Supporters: Left and Right, lion-mask with protruding tongue.
6. Plain seat.
7. Design of oak-leaves and acorns.
8, 9, and 10. Plain seats.
11. Bunch of leaves and berries.
12. Monster, web-footed, winged, and twin-bodied. Supporters: Left and Right, bust of woman wearing a hooded head-dress.

South side from east

1 and 2. Plain seats.
3. Grotesque of an old man, wearing a cap and with a long curly beard, crouching between hunched shoulders, and supporting himself on his hands. Supporters: Left and Right, small dragon, its head close to the man's beard, and its neck clutched by his hand. (PLATE 39*b*.)
4. Vine-leaves and grapes. Supporters: Left and Right, vine-leaf.
5. Lion-mask with pointed ears. In its mouth are the tails of two dragons, the supporters, which have their backs turned to the viewer, and appear to be holding on to the bracket with their teeth.
6. Plain seat.
7. Merman, bearded, and wearing a loose tunic and cowl, supporting the bracket with his shoulders, and holding his tail in his hand. Supporters: Left and Right, oak-leaf. (PLATE 39*c*.)
8. Monster, with female head and bosom, and vulture's wings and claws (a harpy). Supporters: Left and Right, lion-mask.
9. Plain seat.
10. Double-bodied dragon with one head and two long tails. Two vine- or maple-leaves flank its head. Supporters: Left and Right, vine- or maple-leaf.
11. Plain seat.
12. Tumbler in a long cloak, sprawling forward, standing on his head, and supporting the bracket with his feet and buttocks. Supporters: Left and Right, three-lobed leaves.

DATE: Probably *c.* 1290, when the rebuilding of the Hospital was completed. Edward I confirmed the Hospital in its second home in 1285 (*V.C.H., Sussex,* ii. 101).

EAST LAVANT   St. Mary   *Five*

On the north side of the chancel are five stalls with misericords.

1. Head of a man with curled hair on each side, below a banded cap. Supporters: Left and Right, rose and leaves.

2. Head similar to No. 1. Supporters: Left and Right, shield quartered by a cross.

3. Two large-fronded leaves, branching from a common stem. Supporters: Left and Right, a large similar leaf.

4. Head of a man, possibly a bishop, wearing a mitre-shaped head-dress, but this could be a coronet. Supporters: Left and Right, a large rose.

5. Head similar to Nos. 1 and 2. Supporters: Left, an indented, shrivelled leaf. Right, an outspread lizard with forked tail.

DATE: 15th century (*V.C.H., Sussex,* iv, p. 103).

ETCHINGHAM   The Assumption and St. Nicholas   *Eighteen*

Each set of nine has the same carvings in the same order.

North and south from east

1. Ornamented column of scrolled leaves. Supporters: Left and Right, vine-leaf.

2. Column with double-cusped arches. Supporters: Left and Right, a man's head, in square brocaded head-dress.

3. Floriated column. Supporters: Left and Right, a large key, hanging by short chain from the end of the bracket.

4. Hawk, with raised wings, holding fish. Supporters: Left and Right, acanthus-leaf.

5. Column with scrolled leaves. Supporters: Left and Right, rosette.

6. Column with formal leafage. Supporters: Left and Right, leaping dolphin. (PLATE 39*d.*)

7. Plain vaulted column crenellated at base. Supporters: Left and Right, scrolled leaf, possibly of vine.

8. Plain column. Supporters: Left and Right, conventional acanthus-leaf.

9. Fox in centre in friar's cloak holding key, preaching to three geese on each supporter. (PLATE 10*a.*)

DATE: 14th century. The church was rebuilt by Sir William de Echyngham, d. 1388–9 (*V.C.H., Sussex,* ix, p. 215).

HARDHAM   St. Botolph   *One*

There is fitted into a nineteenth-century priest's stall one carved misericord of foliage, a triplet of formal leaves, with single-leaf supporters. The seat is of semi-oval shape and probably early fourteenth century. Probably from the Augustinian Priory of St. Cross, at Hardham. (PLATE 40a.)

WEST TARRING   St. Andrew   *Six*

From north to south

1. Stylized rose, backed by four leaves.
2. Large formal flower and leaves. (PLATE 40b.)
3. Fine bearded head with long, flowing hair.
4. Similar to No. 2.
5. Very fine bearded head with long, flowing hair, and a rosette surmounted by a small cross, on the forehead. (PLATE 40c.)
6. Similar to No. 2.

Supporters in each case, stiff leaf, either vine or acanthus.

DATE: 15th century. The chancel was rebuilt in the early fifteenth century and screen and stalls were then erected (J. L. André, *Sussex Archaeological Collections*, xli, pp. 55 and 59).

WEST WITTERING   St. Peter and St. Paul   *Two*

In the north-west corner of the chancel is a pair of ancient stalls, one side, the western, renewed, with three original arm-rests and two original backs. They were once part of a series, and appear to have been moved from their original position.

1. Western. A mitred head, surmounted by a vaulted corbel. Supporters: Left and Right, a five-petalled rose backed with four leaves.
2. Eastern. A five-petalled rose, surmounted by a vaulted corbel. Supporters: Left and Right, a square arrangement of four leaves not identical in shape.

DATE: Probably 16th century (*V.C.H., Sussex*, iv, p. 22, is incorrect).

WARWICKSHIRE

ASTLEY   St. Mary   *Eighteen*

There are eighteen stalls with misericords.

1 to 7. Ribbed vaulting springing from a rosette. Supporters, varying types of formal flower in lozenge arrangement.
8. Ribbed vaulting springing from a rosette. Supporters: Left and Right: acacia-leaf.

9. Ribbed vaulting springing from a small head with hair arranged in rayed halo. Supporters: Left and Right, formal flower.

10. Main carving as for No. 9. Supporters: Left and Right, large double rosette.

11. A boar passant, with well-defined cloven hooves. Supporters: Left and Right, lozenge-shaped flower pattern.

12. A cat-like beast with well carved claws. Supporters, as for No. 11.

13. Woman's head in flat, frilled head-dress with side-veil. She has a round-necked gown. Supporters as for Nos. 11 and 12. N.B. This type of head-dress seems to confirm the date as fourteenth century.

14. Lion passant regardant to left, with protruding tongue. Supporters: Left and Right, man's head with flowing hair beneath flat cap.

15. Talbot dog passant left. Supporters: Left and Right, formal lozenge-shaped flower.

16. Wyvern rampant, facing right. Supporters, as for No. 15.

17. Wyvern sejant, facing left, with wings raised. Supporters: Left, man's head with flowing hair beneath flat cap. Right, man's head with well-defined curly hair. (PLATE 40d.)

18. Bestiary wolf or hyena with cloven hooves. Supporters: Left and Right, pendant acacia-leaf.

DATE: Early 14th century; a college was founded in 1340 by Sir Thomas Astley and renamed the College of the Assumption in 1343 (*V.C.H., Warwick*, ii, p. 117).

COVENTRY

The existing misericords are divided between Trinity Church and the Grammar School as described below. They came from the White Friars or Carmelite monastery there. They belong to the fifteenth century and are marked by simplicity of design and finely artistic workmanship.

These carvings have undergone many vicissitudes, especially those in the Grammar School.

Many carvings have been lost or destroyed.

This is evidenced by some old drawings in the British Museum (Lansdowne MS. 209 ff, 254–5b) (Coats of Arms under Benches in Coventry Free School).

COVENTRY   Holy Trinity Church   *Twenty*

South side from west

1. Two cockatrices, back to back; monsters with bird's feet, lion's body, cock's head and wings, tail knotted in the centre. Supporters: Left and Right, woman's head with crespine head-dress and high, turned-down dagged collar. (The crespine, which was worn from about 1380 to 1450

consisted of a coronet of goldsmith's work over the forehead, connecting two cauls, one on each side of the face. The cauls were nets of gold wire, in this example ornamented with knobs.)

2. Two eagles back to back. Supporters: Left and Right, two eagles, a smaller one perched on the inner side of the moulding.

3. Stag at bay attacked by a hound. On left a hare, on right a hunter with a long dagger. Supporters: Left and Right, foliage.

4. Wodehouse bearded and clothed with skins. Behind, a sitting lion. Supporters: Left and Right, rose.

5. Foliate mask. Supporters: Left and Right, foliage. (PLATE 6a.)

6. Bearded and moustached face in profile with a kerchief bound over brow. Supporters: Left and Right, foliage. (This resembles the misericord South 2 in St. Katharine's Hospital, London.)

7. Lion-mask. Supporters: Left and Right, lion-mask.

8. Closed door. Supporters: Left and Right, rose. A closed door is emblematic of the virginity of Mary.

9. Wodehouse seated holding a club and a chain attached to a collar round the neck of a lion. Supporters: Left and Right, foliage. (PLATE 16d.)

10. Conventional foliage.

North side from west

11. Shield charged *plain quarterly* (arms of de Say). Supporters: Left, shield charged *a cross sable* (arms of John de Vesci of Alnwick, the founder of the first house of White Friars in England). Right, shield charged *a fess between three crescents* (arms of Hugh de Patteswell, Bishop of Lichfield and Coventry, 1240–1).

12. Foliage. Supporters: Left and Right, foliage.

13. Griffin. Supporters: Left and Right, lion-mask.

14. Double roses. Supporters: Left and Right, double rose.

15. Shield charged with *lion rampant* (arms of FitzAlan). Supporters: Left and Right, foliage.

16. Shield charged with *lion rampant*. Supporters: Left, shield charged *a chief chequy* (arms unidentified). Right, shield charged *fretty* (arms of John FitzAlan, Earl of Arundel, 1434).

17. Oak-foliage with little acorns. Supporters: Left and Right, oak-foliage.

18. Demi-angel. Supporters: Left and Right, vine-foliage.

19. Lion-mask. Supporters: Left and Right, scroll of ivy.

20. Arms of Sir William Walworth, *a bend raguly between two garbes*. Supporters: Left, arms of Walworth impaling Lovekin, *on a chevron between three doves rising, three escallops*. Right, arms of Walworth, *differenced by a border engrailed*. (Walworth and Lovekin were both Lord Mayors of London, *c.* 1366–81.)

COVENTRY   Henry VIII's Grammar School   *Fifteen*

In the Library.

These misericords were taken from the stalls which still line the walls of the old Grammar School in Hales Street. They have been cut and hacked by generations of schoolboys.

1. Lion sitting chained. Supporters: Left and Right, rose.

2. Lion springing. Supporters: Left and Right, lion-mask.

3. Winged lion. Supporters: Left and Right, foliage.

4. Lion-faced winged dragon. Supporters: Left and Right, foliage.

5. Head of bearded man. Supporters: Left and Right, oak-foliage. (Similar to one at Loversall.)

6. Woman's head with perpendicular four-leaved flower ornament round her rolled hair. Supporters: Left and Right, vine-foliage.

7. Foliage.

8. Angel peeping round shield charged, *within a bordure, between two annulets two bendlets and between the bendlets a saltire* (the merchant's mark of John Onley, Mayor of Coventry, 1396 and 1418). Supporters: Left and Right, double quatrefoil.

9. Foliage.

10. Arms of de Ros, *three water-bougets impaling Badlesmere: fesse between two gemel bars.* Supporters: Left, arms of de Ros. Right, arms of Arundel-FitzAlan, *a lion rampant.*

11. Arms of John Stody, *on a saltire engrailed, a leopard's face.* Supporters: Left, shield charged with *a chevron between three pierced mullets* (arms unidentified). Right, arms of William Walworth.

12. Shield charged with *three bars, over all a bend.* Unknown. Supporters: Left, arms of Gorges, *on a lozengy field a chevron.* Right, arms of Camoys, *on a chief three roundels.*

13. Fragment only, charged *three escutcheons*: unknown.

14. Sol in Libra. A long-robed figure holding a balance above the handle of which is a sun in its glory among foliage. The sign for September. Supporters: Left, a mutilated figure in a short tunic picking grapes and putting them into a basket. Right, a mutilated figure who appears to be crushing grapes with a pole, a barrel behind. (Grape-gathering misericords at Gloucester.)

15. Sol in Capricorno. A goat, with a sun in its glory on its flank, standing on its hind legs. The sign for December. Supporters: Left, David playing the harp. Right, man seated at table holding a loaf of bread in his left hand.

COVENTRY   St. Michael's Cathedral

The Cathedral, destroyed by enemy action in the 1939–45 War, had twelve misericords of great interest, dating from the late fifteenth century. The subjects consisted of representations of the Seven Works of Mercy, the Dance of Death, and Biblical subjects. They are fully described by M. D. Harris, 'Misericords in Coventry', *Birmingham Arch. Soc. Trans.* lii (1927), pp. 246–66.

HALFORD   St. Mary   *One*

In the chancel is an early seventeenth-century chair made up partly with a fifteenth-century stall. It has moulded elbow and capping and a tip-up seat with a misericord carved with a bearded man performing a tumbling trick in a pair of breeches, his head between his legs. Supporters: Left and Right, human head. The stall may have come from Kenilworth Abbey.

KNOWLE   St. John the Baptist, St. Lawrence and
St. Anne   *Eleven*

East of the screen are eleven collegiate stalls reset from further west, six on the north side and five on the south.

The easternmost on the north is carved with a lion and foliage. Supporters: Left, a hart. Right, a unicorn.

The opposite south carving is of an ape in a monk's hood holding urine flask. Supporters: Left and Right, ape, one holding a book.

Four of the others are carved with foliage and have leaves as supporters. The remaining five have uncarved centres, also with leaves as supporters.

DATE: Probably 15th century; certainly much of the church was rebuilt in the early part of this century (*V.C.H., Warwick.*, iv, p. 97).

STRATFORD-ON-AVON   Holy Trinity   *Twenty-six*

South side

1. Two hawks supporting in their beaks a crest, a coronet above an eagle displayed. Supporters: Left, winged monster, with hindquarters of a lion, head and shoulders of a monk. Right, the same, but with head of a nun.

2. Woman, in tight-fitting dress and loose mantle, seated with hands out-stretched towards a unicorn into which a man in forester's dress is plunging a spear; between them is a shield charged with *three crosslets patée; on a chief, a crescent* (arms of Peckham). Supporters: Left and Right, oak-foliage and acorns.

3. Two bears counter rampant, muzzled and chained, supporting between them a staff ragulée (the Warwick badge). Supporters: Left, monkey filling jug. Right, monkey drinking from another jug.

4. St. George (a knight in the armour of the period) and the Dragon; on the right a palm tree, on the left a royal maiden praying. Supporters: Left, a monster, hindquarters of a dragon, head and shoulders of a jester. Right, similar figure, but with head of a man arranging his beard into plaits.

5. Satanic mask with four horns. Supporters: Left and Right, comic mask.

6. Ram-headed mask. Supporters: Left, a goat. Right, a dolphin embowed.

7. Grotesque demi-figure of a woman leaning on her right arm. Supporters: Left and Right, harpy.

8. Grotesque mask, with mouth-foliage. Supporters: Left and Right, four-leaved flower.

9. Three comic masks of women, the left with tongue protruding. G. C. Druce suggests this series may represent the career of a scold (*Jour. Brit. Arch. Assoc.*, N.S. xxxvi (1931), p. 258).

10. Vine-foliage

11. Snake-bodied monsters, male and female intertwined, the left playing a pitch pipe; on the left a figure in a nightcap and robe issuing from a fish's mouth.

12. Sphinx with male rider (now headless). Supporters: Left, man and woman fighting; he seizes her by her hair, and she scratches his face. Right, nude woman; a dog seizes her legs and a man in a cloak is beating her with a birch.

13. Man and woman fighting. She tears his beard and raises a saucepan to beat him. Supporters: Left and Right, I H S in an interlaced circle.

North side

1. Man and woman issuing from whelk-shells; he wears a buttoned doublet and collar and holds a flesh-fork; she is in flowing drapery with sleeves, holding a carding instrument in her right hand and a spindle in her left. Supporters: Left and Right, vine-leaf.

2. Eagle perched on a swaddled infant (the Stanley badge). Supporters: Left, a monster, upper part a cowled monk, lower a lion; his left hand holds his tail, his right is raised, Right, a lion coward, sejant.

3. Merman holding a stone, and mermaid combing her hair and holding a looking-glass (damaged).

4. Nude woman riding a stag, holding a branch of four roses in one hand, the other outstretched towards a blank scroll behind two conventional trees (possibly representing Luxuria). Supporters: Left and Right, foliage.

5. Dromedary with palm branches behind. Supporters: Left and Right, horned wyvern.

6. Double four-leaved flower. Supporters: Left and Right, similar single flower.

7. Bicorporate lion with head of a bearded man. Supporters: Left and Right, bat-like dragon.

8. Defaced.

9. Large rush-basket holding head and shoulders of goat-headed devil. Supporters: Left and Right, gourd-leaf.

10. Owl with wings outspread. Supporters: Left and Right, foliage.

11. Double rose with shield in centre. Supporters: Left and Right, similar rose.

12. Vine-foliage.

13. Bearded mask with eastern head-dress. Supporters: Left, ostrich holding horseshoe in its beak. Right, goose. (PLATE 11d.)

DATE: Late 15th century (Bond, *Misericords*, p. 217).

This was a collegiate church, the college having been founded *c.* 1480 (*Bristol and Glos. Arch. Soc. Trans.*, xii, p. 206).

WILTSHIRE

HIGHWORTH   St. Michael   *Three*

North side

1. The head and wings of an angel.

South side

1. Mermaid displaying round mirror. (PLATE 41a.)

2. Male head, somewhat aquiline, and with long moustaches and forked beard.

The supporters of all three misericords are: Left and Right, a rose.

DATE: 15th century (R. L. P. Jowitt, *Wiltshire* (Methuen, London, 1949), p. 115).

MERE   St. Michael the Archangel   *Ten*

On the south side of the chancel are six old stalls with carved misericords.

On the north side of the chancel there are four old stalls which were purchased in 1949 from a local firm who had bought them from the executors of the will of an antique-collector.

South side from the east

1. Face with protruding tongue and mouth-foliage. Supporters: Left and Right, foliage.

2. Large rosette. Supporters: Left and Right, leaf.

3. Face of man wearing chin-beard and hat. Supporters: Left and Right, leaf.

4. Foliage.

5. Angel holding uncharged shield. Supporters: Left and Right, leaf.

6. Foliage covering a fox. (PLATE 41b.)

North side from east

1. Angel holding a shield *à bouche*, charged *three billets, two and one, on each an annulet*. Supporters: grotesque floral head roughly carved.

2. Angel holding a lute. Supporters: Left and Right, heads with flowing hair (PLATE 41c.)

3. Angel holding a shield, on which is a cross flory, possibly the arms of Melton of Lancaster, over a prone child, and with the other hand holding another child. Supporters: Left and Right, head of angel covered by wings.

4. St. George and the Dragon. Supporters: Left and Right, dragon's head.

DATE: Those on the south side, 14th century. A desk-end to this row bears the arms of Gilbert Kymer, Dean of Salisbury, 1449–63. Those on the north side, 16th century. Efforts to trace their origin have been unsuccessful. The arms on North 1 could be those of Ambrose of Lancaster, or of Paynter of Cornwall and Surrey.

SALISBURY   The Cathedral   *One hundred and six*

There are twenty-seven stalls on each side of the choir and four returned on each side. Below them on each side are twenty-two stalls. The Dean's stall on the south side in the returned stalls is fixed. All the other stalls have carved misericords which are all similar (except the fifth stall on the south side from the east), having floral designs with similar supports. The misericord of the fifth stall is a sleepy-looking bicorporate lion. Supporters: Left and Right, rose.

DATE: 13th century. N. Pevsner states: 'In a collection table in the North Aisle is incorporated a misericord with a carving of the virgin and unicorn' (Pevsner, *Wiltshire*, Penguin, 1963, p. 369).

SALISBURY   St. Thomas of Canterbury   *Four*

From north-east

1. Clean-shaven face ,with head crowned with foliage. Supporters: Left and Right, foliage in a quadruple, lozenge-shaped oak-leaf pattern.

2. Formal leaf and fruit pattern. Supporters: Left and Right, lozenge-shaped rosette.

From south-east

1. Clean-shaven, cowled, smiling head, with leaf on each side of cowl. Supporters: Left and Right, oak-leaf.

2. Corbel-shaped oak-leaf pattern. Supporters: Left and Right, oak-leaf.

DATE: Probably 15th century. The chancel was rebuilt *c.* 1447–50.

WORCESTERSHIRE

GREAT MALVERN The Priory Church of St. Mary and
St. Michael *Twenty-two*

North side from west
  Upper Tier

1. Lion-mask.

2. Swineherd, dressed in the usual flat cap, doublet and hose, and pointed shoes, knocking down acorns. Representing October. Supporters: Left and Right, pig.

3. Subject doubtful, it may represent a drunkard being beaten by his wife. There is also a prone figure drinking out of a leather bottle. Supporters: Left and Right, dragon's head.

4. Two long-necked monsters; one, with wings and tail, has the face of a man, and the other, with webbed feet facing and intertwined, has the face of a woman. Supporters: Left and Right, dragon's head.

5. Woman hitting man's head with broken distaff. Supporters: Left and Right, winged head.

6. Man with bag fastened to a strap over his shoulders with a seed-container on his left. He is a seed-sower and represents March. Supporters: Left and Right, bird in flight.

Lower Tier

1. Man seated at a table holding up a wine-cup in each hand. Probably representing January. The round, flat cap is characteristic and is seen in the Worcester Cathedral misericord carvings. Supporters: Left and Right, double rose.

2. Man reaping. In his right hand he has a long forked stick to hold down the corn, and with his left he cuts it with a long-handled hook. Representing August. Supporters: Left and Right, a bird with wings and claws expanded, probably pigeons.

3. Three mice hanging a cat by pulling a rope over a bar. Supporters: Left and Right, owl.

4. Man with a scythe. Representing June. Supporters: Left and Right, conventional leaf.

5. Smiling man carrying a bunch of grapes in his left hand and a basket in his right. Representing September. Supporters: Left and Right, conventional leaf.

6. Cockatrice. Supporters: Left and Right, foliate square.

South side from west

  Upper Tier

1. Monster, with a hooded human head and two-toed feet, stands back to back with another scowling monster with the head of an animal (with something in its mouth) and human feet. Both have turned their heads. Supporters: Left and Right, cowled mask.
2. Merman holding a mirror in his left hand, and a mermaid with a comb in her right hand. Supporters: Left and Right, bird's head.
3. Sick man in bed supported by a woman while a doctor looks at two flasks which he holds in his hands. Supporters: Left and Right, serpent's head.
4. Man in a cowl drives away a demon with bellows. Supporters: Left and Right, bird's head.

Lower Tier

1. Grotesque mask with long hair. Supporters: Left and Right, the same.
2. Head and shoulders of a man in a flat cap with wings of hair on each side. Probably a portrait. Supporters: Left and Right, leaf in lozenge form.
3. Butcher, wearing doublet and hose, killing an ox with a broken pole-axe. Representing December. Supporters: Left and Right, conventional leaf.
4. Angel, with outspread wings and wearing a cope, playing a cither or cittern (an old metal-stringed instrument like a lute or guitar — not to be confused with a zither), with mouth open, singing. Supporters: Left and Right, conventional leaf in lozenge form.
5. Wyvern. Supporters: Left and Right, conventional leaf in lozenge form.
6. Man holding a large bunch of flowers in each hand. Representing May. Supporters: Left and Right, conventional leaf in lozenge form.

DATE: *c.* 1480 (Vera L. Edminson, *Ancient Misericords in the Priory Church*, 1955).

The positions of all these carvings have been changed since Miss Emma Phipson described them in 1896.

RIPPLE St. Mary *Sixteen*

This church is remarkable for having a complete set (and it is believed the only complete set) of misericord carvings showing the monthly agricultural occupations of a village throughout the year. These are:

1. *January.* Two men wooding, i.e. collecting dead branches of trees.
2. *February.* Hedging and ditching. One man is hammering a wedge to split a hedge-stake, the other (whose right leg is broken off) holds a spade-handle. Between them is a bundle of unburned stakes.
3. *March.* Sowing. With his right hand a man is broadcasting seed, holding a basket with his left; a horse walks behind pulling a harrow to cover the seed. (PLATE 41*d*.)

4. *April*. Bird-scaring. One man waves a flag which he holds in his right hand.

5. *May*. Blessing the crops at Rogationtide. In the carving is shown the figure of St. Mary with a large bouquet of flowers in each hand. This figure was carried round the fields.

6. *June*. Hawking. A mounted man with what no doubt was a hawk on his wrist but which has been broken off.

7. *July*. Thought to be Lammas (Loaf-Mass) Eve at the manorial bakery. The mouth of the oven and a loaf are shown.

8. *August*. Reaping. Man with sickle, and woman with crook.

9. *September*. Removing corn for malting. Two men hold partly filled sacks and a long corn bin as they kneel behind a pile of grain.

10. *October*. A man is beating down acorns (which are shown as very large) for pig-food. The man's stick has been broken off.

11. *November*. Pig-killing. A man holds a squealing pig by the ear, another by the tail, while behind another pig squeals. (PLATE 42*a*.)

12. *December*. Man and wife on a curved settle by the fire on which is a pot. The man wears a hood and thick, fingerless gloves; the woman is spinning. The men in all the carvings (except the last) wear the characteristic flat cap that also appears in the Worcester Cathedral carvings, which are dated 1397. In all cases the supporters are conventional leaves.

In addition to the twelve carvings there were four others representing blessings to help the crops:

A. *Day*. A sun, a face with flames round it.

B. *Warmth*. Another sun.

C. *The Moon*, the phases of which were regarded as indicating the time to sow. (PLATE 42*b*.)

D. *Rain*. Aquarius, the sign of the Zodiac called the 'Water Carrier'.

Originally these four were returned stalls, two on each side facing the altar. At present A is between Nos. 3 and 4, C is between Nos. 9 and 10, and the other two are in the vestry.

M. Moore, *Worcestershire*, Methuen, London, 1952, p. 133, records that the stalls are thought to have been brought from Hartlebury Palace.

DATE: 15th century. See E. F. Gray, *The Two Churches of Ripple*, 1946, p. 9.

WORCESTER   The Cathedral   *Forty-two*

North side from east

1. The Temptation in Eden. The Serpent, having the body of a dragon and the head of a beast with long ears, is wound round the tree. Adam and Eve stand on each side, holding fruit. Supporters: Left and Right, a pair of eagles, back to back.

2. The Expulsion from Paradise. Adam and Eve, who are retiring before an angel with a drawn sword, are putting on fig-leaves. Supporters: Left and Right, dove, facing inward.

3. Abraham offering up Isaac. The hand of an angel is grasping the point of Abraham's sword. A ram stands beside Abraham on his left. Supporters: Left and Right, man's bust, with flat cap on his head and a mass of hair sticking out each side horizontally. He wears an embroidered tunic.

4. Moses and a companion, with the Tables of the Law. A devil stands between them on a pedestal (the Brazen Serpent). Supporters: Left and Right, serpent, with calf-like head, entwined.

5. The Judgement of Solomon. The King, with the Queen, is sitting under a canopy. On the King's left, forming the supporter, is an officer of state with a sword about to divide a living child carried by a woman. On the other side is a woman with a dead child wrapped in burial clothes.

6. Samson riding a lion and holding its jaws with both hands. Supporters: Left and Right, an intricate large circular design of leaves.

7. Two men, each holding a long roll of parchment, apparently disputing. They may be Old Testament Prophets. Supporters: Left and Right, fowl, having bald, bearded man's head.

8. Swineherd striking down acorns from a tree; two pigs underneath. October. Supporters: Left and Right, large oak-leaf design.

9. Lion and dragon fighting. Supporters: Left, seated lion. Right, dragon rampant.

10. Sow suckling five piglets. Supporters: Left and Right, large, round double flower.

11. King with a richly caparisoned horse and a page. Supporters: Left and Right, bust of a man with a flat cap and bushy hair.

12. Composite creature with hooded woman's head. Supporters: Left, a hawker with gauntlet. Right, hawk and prey.

13. Lion, with the head of a woman, wearing a square cap. Supporters: Left and Right, dove preening.

14. Basilisk. Supporters: Left and Right, weasel facing inward, holding sprig of rue, which gives it immunity from the basilisk's deadly glance. (PLATE 10c.)

15. Woman, nude except for a large meshed net draped around her, riding a goat and carrying a rabbit under her arm. Illustrates the folk-tale of the 'Clever Daughter' or the Deadly Sin of Lechery. Supporters: Left and Right, floral mask. (PLATE 16c).

16. Woman with a distaff and a man digging. Possibly a reference to 'when Adam delved and Eve span . . .'. Supporters: Left, a man and Right, a woman, with grotesque heads, and with the legs and feet of quadrupeds, wings of birds, and heads and necks of swans.

17. Stag couchant under a tree. Supporters, Right only, a round design of leaves.

18. Wyvern. Supporters: Left and Right, basilisk.

19. Headless robed figure under a canopy. Supporters: Left and Right, double eagle.

20. Dragon devouring man in a girdled tunic; the head has been swallowed. (Judas in the jaws of Satan.) Supporters: Left and Right, hound gorged.

21. Pelican in her piety. Supporters: Left and Right, oak-leaves and acorns.

South side from east

1. Two wyverns in mortal combat. Supporters, wyverns couchant.

2. Abraham, with sword and altar lamp, followed by Isaac, robed and carrying crossed bundles of wood on his shoulders to the place of sacrifice. Supporters: Left and Right, lion with bearded man's head and cap with long plume.

3. Three men mowing with scythes. June. Supporters: Left, an ape riding a hound wearing a collar. Right, a wolf in clerical cloak preaching or saying grace over the head of a sheep on a table or altar. (PLATE 42c.)

4. Three men harvesting, wearingt he usual flat cap and having bushy wings of hair. July. Supporters: Left, a sphinx playing a dulcimer. Right, a sphinx playing a viol.

5. Three men reaping corn with sickles. August. Supporters: Left and Right, triple sheaves.

6. Knight, with helmet, shield, and drawn sword, fighting with two griffins. The shield bears a bear sejant which may refer to Urso d'Abitot or the Earls of Warwick (E. Aldis, *Carvings and Sculptures of Worcester Cathedral*, Bemrose, London, 1873, p. 10). Supporters: Left and Right, mask with curled hair.

7. Huntsman sounding horn wound around him. Supporters: Left and Right, double-headed eagle.

8. Angel playing a lyre or lute. Supporters: Left and Right, curly-headed mask in embroidered collar.

9. Jousting scene. One knight has unhorsed another who has broken his spear, whose foot with a sharp pointed spur is out of his stirrup, and whose horse is on its haunches. Both knights are fully armed. One squire (left), who appears horrified, is falling backwards, and another (right) is blowing a serpentine horn. (PLATE 5a.)

10. Man sowing seed, a bag strapped to his shoulders. On the ground on each side of him is a basket. The toes of his shoes are pointed. March. Supporters: Left and Right, dove.

11. Woman wearing a hood and cape with loose sleeves, sitting on a bench and writing in a book at a desk. A large bird is on the floor with a bottle in its beak from which the woman is taking something in her left hand.

A smaller bird is being seized by a serpent whose head protrudes from the woman's sleeve. This carving resembles early manuscript drawings of Dialectica. Supporters: Left, a boy picking fruit. Right, a hunter carrying a rabbit on a pole.

12. The Presentation of Samuel. Supporters: Left and Right, circular leaf design.

13. Boar. Supporters: Left and Right, large lion-mask.

14. The Circumcision of Isaac. Supporters: Left and Right, fowl, having bald, bearded man's head. (PLATE 4d.)

15. Butcher killing an ox. He wears sharp-pointed shoes. November. Supporters: Left and Right, double rose.

16. Man wearing a cap with a hood drawn over his ears, and a cloak and sword, and bearing in each hand a large branch of foliage. Supporters: Left and Right, crested fowl, with prominent eyes, facing inward. May.

17. Angel playing a viol beneath a canopy. Supporters: Left and Right, curly-headed mask in embroidered collar.

18. Crowned lion. Supporters: Left and Right, a man's face, smiling.

19. Man wearing a cap and playing an instrument like a pipe. Supporters: Left and Right, circular cluster of five roses.

20. Old man stirring a pot over a fire and seated in a semicircular armchair with three legs. There is a chimney, which indicates that he is well-to-do. The man has taken off his boots and is warming his feet. He wears two-fingered gloves. Supporters: Left, a dog or cat is warming itself. Right, two flitches of bacon are hanging. December.

21. Crowned man seated, with birds on either side, probably representing Alexander's Flight. Supporters: Left and Right, eagle with rear part of a lion.

DATE: late 14th century (Lady M. D. Cox, 'The Twelfth Century Design Sources of the Worcester Cathedral Misericords', *Archaeologia* xcvii (1959), pp. 165–78).

YORKSHIRE

BEVERLEY   The Minster   *Sixty-eight*

In ordinances drawn up in 1391 for the 'government of the Collegiate Church of Beverley' the Bishop of York made arrangements for the seating of the clerks, their masters or ecclesiastical superiors, and the choristers in three rows. At that date there were sixty-eight officers of the church, from which it would appear that none of the misericords has been lost.

They were carved in 1520 as shown by the date on misericord No. 12 on the upper row on the north side.

The front of the brackets is enriched with a row of small arches; the supporters are encircled by the bracket moulding, fastened with foliated clasps.

South side

Upper row from west

1. Pelican in her piety; there are six young in the nest. Supporters: Left, a pelican standing with outstretched wings. Right, a pelican turned to the left, pecking its left claw. (The Archbishop's stall.)

2. Ape on horseback, face to tail, holding mane with left hand. Behind, man raises a club (man's arms broken off). Supporters: Left, ape riding cat which he combs with a large comb. Right, boy riding a pig and holding its tail.

3. Winged demi-angel in alb bearing in front the Sacred Heart. Supporters: Left and Right, fruit and foliage.

4. Shield charged, *a fess between three weights, two and one*. Scroll inscribed *William Wight Tempore Cancellarius Hujus Ecclecie*. (Punning heraldry.) Supporters: Left, man with a weight in each hand. Right, a man holding scales and raising his foot from the ground. Wight was Chancellor in 1520 (*Archaeologia*, lxxxv, p. 120).

5. Lion and dragon fighting. Supporters: Left (obviously connected with next misericord), seated ape holding a baby (or perhaps a doll from the pack). Right, seated ape holding bottle.

6. Pedlar asleep while eight apes ransack his pack; one ape is looking at a mirror, another is passing articles to the others. Supporters: Left, ape seated on a leaf holding out his hand for his share. Right, cat in a tree, ape below with stick.

7. Shield charged, *a fess between three weights, two and one*. Supporters: Left, man, in hood and liripipe, lifting two weights. Right, man walking, carrying two weights.

8. Conventional foliage (well carved). Supporters: Left and Right, leaf.

9. Woman standing (upper part broken off); on her right a man kneeling and blowing fire with bellows; on her left man chopping wood with axe. Supporters: Left and Right, fruit and foliage.

10. Two men dragging a wicker cage in which lies a bear. In the centre, man standing, holding a staff with both hands. Supporters: Left, man muzzling crouching bear. Right, man muzzling bear standing on hind legs.

11. Seated man in cap holding a sheep; another man astride a ram that he is shearing. Supporters: Left, shepherd with crook, stroking dog. Right, two rams butting.

12. Shield charged quarterly: 1st and 4th, *three billets below three besants*; 2nd and 3rd, *chevron between three mullets two and one*; supported by griffins. Supporters: Left, pelican in her piety below a scroll with *arma magistri*

Thome. Right, doe gorged and chained, lying on a tun, behind scroll with *donyngto '[n]p' [re] centoris huis ecclie.* Donyngton was Precentor in 1520.

13. Two men pulling rope attached to muzzled bear; from left another wheels a barrow to receive bear. Supporters: Left, man holding dog's muzzle to prevent barking. Right, muzzled bear.

14. Dead stag being cut up by two men. Supporters: Left, man with hound in leash. Right, man with five hounds blowing horn.

15. Huntsman with dogs attacking bear; two men running, one with staff, the other blowing horn. Supporters: Left, man holding whip over cowering ape. Right, bear dancing to bagpipes played by seated ape.

16. Ape on horse leading three muzzled bears, preceded by dog. Supporters: Left, muzzled bear. Right, ape holding dog as if to play it like bagpipes.

17. Man between two dragons whose tails surround him. Supporters: Left, hooded man spearing snail. Right, man entering a sack.

18. Sow on hind legs playing bagpipes, trough in front, four piglets dancing. Supporters: Left, saddled pig. Right, sow playing harp.

19. Three hounds running in front of man with bow and arrow (broken), a fox puts his head out of an earth. Supporters: Left, monkey riding fox. Right, ape nursing or shriving a fox in bed.

20. Fox running away with a goose, chased by women; to left, farmhouse with child standing in doorway; behind, fox and four geese. Supporters: Left, two seated foxes facing each other. Right, fox looking over his shoulder, a goose under his paws.

21. Grapes and foliage. Supporters: Left and Right, bunch of grapes and vine-leaves.

South side

Lower row from west

1. Demon running after woman (damaged). Supporters: Left, hooded man seated before money chest, counting his money; head of demon peeps over shoulder. Right, demon encouraging a glutton. May refer to the Deadly Sins of Avarice and Gluttony.

2. Fruit and foliage. Supporters: Left and Right, flower and leaves.

3. Owl holding mouse. Supporters: Left and Right, leaf.

4. Two cranes eating from a sack. Supporters: Left and Right, crane.

5. Cat seizing mouse. Supporters: Left, cat playing viol to four dancing kittens. Right, cat tossing mouse.

6. Hare riding fox. Supporters: Left, man drawing bow. Right, rabbits.

7. Lion and deer. Supporters; Left, lion crowned couchant. Right, unicorn scratching its head with hind hoof.

8. Two demi-figures of carvers wearing tight jerkins, quarrelling; one raises a mallet, the other holds a chisel. Supporters: Left, man wearing cap

puts his left hand derisively to his nose. Right, man in flat cap raises his hands.

9. Mermaid or dolphin (damaged). Supporters: Left, large fish seizing smaller. Right, three fishes interlaced in a triangle.

10. Foliage. Supporters: Left and Right, foliage.

11. Joshua and Caleb carrying a large bunch of grapes on a branch (Num. 13: 23). The only scriptural subject; copied from block-book, *Biblia Pauperum*. Supporters: Left, vine-leaf and tendril. Right, leaf and grapes.

12. Two lions couchant. Supporters: Left and Right, square foliated ornament.

13. Elephant with large castle on his back, his ears webbed like a bat's, being driven by ape with staff; porcupine leads the way. Supporters: Left, camel couchant. Right, lion.

North side

Upper Row from west

1. Stag chased by hounds with spiked collars, and being pierced with a spear by man in tight jerkin. Supporters: Left, man riding caparisoned horse and winding a horn. Right, doe scratching her head with left foot.

2. Man piercing lion with spear. Supporters: Left and Right, lion, the right one with tongue protruding.

3. Unicorn. Supporters: Left and Right, foliage.

4. Fox in hood in a pulpit preaching to seven geese; behind him is an ape as clerk, with a goose slung on a pole. Supporters: Left, owl. Right, man shoeing a goose.

5. Man in short tunic, gypciere hanging from his belt, holding a hawk on his wrist; another holds two hounds in leash. Supporters: Left, cock, Right, dog with bone, below each is a scroll inscribed, on the left, *Johannes Sperke*, on the right, *clericus fabrici*, John Sperke, Clerk of Works, 1520.

6. Deer browsing. Supporters: Left, hart leaping. Right, doe and fawn.

7. Fox hanged by six geese holding the rope in their beaks. Supporters: Left, fox and two sleeping geese. Right, ape takes the rope from the dead fox.

8. Foliate mask with tongue protruding. Supporters: Left, man chopping branch from tree. Right, conventional foliage.

9. Two monsters, one human-headed. Supporters: Left, dog grasping a pole. Right, dog-headed ape.

10. Man in belted tunic warming hands at fire; woman (broken) chases dog which has stolen meat from the pot. Supporters: Left, man, with apron over short tunic, kneeling before a pot washing platters. Right, man pulling up his hose; shoes on ground, wallet hung on wall.

11. Man on horse; before him a harvest cart (damaged). ('The cart before the horse.') Supporters: Left, cow lying down. Right, girl milking with pail with three hoops. (PLATE 42*d*.)

12. Shield charged, *fess between three birds, two and one*; supported by hawk and hound. Supporters: Left, dove. Right, hawk, below each a scroll inscribed, on the left *arma wilhelmi tait*, on the right, *doctoris thesaurarii huius ecclie 1520*.

13. Man, wearing cote-hardi and round cap, spearing boar; his hound seizes another boar by the ear. Supporters, conventional roses.

14. Wodehouse with long hair fighting dragon. Supporters: Left and Right, fruit.

15. Bust of man, wearing tight-fitting cap with brim turned up at sides, with his fingers stretching the corners of his mouth. Supporters: Left and Right, lion's mask with protruding tongue.

16. Cock crowing. (Emblem of St. Peter.) Supporters: Left, cock pluming himself. Right, two cocks fighting perched on a barrel.

17. Man wheeling virago in a barrow; she wears kerchief on head and full-necked dress, and is holding on to the man's hair (damaged). Supporters: Left, man lifting beam. Right, woman holding dog by its neck. (PLATE 43*a*.)

18. Woman standing and seizing man by his hair, dog helping himself from pot. Supporters: Left, woman grinding hand-mill. Right, man chopping.

19. Dragon-headed bird with a human face carved on its breast. Supporters: Left and Right, small dragon.

20. Demi-angel in alb. Supporters: Left, grapes and vine-leaves. Right, rose and leaves.

21. Three jesters, hand-in-hand, dancing, wearing hoods with long ears and scalloped tunics. Supporters: Left, jester kneeling and holding staff and bladder. Right, jester playing fife and tabor.

North side

Lower row from west

1. Two lions seated, one crowned. Supporters: Left, boar. Right, hawk.

2. Two men fighting; the right-hand one has a shield, sword, and scabbard; the other is nude and holds a dagger. Supporters: Left and Right, leaf.

3. Hawk. Supporters: Left, man seated, feeding hawk on wrist. Right, hawk seizing pigeon.

4. Rose-tree with four roses. Supporters: Left and Right, rose.

5. Hawk flying after a bat. Supporters: Left and Right, bird scratching head.

6. Lion with paw on prostrate man. Supporters: Left, wyvern. Right, griffin.

7. Two birds on jester's head pecking his long-eared hood. Supporters: Left, goose pluming itself. Right, swan swimming.

8. Bust of jester wearing long-eared hood; he is putting right fore-finger in his mouth and left hand over his eye. Supporters: Left, flying goose. Right, goose pluming itself.

9. Owl attacked by four small birds. Supporters: Left and Right, hawk.

10. Two dragons. Supporters: Left, raven on branch. Right, dove on foliage.

11. Bust of jester in eared hood, grinning. Supporters: Left, face laughing. Right, hooded head, mouth puckered.

12. Foliage. Supporters: Left and Right, leaf.

13. Hen and five chickens. Supporters: Left, cock scratching his comb. Right, hen sitting on chickens, one on her back.

BEVERLEY   St. Mary   *Twenty-three*

North side from west

1 and 2. Modern.

3. Ape parodying doctor, holding up bag to an ecclesiastic who holds up a large coin; on the other side is a man holding up what appears to be bread. Supporters: Left and Right, foliate face.

4. Knight (possibly St. George) with sword attacking a wyvern; another wyvern behind him. Supporters: Left and Right, leaf with bird in centre.

5. Two wodehouses with clubs; on either side a dragon. Supporters: Left and Right, leaf with dragon in centre.

6. Knight with spear attacking wild boar with his left hand. He is drawing his dagger to cut its throat. Supporters: Left and Right, leaf.

7. King, sitting cross-legged on throne, holding a sceptre in each hand; a griffin standing on a dragon on each side. Supporters: Left and Right, angel in foliage playing a cithern.

8. A pelican in her piety. Supporters: Left and Right, leaf.

9. King holding a sceptre in his right hand; with his left keeping back a nude woman riding a goat and carrying a small dog or hare under her arm. On the king's right is a man riding an animal and forcing its mouth open (probably Samson and the lion). A dog under each rider. Possibly a variant of the 'Clever Daughter', cf. Worcester, North 15.

10. Valentine and Orson meeting each other. Supporters: Left and Right, foliate face.

11. Foliate mask. Supporters: Left and Right, leaf.

12. Fox in pulpit between two monks, each of whom has a long scroll in his hand. Below are two seated monkeys with scrolls. Supporters: Left and Right, leaf.

13. Head with foliage coming out of its mouth. Supporters: Left and Right, foliate head.

14. Eagle holding an open book from which two foxes are reading. Supporters: Left and Right, leaf.

South side from west

1. Stag lying under tree, a small dog on each side. Supporters: Left and Right, leaf.

2. Modern. Fox and goose.

3. Eagle and dogs.

4. Ecclesiastic in hood and gown, holding a scroll. On either side a fox holding a pastoral staff with a goose hanging out of his cowl behind. Supporters: Left and Right, small dog in leaves.

5. Elephant and castle; at sides vine-leaves and grapes.

6. King's head between two oak-leaves. Supporters: Left and Right, leaf.

7. Tree of Life between two griffins; under each a rabbit. Supporters: Left and Right, leaf.

8. An impassive bear and two dogs, a bear-baiting scene. Supporters: Left and Right, foliate face.

9. Modern.

10. Wodehouse between two lions; dragons under his feet. Supporters: Left and Right, leaf.

11. Head with spray. Supporters: Left and Right, leaf.

12. Modern.

13. Fox transfixed by a large arrow is proffering a bag to a monkey that is pouring liquid on the fox's head. At the side of the fox stands a wodehouse with a bow in his hand. Supporters: Left and Right, foliate face.

14. Head with cap and large curls, bunches of grapes coming out of the corners of his mouth. Supporters: Left and Right, foliate face.

DATE: *c.* 1445 (Cox and Harvey, *English Church Furniture*, p. 261; F. Bond, *Misericords*, p. 227).

DARRINGTON   St. Luke and all Saints   *Four*

There are three stalls with carved misericords on the south side of the chancel, two near the altar, which appear to be used as sedilia, and one on the same side at the west end of the chancel. Opposite on the north side is one stall.

South side from east

1. Floral design. Supporters: Left and Right, leaf.

2. Head. Supporters: Left and Right, square foliate design.

3. Bearded face crudely carved. Supporters: Left and Right, face.

North side

Floral design. Supporters, Left and Right, leaf.

DATE: Late 15th century (information from G. C. Pace).

HACKNESS   St. Mary the Virgin   *Fourteen*

On the north side the misericords are plain, except the second, which is carved with grapes and fruit.

South side

1. Grotesque face.
2. Large scalloped shell.
3. Foliage.
4. Grotesque face.
5. Angel with shield charged with *a maunch* (probably the arms of Conyers).
6. Foliage and fruit.
7. The Percy badge of a crescent and shackle.

All supporters, conventional foliage.

DATE: 15th century (*V.C.H., North Riding*, ii, p. 531).

HALIFAX   St. John   *Nine*

There are nine stalls with misericords in the chancel, in three groups of three. One group formed sedilia, and there is a group of three on each side of the chancel.

North side

1. Figure climbing a tree. Supporters: Left and Right, rose.
2. Clean-shaven face. Supporters: Left and Right, rose.
3. Angel holding a plain shield. Supporters: Left and Right, rose.

South side

(*Returned stalls*)

1. Pelican in her piety. Supporters: Left and Right, lion-mask.
2. Grotesque head with cat's ears, and foliage issuing from the mouth and trailing round to form supporters.
3. Angel bust. Supporters: Left and Right, formal leaf.

Sedilia (These appear to be of rather later date.)

1. Mermaid with comb and mirror. Supporters: Left and Right, vine-leaves and grapes.
2. Grotesque face with protruding tongue and cat's ears. Supporters: Left and Right, vine-leaves.

3. Angel holding a plain shield. Supporters: Left and Right, vine-leaves.

DATE: 15th century (H. E. Savage, 'The Woodwork of Halifax Church', *Hal. A. Soc. Proc.* v (1909), p. 374).

HEMINGBOROUGH   Blessed Virgin Mary   *One*

There were formerly four stalls with misericords, but only one remains. The carving is a symmetrical design of conventional trefoil foliage springing from a central base. The seat is simple semi-oval, with a trefoil leaf at each end. The misericord is of 13th-century date, and one of the oldest in England, although Hemingborough did not become collegiate until 1426. (*V.C.H.*, *Yorkshire*, iii, p. 359.) (PLATE 43*b*.)

LOVERSALL   St. Katherine   *Two*

In the Wyrrall Chapel are four old stalls in two pairs. One stall in each pair has the seat missing. The other two have carved misericords of foliate masks. Supporters: Left and Right, leaf. (PLATE 43*c*.)

It has been suggested that the stalls were brought from Roche Abbey or from the parish church at Doncaster to which Loversall Church was a Chapel of Ease. They are said to be by the same carvers as those at Lincoln and Chester (M. D. Anderson, *Lincoln Choir Stalls*, p. 10).

DATE: Probably 14th century.

MIDDLETON BY PICKERING   St. Andrew   *One*

The motif is a head and shoulders of a man holding his arms aloft, so that his head and hands support the bracket. He wears a caped tunic, with long, wrist-length buttoned sleeves, and a turbaned cap with a clasp or ornament in the centre of the forehead. He has a curly forked beard, moustache, and side-whiskers.

The adjoining stall is worthy of note, having two shields carved in relief on the insides of the wings, the arms on which have defied identification. They are: west side, *fretty on a chief three annulets*; east side, *two annulets and a canton*.

DATE: Probably 15th century.

OLD MALTON   St. Mary   *Eight*

This fine church, which is part of the Priory Church, and the only Gilbertine church remaining, has thirty-five stalls on three ranges on each side of the chancel, seventeen on the north side, and eighteen on the south side. A major restoration took place in the nineteenth century, and many of the misericords which were in decay were replaced by very good copies. Eight original misericords remain, dating from the late fifteenth (*V.C.H.*, *North Riding*, i, p. 541) or early sixteenth century.

North side from east

Top Range

2. Hare or rabbit in crouching position, facing west with head turned back. (PLATE 43*d*.)

3. Heraldic lion passant regardant to east, with tail passing between rear legs and upturned over its back.

4. Griffin facing east with upraised wings and tail. (PLATE 44*a*.)

South side from east

Top Range

2. Eagle facing east with upraised wings.

3. Owl facing west with upraised wings. (PLATE 44*b*.)

4. Elaborate design of pomegranate or pineapple.

5. Kneeling camel facing east with tail upraised over back, and haltered. (PLATE 44*c*.)

Single seat only on display at west end of church

Antelope, with long, serrated horns and raised, tufted tail, facing right in leaping position. This is in bad condition, and was evidently worth preserving at the restoration but too far gone to replace in a stall.

One amusing incongruity among the replaced carvings may be seen at top range, North 5, that of a tumbler in *Victorian* clothes. He has a fox's head with protruding tongue.

RICHMOND   St. Mary   *Twelve*

North side from west

1 and 2. Modern.

3. Grotesque mask with tongue protruding. Supporters: Left and Right, leaf.

4. Spray of roses and leaves. Supporters: Left and Right, leaf.

5. Dragon carrying goose by the neck. No supporters.

6. Grotesque animal, crowned and crouching.

7. Basket of flowers. Supporters: Left and Right, foliage.

8. Cockatrice. No supporters.

South side from west

1. Fruit and foliage. No supporters.

2. Hart, lodged, gorged, and chained. No supporters.

3. Pig playing the bagpipes; two little ones dancing. No supporters.

4. Man's head wearing a cap.

5. Dragon. Supporters: Left and Right, foliage.

6. Dragon. No supporters.

7 and 8. Modern.

These stalls came from Easby Abbey, being brought to the church at the time of the Dissolution.

Their date can be fixed, as over the Abbot's stall is a shield on which is carved the rebus or picture-name of Abbot Bampton, the last of the Abbots of Easby, who succeeded to the position in 1515. It shows a crozier fixed in a tun inscribed B.A., i.e. Bamtun. (F. Bond, *Misericords*, p. 215.)

RIPON   The Minster   *Thirty-five*

North side from west

1. Lion attacked by two dogs, who stand one on each of two large leaves which form the supporters.

2. Dragon attacked by two dogs, who stand one on each of two large leaves which form the supporters.

3. Demi-angel holding a blank shield. Supporters: Left and Right, rose.

4. The Tree of Life represented only by large leaves which form the supporters, and on each of which stands a bird. A wyvern in the centre. (If the birds remain in the shelter of the Tree they are safe from attack by the wyvern; symbolism for the safety of souls in the shadow of the Almighty.)

5. Hart's-tongue ferns. Supporters: Left and Right, vine-leaf.

6. Conventional flowers. Supporters: Left and Right, conventional flower.

7. Ape attacked by lion. Supporters: Left and Right, conventional flower.

8. Vine with grapes. Supporters: Left and right, vine-leaf.

9. Birds pecking fruit. Supporters: Left and Right, cluster of fruit.

10. Two antelopes. Supporters: Left and Right, elaborate flower foliage.

11. Fox in pulpit preaching to goose and cock. Supporters: Left and Right, sycamore-leaf.

12. Fox running off with two geese. Supporters: Left and Right, triple sycamore-leaves.

13. Fox caught by dogs. Supporters: Left and Right, five-petalled rose.

14. Dragons fighting. Supporters: Left and Right, rose.

15. Grotesque mask, with fruit and flowers issuing from mouth. The head is inverted. Supporters: Left and Right, fruit.

16. Man holding club and wearing chaplet of oak-leaves and acorns. May be meant to represent Orson. Supporters: Left and Right, triple fruit design.

17. Hawk catching rabbit. Supporters: Left and Right, fruit. (Mayor's stall.)

South side

1. Angel with book. Supporters: Left, unicorn. Right, rose.

2. Demi-angel with label bearing date 1489. Supporters: Left and Right, leaf.

3. Lion fighting dragon. Supporters: Left and Right, leaf.

4. Griffin eating human being. Supporters: Left and Right, leaf.

5. Owl with outspread wings. Supporters: Left and Right, rose.

6. Mermaid with mirror and brush. Supporters: Left and Right, fruit.

7. Two piglets dancing to bagpipe played by a sow. Supporters: Left, rose, Right, rose reversed.

8. Jonah cast overboard. Supporters: Left and Right, flower in profile. (PLATE 8d.)

9. Man wheeling in a wheelbarrow another figure, which holds out a reed or bag. This may be either (1) a scold being taken to the ducking stool, the man resisting the temptation of a reward held out to him, or (2) a man wheeling his bride to church. The barrow has three wheels, a rare example. Supporters: Left and Right, formal foliage. The main subject is identified with a woodcut reproduced by Ottley in *Collection of Facsimiles of Prints*, London, 1826.

10. Fox carrying off a goose, caught by a dog, on left supporter, and a woman with distaff, on right supporter.

11. Griffin in profile. Supporters: Left and Right, leaf.

12. Hart gorged and chained. Supporters: Left and Right, leaf.

13. Pelican in her piety. Supporters: Left and Right, grotesque head with protruding tongue.

14. Jonah coming out of the whale. Supporters: Left, fruit. Right, a small animal with long tail. (PLATE 9a.)

15. Samson carrying the gates of Gaza. Supporters, Left and Right, leaf. (PLATE 9c.)

16. Head with flowing hair and beard. Supporters, Left and Right, rose. (This may be modern.)

17. Caleb and Joshua carrying the grapes on their return from the Promised Land. Supporters: Left and Right, blemya. (These may be meant to represent Anakim). (Bishop's Throne.)

With regard to the modern misericord South 16, the Bishop's Throne was originally occupied by the Archbishops of York and it was then the width of two stalls. The old misericord was probably removed when the Throne was made and a copy made when reconverted later.

South 8, 14, 15, and 17 are copied from the block-book *Biblia Pauperum*.

DATE: 1489–94. (J. S. Purvis, *Archaeologia*, lxxxv, p. 108.)

In 1958 the Minster accepted a bequest of a misericord said to be one of the set removed from the stalls when the 15th-century set was installed. It it undoubtedly of early date, having a round shelf and no supporters. Two men in armour face each other in combat; he on the left thrusts with a lance, which his opponent grasps with his right hand whilst threatening with a dagger held in his left hand. Their visors are lifted. In the centre background a tall tree spreads its branches about them. (PLATE 44*d*.)

DATE: Probably late 13th century.

ROTHERHAM   All Saints   *Two*

The ascribed date is 1483. The stalls themselves are richly carved with arcading and geometrical designs.

1. Head of a man, beneath a corbel-shaped bracket. He has curled hair and a combed, pointed beard, also what may be either combed, full side-whiskers or a frilled collar. Supporters: Left and Right, formal vine-leaf pendant.

2. Head of a man, beneath a corbel-shaped bracket. He is clean shaven and has a close-fitting hood, from which what appear to be horns emerge. Supporters: Left and Right, formal vine-leaf pendant.

F. Bond, *Misericords*, p. 227, ascribes their installation to Archbishop Rother-ham of York, 1480–1501.

SPROTBOROUGH   St. Mary the Virgin   *Three*

The carvings have been badly damaged and it is almost impossible to identify their subjects. Professor Rix of Birmingham University considers that one is a typical autumn scene, possibly October, with a man and a boy feeding his pigs, and that another is the devil taking off a man and a woman.

No identification of the third carving is possible.

DATE: Late 14th or early 15th century. J. E. Morris, *West Riding of Yorkshire*, 2nd ed., 1923, p. 488 and note, suggests they are of the same date as old pewing, on a bench-end of which are the arms of Gascoigne and initials W. C. for William Copley (d. 1556).

SWINE   St. Mary   *Eight*

The church was attached to a priory of Cistercian nuns and was rebuilt in the twelfth century, the priory church and parish church being on opposite sides of a central tower. There were originally sixteen seats with misericords for the prioress and fifteen nuns, increasing later to thirty-six (J. Rilson, *E. Riding Ant. Soc. Trans.* iv. pp. xx f.). The exact site of the priory chapel is in some doubt.

North side from West

1. Bearded man lying prostrate, looking through his legs which are held up in the air.

2. Man's head with forked beard.

3. Griffin with large claws biting its tail.

4. Knight's head in profile with helmet and pointed beard.

South side from west

1. Nun's head in wimple between two creatures back to back. The nun's veil is drawn half across her face, and she appears to be winking.

2. Grotesque, with human face and long ears, wearing bishop's mitre.

3. Head with foliage coming from the mouth.

4. Female head in head-dress of the period.

There are no supporters.

DATE: Probably c. 1500. G. Poulson, *Hist. and Antiquities of . . . Holderness*, Hull, 1841, p. 211, suggests similar to Beverley Minster (1520 by William Brounflete). J. E. Morris, *East Riding, Yorkshire*, 2nd edition, 1919, p. 311. suggests same date as old screen dated 1531.

WAKEFIELD   Cathedral Church of All Saints   *Ten*

There are twenty-five stalls in the choir, all of which have misericords, but only ten of the latter are original, and these are of late fifteenth-century date. The old carvings are described below. Some of the stalls bear the arms of Thomas Savile and his wife, Margaret Basworth, who married in 1482.

North side

1. Fruit and leaves in formal design.

2. Pelican in her piety.

3. Formal foliage.

South side

2. Flower design.

3. Flower and leaves.

4. Grotesque face.

5. Rose.

6. Crescent and fetterlock; the badge of the House of Percy.

7. Grotesque face.

8. Rose.

There are no supporters.

YORK   The Minster   *Two*

The stalls were almost all destroyed in 1829, when the choir was set on fire by a lunatic and gutted. Two misericords were saved, and are in the Zouche Chapel.

1. Little bearded man seated, wearing a peaked cap. He supports the bracket with his head, which is turned on one side, and his hands. Supporters: Left and Right, lion-mask.

2. Eagle. Supporters: Left and Right, foliage.

DATE: Late 15th century. (J. B. Morrell, *Woodwork in York*, Batsford, 1949, pp. 155, 156, and 158.)

YORK   All Saints, North Street   *One*

1. Pelican in her piety with three chicks. Supporters: Left, monogram initial feature *Im* in centre of large letter *G*, with cresting above, backed by large formal leaf. This refers to John Gilliot, Mayor in 1463 and 1464 and again in 1474. He was a member of Corpus Christi Guild, hence the pelican device. Right, a shield charged, *on a bend three fishes heads erased* (for Gilliot). The same device is on a boss of the hammer-beam roof.

DATE: Late 15th century. (J. B. Morrell, pp. 155 and 158.)

YORK   St. Mary, Castlegate   *One*

1. Full face, head and shoulders of a man in hood and robe. His upraised hand and head support the shelf. Supporters: Left and Right, animal head in roundel.

DATE: Early 15th century. (J. B. Morrell, op. cit., pp. 155 and 158.)

YORK   St. Saviour   *Two*

St. Saviour's Church is no longer used for religious purposes. In 1955 the building was leased to the Corporation as a store for the Castle Museum. The misericords are now in the care of the Clerk of Works of York Minster, but are not on view to the public. The date is said to be 1475, and the style is similar to that of those in the Minster.

The misericords are identical in design, and consist of a central vaulted moulding based on a corbel, plainly carved. The supporters are square geometric representations of an oak-leaf. (J. B. Morrell, op. cit., pp. 156 and 158.)

SCOTLAND

ABERDEENSHIRE

ABERDEEN King's College Chapel *Seven*

There are fifty-two stalls in the choir, of which only seven have misericords.

North side from east

2. Bunch of grapes, with triple vine-leaves in square format flanking on each side. No supporters.
3. As for 2, but surmounting two rosettes, which are flanked by rose-leaves.
4. Vine arising from a corbel moulding, and having a bunch of grapes horizontally on each side, and a leaf pattern above.

South side from east

1. Three thistles with appropriate foliage arranged in a symmetrical pattern.
2. Intricate pattern of roses and thistles and their appropriate foliage in a square format.
3. Coronet surmounting an inverted chevron, between the arms of which is a triple leaf.
4. Initials IHS in decorative form.

None of the misericords has supporters.

The carvings are fully described and illustrated by F. C. Eeles in 'King's College Chapel, Aberdeen' (Oliver and Boyd, 1956).

DATE: Early 16th century.

NORTH BERWICK *One*

There is in the possession of Dr. James S. Richardson, of 7a Tantallon Terrace, North Berwick, East Lothian, a single misericord from an unspecified church in South Scotland. Dr. Richardson was formerly curator of the Society of Antiquaries of Scotland, and described this misericord in the Society's *Proceedings*, Fifth Series, (1926), lx, pp. 384 ff. He has kindly given permission for his description to be quoted here.

> The carving represents the Adoration of the Magi. The Virgin wears a full robe, and has long curling tresses. Behind her appear the head and shoulders of an ox and the head of an ass. A wise man kneels before her, holding a cup in his right hand, and removing the lid with the help of the Child. He wears a gown girdled, and a hood on his head. Behind is a young man wearing a tunic girdled, a short

surcoat and tippet. He wears a round low-crowned hat ornamented with a chevron pattern, over hair in ringlets, and holds a tall moulded cup in his left hand, and grasps the lid with his right hand. The supporters are missing, but it is presumed that they would have been St. Joseph and one of the Three Kings. PLATE 45a.)

MIDLOTHIAN

EDINBURGH   National Museum of Antiquities of Scotland

Seven

(a) Two misericords from Lincluden, Kirkcudbrightshire, formerly in the 'Queir' at Terregles. Date *c.* 1400, believed transferred to Terregles in about 1585 from original unknown situation.

1. Serpent. Its face has curved chin, staring eyes, and pointed ears. It has an M-shaped body and two webbed front claws. Underside of body stamped with six-pointed stars with blunt points.

2. Full-maned lion-head with human features and staring eyes, no front legs and webbed rear claws. The tail ends in an amphisbaena head. There are no supporters to either misericord.

(b) Three misericords from the Cathedral of Moray, Elgin. DATE: Probably 14th century.

1. Demi-angel with raised wings holding a shield *parted per pale.* (PLATE 45b.)

2. Two four-legged beasts, with human features, and hands instead of forepaws, supporting between them a tree-trunk with side-branches lopped close to the trunk to form steps, the top supporting the bracket. (PLATE 45c.)

3. Dragon with raised wings, and a tail ending in an amphisbaena head, trampling on a prone beast with dog-like head. The whole is crudely carved. (PLATE 45d.)

Supporters in all cases are pendant vine-leaf.

(c) Two misericords, probably English, but of unknown origin. They appear to be late thirteenth- or early fourteenth- century in date, and have interesting resemblances to examples of those dates in Chichester Cathedral, Sussex.

1. Two branches of acanthus-leaf, leading from the corners of the bracket and meeting in the centre; that on the left curving down and upward, that on the right pendant. Supporters: Left, missing. Right, a woman's head in a wimple.

2. Beast walking to right, with arms instead of forelegs, the right arm stretching along its back to grasp the tails which curve forward. The feet of the hind legs are human. The head is a well-carved mitred face. The beast appears to stand upon a rock. Supporters: Left, a mitred head with flowing side-locks of hair. Right, missing.

PERTHSHIRE

DUNBLANE The Cathedral *Eighteen*

There are eighteen misericords in the Cathedral, in three groups, and these have been fully described and well illustrated by Dr. James Hutchinson Cockburn in publications of the *Society of Friends of Dunblane Cathedral*, viii, pts. III and IV, and ix, pt. I. The illustrations are by Mr. John Dickie and Mr. W. D. Leask.

(a) *East end of the choir*

Here are ten stalls, known traditionally as the Ochiltree stalls (Bishop Ochiltree (1429–47) was their donor). There were at the end of the eight-eenth century thirty-two stalls in the Cathedral, and among the few remain-ing some may be of later date than that ascribed to them.

North side from west to east

1. Intertwined branches with trefoil and curly-tailed ends. No supporters.
2. Leopard, spotted with curly tail, facing left in kneeling posture. Sup-porters: Left and Right, simple annulet. (PLATE 46*a*.)
3. Intertwined flowering thistles, emanating from a central crown. The carving is strong but stylized. No supporters. (PLATE 46*b*.)

South side from west to east

1. Foliate mask wearing a crown. From his mouth issue bunches of grapes and spread vine-leaves. The bevelled ends of the bracket are curled back. No supporters.
2. Intertwined branches of vine with leaves and bunches of grapes. The curled ends of the bracket end in small trefoils.
3. Floral design of intertwined branches, with fruit, probably grapes. In the centre, superimposed, an elaborate armorial shield, uncharged. Bracket-ends as for No. 2 above.
4. Two thistle-leaves outspread, with central flowering thistle. Bracket-ends, simple annulets. (PLATE 46*c*.)
5. The same design as No. 3 above, but the shield is *parted per pale*.
6. Triple lierne vaulting, the centre shaft being larger than those flanking it. The bracket-ends are simple roundlets, pierced, and bearing a small billet.
7. Bat in flight with outspread wings. This is a very realistic carving, con-trary to most medieval representations of the creature. (PLATE 46*d*.)

(b) *Six canopied stalls at west wall of Nave*

These stalls are associated with Bishop Chisholm (1487–1526), who, it is thought, transferred them to new canopies erected by him *c.* 1520. Nos. 1 and 6 bear his symbol of a boar's head.

1. At each side a growing tree in leaf; in the centre a shield bearing a *boar's head erased*, the shield surmounted by a mitre and supported by two winged angels with flowing robes. The bracket-ends have roundlets as for No. 6 of the chancel stalls.

2. As for Nos. 3 and 5, south side of the chancel.

3. Wyvern in flight facing left. Bracket-ends as for No. 1 above.

4. An elaboration of the monogram IHS. From the top of the central I come two scrolls curving outward as supporters and ending in a vine-leaf. Four flower patterns adorn the centre.

5. Elaborate carved letters forming the words *GRACIA DEI*. Bracket-ends, pierced annulets.

6. At sides a floral design with fruits; in the centre Bishop Chisholm's badge of a boar's head on a shield surmounted by a mitre. The angels are omitted, but a bishop's stole or scarf is added. The bracket-ends are curled.

(c) *Two detached misericords in Cathedral Museum*

1. Grotesque demoniac face, with horns, protruding ears, and staring eyes. From his mouth emerge two diverging fleurs-de-lis. The bracket-ends are simple pierced roundlets.

2. An elaborate design of unidentifiable leaves and branches, with four-leaved and five-leaved flowers inserted, the latter being repeated in the bracket-ends. This is undoubtedly of somewhat later date than the other examples in the Cathedral.

Both these misericords were probably in the choir at some earlier date.

WALES

ANGLESEY

BEAUMARIS   St. Catherine   *Twenty*

The centre motif is the same in all cases and is a demi-angel with outspread wings, carrying a blank shield. The supporters vary as detailed below.

North side

1. Left, large, bald head with long, curled moustache and beard. Right, large head with long, curly hair, long moustache and beard.

2. Left, small female head, draped, bearing milk-pail. Right, small head, with moustache and beard, cowled or hooded, bearing cask.

3. Left, bust of bishop with mitre and vestment. Right, tonsured bust of priest in collar and vestment.

4. Left, large tonsured head with long, curled moustache and beard. Right, tonsured bust of monk, with cowl or hood around neck.

5. Left, bust of nun veiled, with open collar to gown. Right, bust of nun, long veil covering head and shoulders, wimple over chin, neck, and breast.

6. Left, large, male clean-shaven head, with short, curly hair. Right, Female bust, hair trussed, with turban head-dress, and gown with open collar.

7. Left, large head with long straight, flowing hair, moustache, and beard. Right, Large head with beard and moustache, wearing Plantagenet cap, with tippet falling to right.

8. Left, female bust, carrying two flagons connected by a rope, and wearing low-necked dress buttoned down front. Right, female bust in veil and low-necked gown, bearing sheaf of corn.

9. Left, large head with flowing hair bunched at sides, moustached and bearded, wearing papal crown. Right, large head, clean shaven, long hair bunched at sides, wearing crown.

10. Left, bust of female with crown, in veil, hood, and wimple. Right, male bust with high cap with jewel in front, collar of vestment fastened with large jewelled brooch.

South side

11. Similar to No. 3.

12. Left, female bust with veil, hood, and wimple. Right, bust of nun, with veil, and open collar to gown.

13. Similar to No. 4.

14. Left, bust of man with cowl, wearing turban, which has shield or tippet over front. He is moustached and bearded. Right, bust of man with long beard and moustache, having the hair bunched at the sides, and wearing a turban, on which a tied sack is borne.

15. Similar to No. 1.

16. Similar to No. 6, but smaller.

17. Similar to No. 7.

18. Left, large head in three-quarter view, with long moustache and beard, and wearing cap with long tippet. Right, female bust, with long, flowing hair, and having a rose crown on her head, and a chain on her neck, from which a locket or pendant is suspended.

19. Similar to No. 9.

20. Similar to No. 10.

DATE: *c.* 1500 (*R.C.H.M., Anglesey*, p. 8).

LLANEDWEN *Three*

(a) Aberbraint House, with variety of old woodwork built in, including two misericords above the front entrance.

1. Angel, with outspread wings, holding a shield uncharged. Supporters: Left and Right, oak-leaf in formal pattern.

2. Figure riding a horse and seated facing rearward. The head appears to have a halo surrounding it. One hand holds the rein, the other the horse's tail.

(b) Moel-y-Don Cottage, dated 1717, lies 400 yards from the church. It has built-in woodwork, and has been much restored. There is one misericord over the doorway, having a group of grotesque figures.

DATE: All the above three misericords appear to be of late 15th or early 16th-century date, and are believed to have come from Bangor Cathedral (*R.C.H.M., Anglesey*, p. 56).

BRECONSHIRE

BRECON Christ College *Six*

A small Dominican priory was founded before 1269, and dissolved in 1538. In 1540–1 a secular college was founded on the site, but dissolved *c.* 1645. A college exists now, and six stalls with misericords are preserved in the ante-room of the school chapel, which is itself part of the nave of the original friary.

F. H. Crossley and M. H. Ridgeway (*Arch. Camb.* 102 (1952/3), pp. 55 f.) describe them and assess their date as post-Reformation. The carvings are crude and look much older than this.

Pair 1. Left seat: A dog resembling a Talbot.
Right seat: A skeleton.

Pair 2. Left seat: A unicorn.
Right seat: An owl's head.

Pair 3. Left seat: An angel.
Right seat: A lion.

There are no supporters.

CAERNARVONSHIRE

ABER-ERCH   St. Cawrdaf   *Five*

The subjects of these five misericords are alternately a double water-leaf between two six-petalled double roses as supporters, and a similar rose between two water-leaves. The stalls are situated on the north side of the chancel.

DATE: Early 16th century (*R.C.H.M., Caernarvonshire*, iii, p. 11).

BANGOR   *One*

The misericords in the Cathedral have all disappeared, but see under Anglesey, Llanedwen.

In Bangor Museum there is a misericord said to have come from the Cathedral. It represents a tonsured, clean-shaven head being devoured by twin wyverns, one on each side. The supporters are missing. (Illustrated in *Archaeologia Cambriensis*, 5th Series, x (1893), p. 343.)

CLYNNOG   St. Beuno   *Fourteen*

There are seven stalls on each side of the chancel of this old church, of which three on each side are returned. All have misericords.

These are all alike, and consist of a moulded bracket, pointed at the base, carved with three ogee-headed arches. The supporters are in each case a lozenge-shaped formation of four small leaves, each leaf having three fronds. (*R.C.H.M., Caernarvonshire*, ii, p. 41.)

DATE: *c.* 1500.

DENBIGHSHIRE

GRESFORD   All Saints   *Eleven*

From south-east end

1. Three men in tunics, holding horizontally on their shoulders a long pole, on which a fourth man performs an acrobatic feat. Supporters: Left, a hog. Right, a hound.

2. Two lions facing inwards, grasping a fox squatting between them. The head of the lion on left is missing. Supporters: Left, a twined ribbon or scroll. Right, a bowl-shaped flower with large pistil.

3. Mutilation renders the identification of this carving difficult, but it appears to represent a bull, erect, driven by a man or woman in long kilted garment, facing left, and, on the left side, facing inwards, an owl with two owlets in a nest; the whole apparently in a stable or shed. Supporters: Left and Right, rosette.

4. Two demi-angels with raised wings and cowled robes, bearing between them a shield having a *pale wavy* (probably arms of Upthomas of Wales). Supporters: Left and Right, formal leaf.

5. Gowned fox in pulpit, preaching to assembly of ten birds, five on each side, including some geese and one cockerel. Supporters: Left and Right, stiff leaf.

6. Corbel, broken away, which may have supported a crucifix (missing). Supporters: Left, an angel in flowing robes, wearing a kind of shallow mitre, and bearing what appears to be a musical instrument. Right, a kneeling woman in a long-flowing robe, crowned, and before a *prie-dieu*, on which is a book (a psalter). The desk is covered with a cloth, and by the head of the figure is a formal flower, which forms part of the supporters. N.B. F. H. Crossley suggests that this may be an Annunciation, but this explanation does not account for the missing centre, which may, however, have been a Lily crucifix.

7. Griffin with raised wings facing left. On either side facing inward is a unicorn; the head of that on the left is missing. Supporters: Left and Right, five-petalled flower with long central pistils.

8. Cowled figure astride a beast, possibly an elephant (the head is broken off), facing left. Two other figures to left and right have been broken off. Supporters: Left and Right, rosette.

9. Badly mutilated figures of two cats walking upright, one leading the other by the forepaw, facing right. Beyond, to the right, appears to be a mousehole with mouse peering out. Supporters, missing.

10. Demi-angel in robe and cowled, bearing a plain shield *parted per pale* (probably arms of Upthomas). Supporters, missing.

11. Pattern of lierne vaulting, with rosettes at junctions, rising from a corbel mask of grotesque lion (or cat). Supporters, missing.

DATE: Late 15th or early 16th century. F. H. Crossley, 'Remains of Medieval Stallwork in Lancashire', *Trans. Lancs. & Cheshire Hist. Soc.* lxx. N.S. 34 (1919), p. 9, states that a strong resemblance between these carvings and those at Halsall, Lancs. suggests that the same carver was employed. The church was rebuilt by patronage of the Stanley family at the end of the fifteenth century.

FLINTSHIRE

ST. ASAPH   The Cathedral   *Twenty*

There are twenty-two stalls in the choir, eleven on each side, of which one is returned; both returned stalls are modern.

The misericords on the original stalls are all alike, and consist of a hollow moulding tapering downward to a pointed bracket, and having cusped tracery at the head. Supporters: Left and Right, single leaf.

DATE: Late 15th century. F. H. Crossley, ('Screens, Lofts and Stalls in Wales and Monmouthshire', *Arch. Camb.* xcviii (1945), pp. 64–112) states that the stalls were erected by Bishop Redman in 1482.

MONMOUTHSHIRE

ABERGAVENNY   St. Mary   *Sixteen*

The south stalls bear the name of Wynchester, who was Prior at the end of the fifteenth century; probable date, 1493. (Revd. Morgan Gilbert, *Guide to the Priory Church of St. Mary*, 1910).

North side from east

1, 4, 9, and 10 have plain fixed seats.

2, 3, 5, 6, and 8 consist of a plain vaulting ending in a point at the base.

7. Plain vaulting ending at the base in a small five-petalled flower.

11. Plain capital with three transverse ribs.

South side from east

1. Double rose surmounted by a crown and flanked by small roses. Supporters: Left and Right, vine-leaf.

2. Dragon with long, curled tail and wings raised, the head looking back over the shoulder. Supporters: Left and Right, vine-leaf. (PLATE 47c.)

3. Capital as for North 11.

4. The same. Supporters: Left and Right, vine-leaf.

5 and 6. Similar to No. 4.

7. Fixed plain seat.

8. Similar to No. 3.

9. Fixed plain seat.

10 and 11. Similar to No. 3.

12. Fixed plain seat.

MONTGOMERYSHIRE

MONTGOMERY   St. Nicholas   *Nine*

There are twelve stalls in the chancel, four on each side of the screen doorway and four on the north side. They are said to have come from Chirbury Priory, three miles away, now in Shropshire, but formerly in Montgomeryshire. They are badly mutilated, not one having escaped serious damage.

From south-west corner

1. Animal and man, much broken.
2. Man, looking between his legs, and dog.
3. Female bust with horned head-dress. Supporters, missing.
4. Leaves. Supporters: Left and Right, similar leaf.
5. Feathered bird (hawk or eagle) with outspread wings. Supporters, destroyed.
6. Animal with smaller beast on its back, much damaged.
7. Judgement. The damned led to the mouth of hell.
8. Duel with swords. Supporters: Left and Right, figures; one on right holding a cloak.
9. Two women, one with a child on her knee.

10 to 12. Missing.

F. H. Crossley and M. H. Ridgway, 'Screens, lofts and stalls in Wales and Monmouthshire', Part Five (*Arch. Camb.* xcix, pp. 206 ff.), state: 'The stalls bear remarkable similarity to those at Leintwardine (ex Wigmore) and Ludlow . . . there is little doubt that all three sets are the work of a single shop.'

DATE: Probably early 15th century.

PEMBROKESHIRE

ST. DAVID'S   The Cathedral   *Twenty-eight*

There are twenty-eight stalls with misericords, fourteen on each side of the choir. They date from 1470. The first prebend belongs to the reigning sovereign and bears the royal arms, an honour peculiar to this cathedral.

North side from east

1. Dragon facing left, its head turned to the rear, and its tail curved over its back. Supporters: Left and Right, oak-leaf.
2. Fox-headed human creature in woman's dress, seated on a bench, holding a platter in one hand and (?) bread in the other. On the bench beside her is a ewer. Running towards her from the left is a fowl with man's head wearing a cap. Supporters: Left and Right, diamond-shaped floral design.
3. Boar, sow, and three piglets seizing by its feet a fox lying on its back; one has it by the throat. Supporters: Left and Right, oak-leaf.
4. Pair of intertwined serpents, with prominent ears (probably asps). Supporters: Left and Right, stiff leaf.

5. Interlaced design of bunches of grapes and vine-leaves. Supporters: Left and Right, vine-leaf.

6. Large, grotesque mask, with prominent pointed ears. Supporters: Left and Right, vine-leaf.

7. Boat-building. Two men are seated on the ground beside a clinker-built hull; they appear to be caulking. On the ground between them is a jug, and one appears to be sipping from a bowl. Behind him on the ground is a setsquare. Supporters: Left and Right, vine-leaf. (PLATE 2*d*.)

8. Two dancers, back to back, leaning forward and supporting the ledge with their backs; their hands rest on their thighs. Supporters: Left and Right, vine-leaf.

9. Two dogs quarrelling over bones. Supporters: Left and Right, leaf with rounded fronds. (PLATE 47*d*.)

10. Woman's head wearing a head-dress with frilled edge. She has downcast eyes, and displays irregular teeth. Supporters: Left and Right, vine-leaf.

11. Double-faced man's head, perhaps Janus, wearing a round hat with the brim turned up over the forehead of each face. A buckled strap conceals any ears. Supporters: Left and Right, vine-leaf.

12. Man seated on a bench at a table on which his wife places a platter bearing a calf's head. The man wears a bag-sleeved, girdled gown. Supporters: Left and Right, vine-leaf. (PLATE 48*a*.)

13. Four men in a boat; one appears to be seasick. This is said to represent the seasickness of St. Govan, uncle of St. David, who was sent with two disciples to Rome by St. Elfynt to obtain a correct form of the mass. Supporters: Left and Right, vine-leaf. (PLATE 2*b*.)

14. Heraldic angel with outspread wings, holding an uncharged shield. Supporters: Left and Right, vine-leaf.

South side from west

15. Interlaced branches, bearing oak-leaves and acorns. Supporters: Left and Right, oak-leaf.

16. Two large oak-leaves sprouting from the branches which carry the supporters: Left and Right, oak-leaf.

17. Owl sitting on an oak-branch, flanked by large oak-leaves. Supporters: Left and Right, vine-leaf.

18. Fowl being seized by the throat by an animal, possibly a hound. Supporters: Left and Right, stiff leaf.

19. Heraldic angel holding a shield, *parted per pale*, left, *lion rampant, under a bend sinister*, (possibly the arms of Meredith); right, *two eagles in combat above a chevron, and below, another eagle*, (probably the arms of Child of Bigelly House). Supporters: Left and Right, a diamond-shaped leaf pattern.

20. Lion seizing by the throat a prostrate dragon. Supporters, vine-leaf. (PLATE 48*b*.)

21. Bust of a fox in monk's cowl. Supporters: Left and Right, vine-leaf. (PLATE 48*c*.)

22. Clean-shaven man's head. From his mouth issue at each side branches of leaves. Supporters: Left and Right, vine-leaf.

23. Pattern of oak-leaves and acorns, similar to No. 15. Supporters: Left and Right, oak-leaf.

24. Wyvern swallowing head-first a man dressed in belted, kilted jacket and long hose, with pointed shoes, probably representing Judas in the jaws of Satan. Supporters: Left and Right, vine-leaf.

25. Similar to No. 22.

26. Sleeping man lying on his side with his feet crossed. He wears a hood, a bag-sleeved gown, and a hanging purse. One hand supports his head and the other rests upon his knee. Supporters: Left and Right, oak-leaf. (PLATE 48*d*.)

27. Horse-head mask with a hooded head-dress draped over its ears, and held by an ornament at the forehead. Supporters: Left and Right, vine-leaf.

28. Heraldic angel, holding a shield, *parted per pale*; left, *on a cross five cinquefoils* (arms of See of St. David's); and right, *chevron between three boars' heads* (said to be arms of Bishop Tully, 1460–81).

IRELAND

LIMERICK

The Cathedral *Twenty*

In the choir are twenty-three stalls, of which twenty-one contain misericords, but one is damaged and indefinable.

South side from west

1. Bust of bearded man, wearing 'chaperon' head-dress.
2. Amphisbaena.
3. Seated antelope with serrated horns, plumed tail, and collar ornamented with trefoils.
4. Mantichora, having man's head, lion's body, eagle's wings and scorpion's tail.
5. Bust of young man, wearing head-dress similar to No. 1.
6. Lion and wyvern in combat.
7. Unicorn passant, looking back at its floriated tail.
8. Wyvern with twisted tail.
9. Wyvern, apparently biting at its tail.
10. Similar to No. 3.
11. Similar to No. 4.
12. Habited angel issuing from ducal coronet, with hands clasped and wings displayed. (The crest of the Harold family.) (PLATE 47*b*.)
13. A lindworm, i.e. a beast similar to a wyvern, but without wings.
14. Two unicorns counter passant with necks entwined. There is a carving resembling this on an ancient font at Oughtmana, co. Clare.
15. A swan passant. (PLATE 47*a*.)
16. Damaged.
17. Griffin sejant, with wings displayed.
18. Similar to No. 6.
19. Eagle displayed.
20. Similar to No. 17.
21. No carving. New seat.
22. Wild boar passant, with tusks visible, and ridge of bristles on its spine.

23. No carving. New seat.

All supporters: Left and Right, square design of acanthus leaf.

DATE: Late 15th century (D. Alleyne Walter, *Reliquary*, July, 1893, N.S. vii, p. 129). Since Walter described the stalls, a major rearrangement of position took place in 1906. *Misericords in St. Mary's Cathedral, Limerick*, J. A. Haydn, revised M. J. Talbot, 1963, Limerick, dates the misericords at the end of the fifteenth century—1480–1500, the period when the Cathedral was renovated and enlarged under Bishop Folan.

APPENDIX

MISERICORDS MOVED FROM ORIGINAL LOCATIONS

THE following list is of misericords said to have been brought from other churches, e.g. monasteries dismantled at the Dissolution. There is, however, normally no written evidence of such movement, and most assertions are based on local tradition, the reliability of which is difficult to assess.

County	*Church*	*Place of origin*
Bedfordshire	Leighton Buzzard	St. Alban's Abbey
Cambridgeshire	Gamlingay	Queens' College, Cambridge
	Landbeach	Jesus College, Cambridge
	Milton	King's College, Cambridge
	Over	Ramsey Abbey
Derbyshire	Church Gresley	Drakelow Hall
Devonshire	Cockington	Torre Abbey and Tormohun Church
Durham	Durham Castle Chapel	Auckland Castle Chapel
Essex	Belchamp St. Paul	Clare Priory
Gloucester	Duntisbourne Rous	Cirencester Abbey
Hereford	Leintwardine	Wigmore Abbey
Hertfordshire	Stevenage	Little Wymondley Priory
Kent	Faversham	Faversham Abbey
Lancashire	Blackburn	Whalley Abbey
	Lancaster	Cockersand Abbey
	Whalley	Whalley Abbey
Lincolnshire	Stamford, Browne's Hospital	Fotheringay Abbey
Norfolk	East Lexham	Castle Acre Priory
	Norwich, St. Margaret	Norwich, St. Swithin

County	*Church*	*Place of origin*
Northamptonshire	Benefield	Fotheringay Abbey
	Gayton	Dunston Abbey
	Hemington	Fotheringay Abbey
	Holdenby	Lincoln Cathedral
	Tansor	Fotheringay Abbey
Nottinghamshire	Nottingham, Sneinton	Nottingham, St. Mary
Somerset	Weston-in-Gordano	Portbury Priory
	Worle	Woodspring Priory
Staffordshire	Colton	origin not known
Suffolk	Oulton	origin not known
Sussex	Hardham	Hardham Priory
Warwickshire	Coventry, Holy Trinity	White Friars
	Coventry, Henry VIII Grammar School	White Friars
Wiltshire	Mere	origin not known
Worcestershire	Ripple	Hartlebury Palace
Yorkshire	Loversal	Roche Abbey *or* Doncaster
	Richmond	Easby Abbey
Anglesey	Llanedwen	Bangor Cathedral

BIBLIOGRAPHY

ANDERSON, M. D., *The Medieval Carver* (C.U.P., Cambridge, 1935).

—— *Animal Carvings in British Churches* (C.U.P., Cambridge, 1938).

—— *The Choir Stalls of Lincoln Minster* (Friends of Lincoln Cathedral, Lincoln, 1951).

—— *Misericords* (Penguin, London, 1954).

—— *The Imagery of British Churches* (Murray, London, 1955).

—— *Drama and Imagery in English Medieval Churches* (C.U.P., Cambridge, 1963).

—— 'Twelfth century design sources of Worcester Cathedral misericords', *Archaeologia*, xcvii (1959), pp. 165–78.

BOND, F., *Woodcarvings in English Churches*: I. *Misericords*; II, *Stalls* (O.U.P., Oxford, 1910).

BROWN, C., *History of Newark* (S. Whiles, Newark, 1904).

CAUTLEY, H. M., *Suffolk Churches and Their Treasures* (Batsford, London, 1937).

—— *Norfolk Churches* (Adlard, Ipswich, 1949).

CLARKE, K. M., 'Misericords of Exeter Cathedral', *Devon and Cornwall Notes and queries*, xi, II (1920), p. 1.

COCKBURN, J. H., 'The Ochiltree stalls and other medieval carvings in Dunblane Cathedral', *Soc. of Friends of Dunblane Cathderal*, viii (1961) III and IV, ix (1962) I.

COLLINS, A. H., *Symbolism of Animals and Birds in English Architecture* (Pitman, London, 1913).

COX, J. C., *Churches of Derbyshire*, 4 vols. (Bemrose, London, 1875–9).

COX, J. C., and HARVEY, A., *English Church Furniture* (Methuen, London, 1907).

CRANAGE, D. H. S., *Churches of Shropshire* (Hobson, Wellington, 1901).

CROSSLEY, F. H., *English Church Craftsmanship* (Batsford, London, 1941).

—— 'Stallwork in Cheshire', *Trans. Lancs. & Cheshire Hist. Soc.* lxviii (1916), pp. 85–106.

—— 'Remains of medieval stallwork in Lancashire', *Trans. Lancs. & Cheshire Hist. Soc.*, lxx (1919), pp. 1–42.

—— 'Screens, Lofts & Stalls in Wales & Monmouthshire', *Arch. Camb.*, xcviii, (1945).

DAY, L. F., *Nature in Ornament* (Batsford, London, 1892).

DRUCE, G. C., 'Animals in English woodcarvings', *Walpole Soc. Annual.* iii (1913–14), p. 57.

—— 'Misericords: Their form and decoration', *Jour. Brit. Arch. Assoc.*, N.S. xxxvi (1931), pp. 244–64.

—— 'Stalls and misericords in Hertfordshire churches', *E. Herts. Arch. Soc. Trans.* x, II (1938), pp. 131–40.

—— 'Stall Carvings in the Church of St. Mary of Charity, Faversham', *Arch. Cantiana*, l (1939), pp. 11–32.

EELES, F. C., *King's College Chapel, Aberdeen* (Oliver & Boyd, Edinburgh, 1956).

GARDNER, A., *English Medieval Sculpture* (C.U.P., Cambridge, 1951).

—— *Minor English Wood Sculpture* (Tiranti, London, 1958).

GARDNER, S. *English Gothic Foliage Sculpture* (C.U.P., Cambridge, 1927).

GRANT, F. J., *Manual of Heraldry* (John Grant, Edinburgh, 1904).

HARRIS, M. D., 'Misericords in Coventry', *Birmingham Arch. Soc. Trans.* lii (1927), pp. 246–66.

HART, R., 'Norwich Cathedral', *Norfolk & Norwich Arch. Soc.* ii (1849), pp. 234–52.

HENDERSON, R. and K., 'Misericords of Carlisle Cathedral', *Cumberland & Westmorland Trans.*, O.S., xii, (1891), pp. 103–4.

HOWARD, F. E. and CROSSLEY, F. H., *English Church Woodwork* (Batsford, London, 1927).

HUGHES, T. C., 'Gresford', *Trans. Lancs. & Cheshire Ant. Soc.* xii (1894), pp. 110–14.

JAMES, M. R., *Windsor, St. George's Chapel, Woodwork of the Choir* (Windsor, 1933).

JEAVONS, S. A., 'Medieval Stallwork in South Staffordshire', *Birmingham Arch. Jour.*, lxvii–lxviii (1947–8), pp. 42–54.

KEYSER, C. E., 'Bampton Church', *Brit. Arch. Assoc. Jour.*, N.S. xxii (1916), pp. 1–12.

LETTS, E. F., 'Misericords in Manchester Cathedral', *Trans. Lancs. & Cheshire Ant. Soc.* iv (1886), pp. 130–44.

MACCOLL, D. S., 'Grania in Church, or the Clever Daughter', *Burlington Magazine*, viii (Nov. 1905), p. 80.

MARTIN, A. R., 'The Church at Cliffe-at-Hoo', *Arch. Cantiana*, xli (1929), pp. 71–88.

MIDDLETON, J. H., 'Notes on three Misericords from Brampton', *Camb. Ant. Soc. Pubns.* vii (1888–91), pp. 28–30.

MORRELL, J. B., *Woodwork in York* (Batsford, London, 1950).

PAPWORTH, J. W., *Ordinary of British Armorials* (Richards, London, 1874).

PEARMAN, A. J., 'Ashford Church', *Arch. Cantiana*, xxviii (1909), pp. 78–88.

PHIPSON, E., *Choir Stalls and their Carvings* (Batsford, London, 1896).

POLWHELE, J., *History of Cornwall* (Cadell & Davies, London, 1803).

PRATT-BOORMAN, H. R., and TORR, V. J., *Kent Churches* (Kent Messenger, Maidstone, 1954).

PURVIS, J. S., 'The Use of Continental Woodcuts and Prints by the Ripon School of Woodcarvers', *Archaeologia*, lxxxv (1936), pp. 107–28.

ROE, F., 'Misericords', *The Connoisseur*, lxxvii (Feb. 1927), p. 80, and lxxviii (May 1927), p. 18.

ROYAL COMMISSION ON HISTORICAL MONUMENTS: *Buckinghamshire*, i and ii; *Cambridgeshire*, i and ii; *Essex, Northwest*; *Herefordshire*, i, ii, and iii; *Huntingdonshire*; *London*, ii; *Anglesey*; and *Caernarvonshire*, ii.

SAVAGE, Canon, 'The Woodwork of Halifax Church' (Halifax, 1909).

VICTORIA COUNTY HISTORIES: *Bedfordshire*, i and iii; *Berkshire*, iv; *Cumberland*, ii; *Cambridgeshire*, iv; *Hampshire*, ii; *Kent*, ii; *Norfolk*, ii; *Sussex*, iv; *Warwickshire*, iv; *Yorkshire North Riding*, i, ii, and iii.

WARD, J., *Historic Ornament* (Chapman & Hall, London, 1897).

WHITE, T. H., *The Book of Beasts* (Cape, London, 1954).

WHITTINGHAM, A. B., 'Norwich Cathedral', *Friends of Norwich Cathedral 19th Annual Report* (1948).

WILDRIDGE, T. T., *The Grotesque in Church Art* (Brown, London, 1890).

WOLFGANG, A., 'Misericords in Lancashire and Cheshire Churches', *Trans. Hist. Soc. of Lancs. & Cheshire*, lxiii (1911), pp. 79–87.

CHURCH GUIDES

CHURCH guides are largely intended to inspire in the casual visitor some appreciation of church architecture and history, and to encourage him to contribute to the expenses of maintenance. They should not be regarded as reliable works of reference, and few give more than a cursory mention of such details as misericords. Those listed below, however, have been selected because they give useful information.

Bishops Stortford, Herts.: *St. Michael's Church*, ed. J. Clarke, 1956.

Boston, Lincs.: *St. Botolph's Church*, John Boulton.

Christchurch, Hants: *Christchurch Choir Stalls and Misericords*, K. F. Wiltshire.

Cartmel, Lancs.: *New Guide to Cartmel Priory Church*, J. C. Dickinson, (2nd edition).

Etchingham, Sussex: *Etchingham Church*, H. Lethbridge, 1960.

Godmanchester, Hunts.; *Little History of St. Mary's Church*, P. G. M. Dickinson.

Great Malvern, Worcs.: *Ancient Misericords in the Priory Church*, Vera L. Edminson.

King's Lynn, Norfolk: *Handbook for Visitors to St. Margaret's Church*, L. Galley.

Lancaster: *Lancaster Priory*, L. I. and M. E. M. J. Cowper.

Peterborough, Northants.: *Short Guide to the Cathedral*, R. E. Sibthorp.

Ripple, Worcs.: *The Two Churches of Ripple*, E. F. Gray, 1953.

St. Neots, Hunts.: *Parish Church of St. Mary the Virgin*, L. Galley.

Tewkesbury, Glos.: *Short Guide to the Abbey Church*, Lionel Gough.

Wakefield, Yorks.: *Guide to All Saints Church*, N. T. Hopkins and J. W. Walker.

ADDENDA

DEVONSHIRE

EXETER   Royal Albert Memorial Museum   *Nine*

In the Harry Hems Collection of antiquities are nine misericords, which are displayed on a wall of the lower ground floor.

Six are stated to have been brought from North Cadbury, near Yeovil, Somerset, and there is a note in the church guide there that misericords which had been taken away were found in Exeter in 1910. The present writer doubts the validity of this claim for the following reasons:

1. The church at North Cadbury was built between 1407 and 1417 by Lady Elizabeth Botreaux (*Somerset Arch. & Nat. Hist. Soc. Proc.* lxxxi, p. 38), but the misericords appear to be of much earlier date.
2. Lady Elizabeth Botreaux obtained a licence in 1417 to found a college of seven chaplains and four clerks (*Som. A. & N.H.S. Proc.* xxxvi, p. 54), 'but her intention was never carried out' (op. cit., lxxxi, p. 38).
3. *Som. A. & N.H.S. Proc.* xxxvi, p. 56 states '. . . the canopy work of the stalls, part of which survived until recently, but all has now unfortunately been destroyed'.

The writer considers that they probably came from Cadbury, Devon, a few miles north of Exeter. There is in the Reference Library at Exeter a manuscript copy of *Notes on Devon Churches*, by Beatrix F. Cresswell (1910), which states that the church of Cadbury was given *c.* 1163 by William Fitz-Ralph and his wife to the Prior and Convent of St. Nicholas, Exeter, who continued to be patrons until the Dissolution. It also states that the church was restored in 1860, and that to this period belong 'the . . . pulpit; the choir stalls are new'. Harry Hems is known to have done restoration work in many local churches about that time, and brought back a good deal of the medieval work he replaced, subsequently giving his collection to the Museum. In addition to the six misericords ascribed as above, two more much-damaged examples appear to be part of the same set; all eight have various designs of early flowers or foliage in both centrepieces and supporters.

DATE: early 14th century.

The ninth misericord, whose origin is unknown, consists of a plain vaulted corbel below a ledge of multiple moulding. Supporters: Left and Right, formal vine-leaf.

DATE: late 15th or early 16th century.

SOMERSET

MIDDLEZOY Holy Cross *One*

Built into the priest's chair on the south side of the chancel is a misericord, the main subject of which is a crouching dragon, one of whose forelegs rests on a small human head. Supporters: Left and Right, formal leaf.

DATE: 14th century.

ICONOGRAPHICAL INDEX

I. RELIGIOUS SUBJECTS

OLD TESTAMENT

Adam and Eve:
Temptation, 16, 46, 76, 169.
Expulsion, 18, 76, 170. Pl. 18b.
Toiling, 18, 170.
Noah, 17. Pl. 18a.
Isaac:
Circumcision of, xxx, 172. Pl. 4d.
Bearing faggots, 171.
Sacrifice of, 50, 170.
Moses:
Rebuking the Israelites, 50.
With brazen serpent, 170.
Joshua and Caleb:
Returning from Canaan, xxxiv, 81, 175, 183.
Samson:
With lion, xxxv, 8, 18, 27, 91, 97, 107, 170, 177. Pl. 6c.
With gates of Gaza, xxxiv, 183. Pl. 9c.
With Delilah, 49.
Samuel presented at Shiloh, 172.
Jesse, Tree of, 90.
Judith and Holofernes, 90.
David, 97, 162.
Solomon, Judgement of, 96, 170.
Jonah, 183. Pls. 8d, 9a.
Elijah, 71.
Prophets, unidentified, 170.

NEW TESTAMENT

Nativity, 90.
Shepherds going to Bethlehem, xxiv, 50.
Magi, 49, 90, 187. Pl. 45a.
Good Shepherd, 59.
Entry into Jerusalem, 114.
Resurrection, xxxix, 64, 91. Pl. 16a.
Ascension, 87.
Last Judgement, 38, 114, 196.
Benediction, 19.
Crucifixion allegory, 74.
Sacred Heart, 173.
Locust of the Apocalypse, xxviii, 36. Pl. 3d.
Passion emblems, 24, 86.
The Vernicle (Veronica's kerchief), 116.

Life of the Virgin (see also above):
Annunciation, xxiv, 64, 135, 194. Pl. 1c.

Virgin and Child, 25, 64.
Emblems of the Virigin, xxvi, 133, 161.
At the sepulchre, 114.
Assumption, 87, 147. Pl. 36d.
Coronation, 26, 29, 49, 91, 107.
Protecting souls, 113.

SAINTS

Andrew, 147. Pl. 36c.
Catherine (wheel only), 61.
Edmund, King, xxv, 147. Pl. 2c.
Etheldreda, 16.
George, xxv, 7, 27, 83, 84, 85, 91, 105, 164, 177.
Giles, xxv, 19. Pl. 2a.
Godric, 40.
Govan, xxv, 197. Pl. 2b.
John Baptist (Herodias' daughter before Herod) 18.
John the Evangelist, 88.
Luke, 34.
Margaret, xxv, 38. Pl. 1d.
Martin of Tours, 145.
Mary of Egypt, 6.
Mary Magdalene, 91.
Matthew, 34.
Michael and dragon, 30, 31, 51, 107.
Peter, 122.
Thomas of Canterbury, 145.
Werburgh, xxv, xxxii, 24.
Zosimus, 6.

Symbols of the Evangelists:
Matthew, 9, 34, 54, 76, 106, 149. Pl. 23b.
Mark, xxv, 9, 54, 76, 103, 106, 119, 149. Pls. 3a, 23a.
Luke, xxv, 9, 34, 67, 68, 76, 103, 149.
John, xxv, 9, 15, 67, 68, 106, 149.

ANGELS

Cherub or putto, 33, 43, 54, 56, 100, 117, 118, 119. Pl. 34b.
Gabriel, 87.
With censer, 19, 86.
With flaming sword, 71, 119.
With keys, 79.
With musical instruments, 24, 29, 30, 74, 90, 91, 93, 107, 120, 134, 141, 147, 166, 168, 171, 172, 177. Pls. 30c, 41c.

II. ALLEGORIES, MORALITIES, AND WARNING TALES

III. LITERARY THEMES

IV. SCENES FROM DAILY LIFE

V. ANIMALS

— with eagle, 178.
— with prey (including geese), 9, 16, 24, 30, 34, 48, 51, 60, 61, 68, 71, 74, 79, 82, 83, 107, 119, 120, 137, 144, 174, 178, 182, 183. Pl. 21c.
— charming goose with music, 156.
— preaching, xxxv, 6, 16, 46, 76, 86, 129, 134, 137, 144, 158, 171, 175, 177, 178, 182, 194. Pls. 10a. 35c.
— as schoolmaster, 82.
— with monk victim, 45.

— riding another animal, 81, 125. Pl. 35a.
— ridden by other animals, 96, 174.
— hanging of, 45, 46, 175.
— other identified scenes from Reynard the Fox, xxxiv, 5, 6, 7, 45, 46, 47, 51, 55, 58, 71, 76, 81, 82, 84, 86, 163, 166, 171, 173, 174, 177, 178, 194. Pl. 9d.
Cat, hanged by mice, 167.
Hare, roasting huntsmen, 82.
Animal musicians, 10, 41, 62, 83, 85, 96, 156, 174, 181, 183.

VI. FOLIAGE AND FLOWERS

(The commonest types of foliage portrayed—Oak, Vine, Acanthus, and a conventionalized sea-weed—are not indexed.)

Beech, 56.
Columbine, 81.
Cypress, 69.
Fleur-de-lis, 3, 25, 36, 68.
Hart's-tongue fern, 182.
Hawthorn, 110, 140.
Holly, 132.
Honeysuckle, 110.
Ivy, 138.
Juniper, 69, 70.
Lily, 97, 109, 110, 111.
Maple, 35, 36, 37, 70, 138.
Marshmallow, 138.
Rose, 2, 6, 13, 27, 84, 89, 105, 110, 114, 122, 124, 130, 131, 132, 138, 153, 176, 181. Pls. 32c, 33c.
Sunflower, 110, 114.
Sycamore, 69, 70, 110.

Thistle, 187, 189. Pl. 46b, c.
Thorn, 24.
Water-lily, 111. Pl. 32d.

Foliate mask, xxiii, xxxii, 1, 6, 8, 12, 13, 16, 25, 35, 36, 42, 44, 57, 58, 60, 62, 63, 74, 76, 77, 78, 84, 87, 88, 89, 90, 92, 93, 97, 103, 104, 106, 108, 114, 117, 121, 122, 123, 125, 126, 130, 131, 135, 157, 161, 162, 164, 165, 166, 175, 177, 178, 179, 180, 182, 185, 189, 190, 198. Pls. 6a, 6b, 34d 43c.

Fruit:
Fig, 4.
Grapes, 6, 67, 69, 70, 76, 114, 124, 139, 155, 156, 174, 175, 182, 187, 189, 197.
Pomegranate, 15, 28, 84, 97, 108, 110, 111.
Strawberry, 37, 44, 110.

VII. MUSICAL INSTRUMENTS

Percussion, 17, 35, 85, 96, 98, 128, 131, 156, 176.
Stringed instruments, 17, 24, 30, 57, 59, 62, 74, 83, 91, 96, 107, 120, 137, 141, 146, 154, 155, 156, 166, 168, 171, 172,

174, 177. Pl. 38b.
Wind instruments, 5, 17, 35, 41, 56, 58, 59, 71, 83, 85, 90, 93, 96, 106, 128, 131, 143, 155, 164, 174, 176, 181, 183.

VIII. HERALDRY

(All but a few of the carvings are without tinctures. Thus, where there is no documentary authentication, identity is based on the insignia coupled with the owner's probable connection with the parish.)

SHIELDS

Arundel, Bishop, 21. Pl. 18d.
Aynel, 2.
Badlesmere, 124, 162.
Banastre, Sir Robert, 118.
Bardolph, 21, 152.
Beauchamp, 2, 21, 130. Pl. 18c.

Bedford Town, 1.
Bernard, Margaret, 21.
Boville, 107.
Boynton (or Bonyton) of Suffolk, 101. Pl. 32b.
Brooke family, 114.
Calverley, 130.

IX. PERSONS

X. INSCRIPTIONS

INDEX OF PROPER NAMES

PLATES

PLATE 1

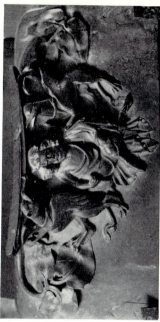

b. Wells Cathedral: Alexander's Flight

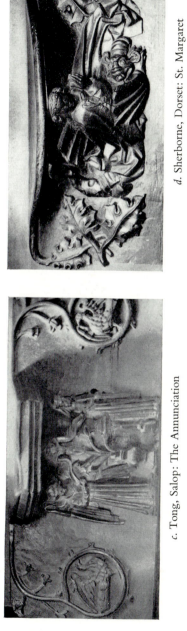

d. Sherborne, Dorset: St. Margaret

a. Windsor, Berks., St. George's Chapel: The Meeting at Picquigny

c. Tong, Salop: The Annunciation

PLATE 2

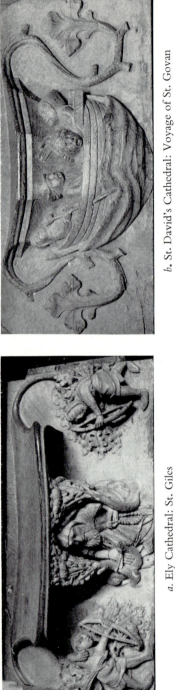

b. St. David's Cathedral: Voyage of St. Govan

d. St. David's Cathedral: Boat building

a. Ely Cathedral: St. Giles

c. Norton, Suffolk: Martyrdom of St. Edmund

PLATE 3

b. Exeter Cathedral: Decoration

d. Exeter Cathedral: Locust of the Apocalypse

a. Norwich, St. Gregory: Lion of St. Mark

c. Exeter Cathedral: Mermaid

PLATE 4

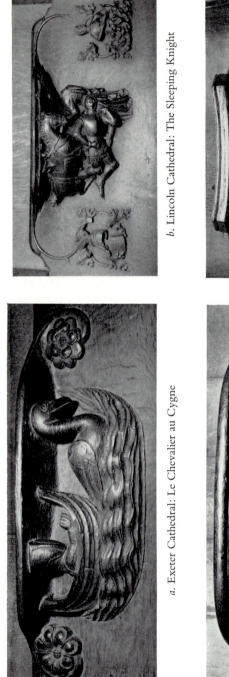

a. Exeter Cathedral: Le Chevalier au Cygne

b. Lincoln Cathedral: The Sleeping Knight

c. Exeter Cathedral: Elephant

d. Worcester Cathedral: Circumcision of Isaac

PLATE 5

b. Chester Cathedral: Foiling the Tigress

d. Marginal Ornament from early printed book

a. Worcester Cathedral: Jousting

c. Throwley, Kent: Design copied from Marginal Ornament

PLATE 6

a. Coventry, Holy Trinity: Foliate mask

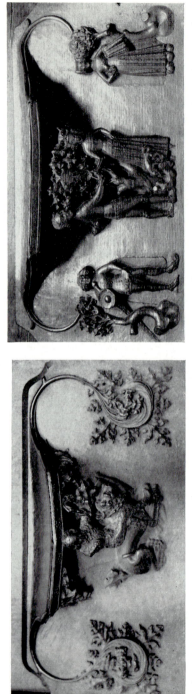

b. Lincoln Cathedral: Foliate mask

c. Lincoln Cathedral: Samson and the Lion

d. Chester Cathedral: Tristan and Iseult

PLATE 7

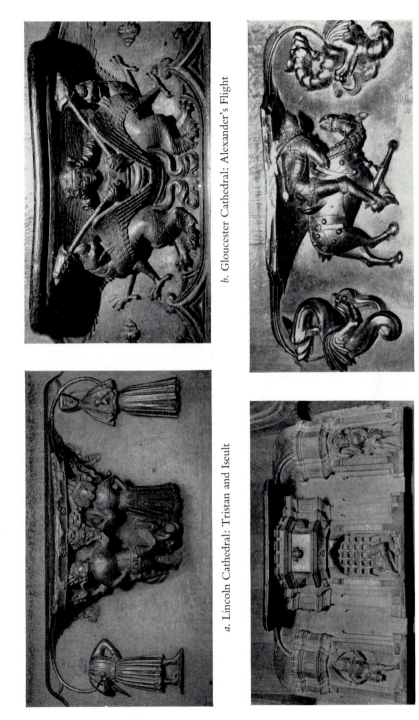

b. Gloucester Cathedral: Alexander's Flight

d. Lincoln Cathedral: The Falling Knight

a. Lincoln Cathedral: Tristan and Iseult

c. Enville, Staffs.: Sir Ywain

PLATE 8

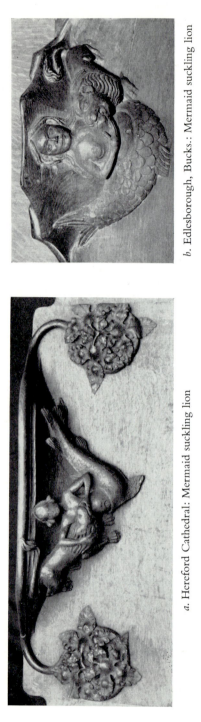

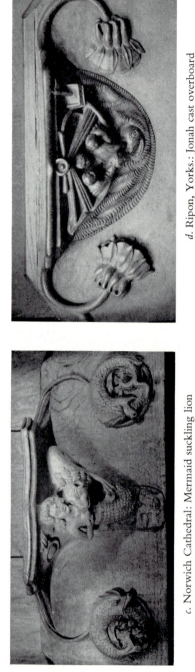

b. Edlesborough, Bucks.: Mermaid suckling lion

d. Ripon, Yorks.: Jonah cast overboard

a. Hereford Cathedral: Mermaid suckling lion

c. Norwich Cathedral: Mermaid suckling lion

PLATE 9

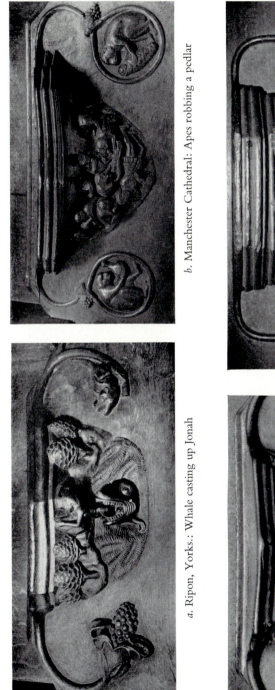

a. Ripon, Yorks.: Whale casting up Jonah

b. Manchester Cathedral: Apes robbing a pedlar

c. Ripon, Yorks.: Samson and the gates of Gaza

d. Bristol Cathedral: Reynard led to execution

PLATE 10

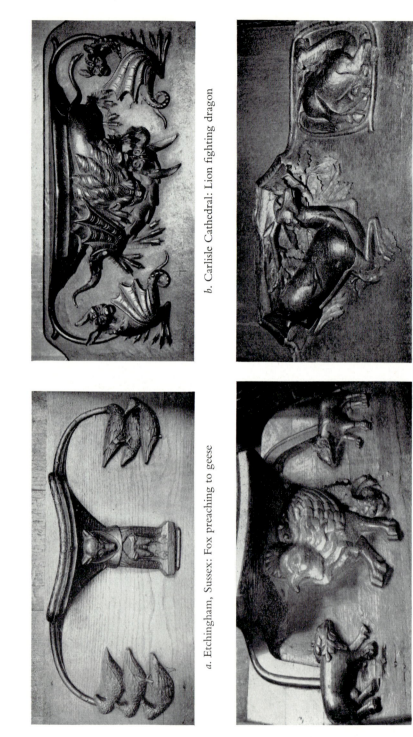

b. Carlisle Cathedral: Lion fighting dragon

d. Boston, Lincs.: Kneeling camel (supporter)

a. Etchingham, Sussex: Fox preaching to geese

c. Worcester Cathedral: Basilisk

PLATE 11

b. Carlisle Cathedral: Hyena and corpse

d. Stratford-on-Avon: Ostrich (supporter)

a. Denston, Suffolk: Crane

c. Lavenham, Suffolk: Ibis and head

PLATE 12

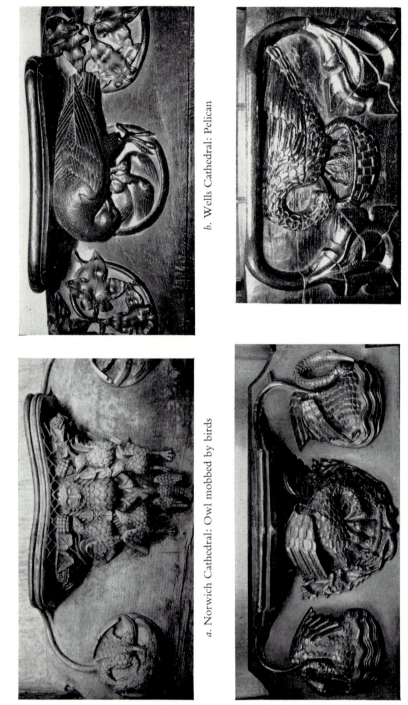

b. Wells Cathedral: Pelican

d. Wantage, Berks.: Pelican

a. Norwich Cathedral: Owl mobbed by birds

c. London, St. Katherine's Foundation: Pelican

PLATE 13

b. Durham Castle Chapel: Unicorn trampling serpent

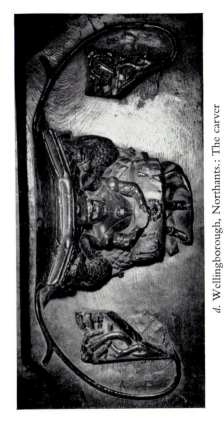

d. Wellingborough, Northants.: The carver

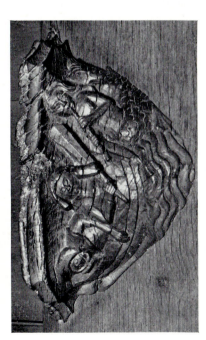

a. Boston, Lincs.: Mermaid and sailors

c. Faversham, Kent: Wolf licking its foot

PLATE 14

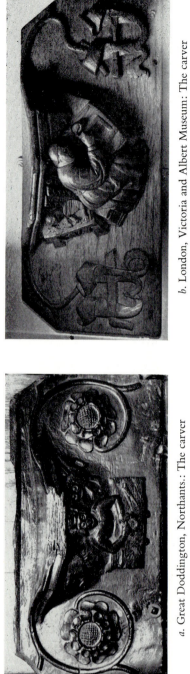

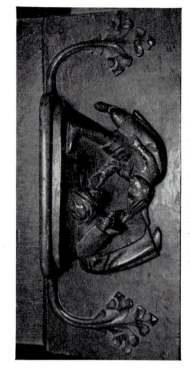

b. London, Victoria and Albert Museum: The carver

d. Fairford, Glos.: Domestic quarrel

a. Great Doddington, Northants.: The carver

c. Brampton, Hunts.: Clothmakers (on supporters)

PLATE 15

b. Oxford, New College: The Seven Deadly Sins

d. Ludlow, Salop: Fate of the dishonest alewife

a. Minster-in-Thanet, Kent: Horned head-dress

c. London, St. Katharine's Foundation: Devil eavesdropping

PLATE 16

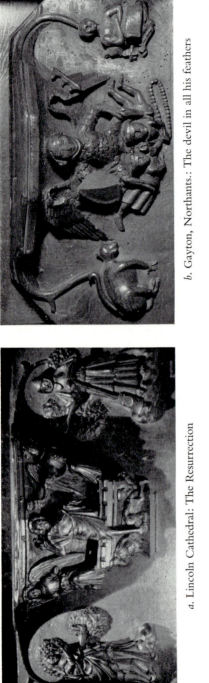

b. Gayton, Northants.: The devil in all his feathers

d. Coventry, Holy Trinity: Wodehouse and lion

a. Lincoln Cathedral: The Resurrection

c. Worcester Cathedral: The Clever Daughter

PLATE 17

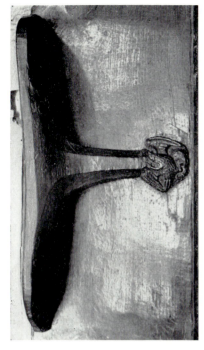

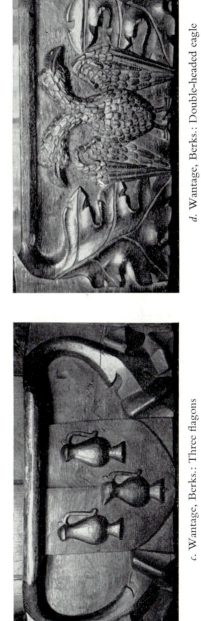

b. Sutton Courtenay, Berks.: Hawk

a. Swineshead, Beds.: Crude village carpentry

d. Wantage, Berks.: Double-headed eagle

c. Wantage, Berks.: Three flagons

PLATE 18

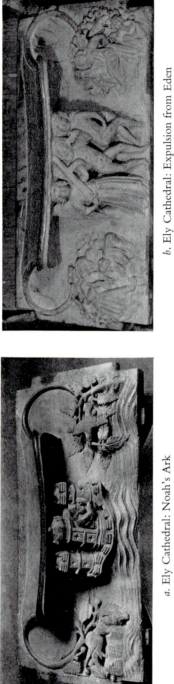

b. Ely Cathedral: Expulsion from Eden

d. Landbeach, Cambs.: Arms of Bishop Arundel

a. Ely Cathedral: Noah's Ark

c. Great Eversden, Cambs.: Arms of Beauchamp

PLATE 19

e. Church Gresley, Derbyshire: Post-Reformation

c. Greystoke, Cumberland: Shoeing the horse

d. Church Gresley, Derbyshire: Post-Reformation

a. Bodmin, Cornwall: Two gowned figures

b. Greystoke, Cumberland: Post-Reformation work

PLATE 20

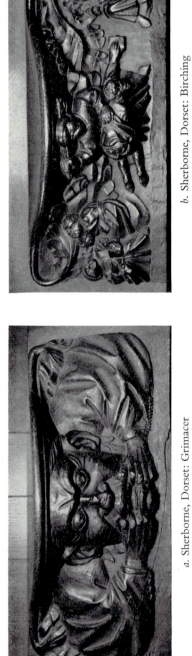

b. Sherborne, Dorset: Birching

d. Darlington, Durham: Bear leading

a. Sherborne, Dorset: Grimacer

c. Sherborne, Dorset: Archery

PLATE 21

b. Bristol Cathedral: Dragon driving souls to Hell

a. Darlington, Durham: Alexander's flight

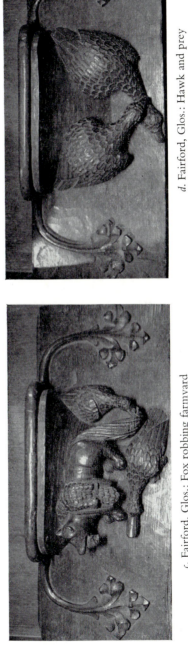

d. Fairford, Glos.: Hawk and prey

c. Fairford, Glos.: Fox robbing farmyard

PLATE 22

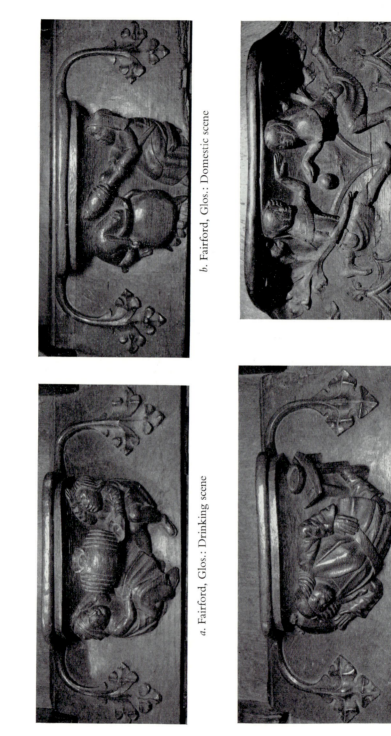

a. Fairford, Glos.: Drinking scene

b. Fairford, Glos.: Domestic scene

c. Fairford, Glos.: Sleeping it off

d. Gloucester Cathedral: Ball game

PLATE 23

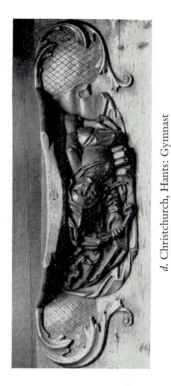

b. Christchurch, Hants: Angel of St. Matthew

d. Christchurch, Hants: Gymnast

a. Christchurch, Hants: Lion of St. Mark

c. Christchurch, Hants: Robed jester

PLATE 24

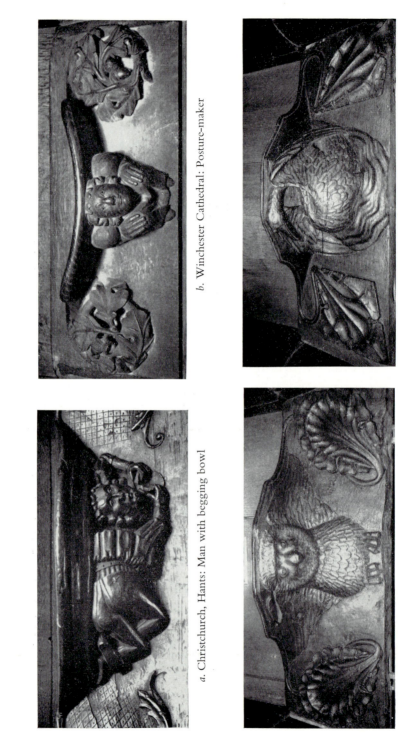

b. Winchester Cathedral: Posture-maker

d. Bishops Stortford, Herts.: Swan

a. Christchurch, Hants: Man with begging bowl

c. Bishops Stortford, Herts.: Owl

PLATE 25

b. Stevenage, Herts.: Foliage

d. Godmanchester, Hunts.: Hare

a. Bishops Stortford, Herts.: Serra or sawfish

c. Stevenage, Herts.: Vine and Grapes

PLATE 26

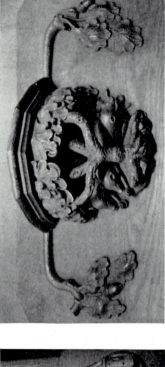

b. St. Neots, Hunts.: Ecclesiastical heraldry

d. Ashford, Kent: Pigs and acorns

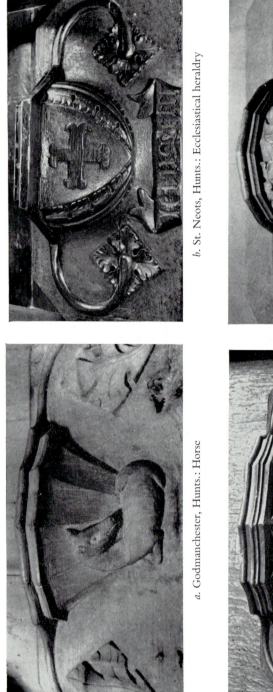

a. Godmanchester, Hunts.: Horse

c. Aldington, Kent: Architectural subject

PLATE 27

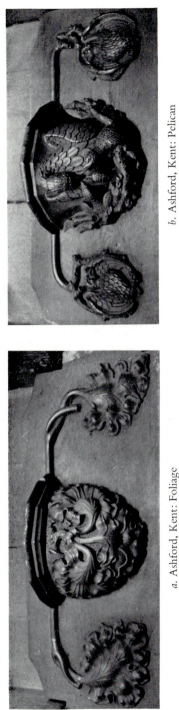

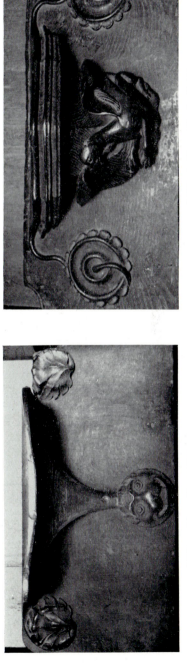

b. Ashford, Kent: Pelican

d. Herne, Kent: Duck alighting

a. Ashford, Kent: Foliage

c. Cliffe-at-Hoo, Kent: Grotesque

PLATE 28

b. Minster-in-Thanet, Kent: Woman with distaff

d. Sandwich, Kent: Heraldry

a. Herne, Kent: Crowned angel

c. Minster-in-Thanet, Kent: The cook

PLATE 29

a. Wingham, Kent: Leaves and acorns

b. Wingham, Kent: Vine and grapes

c. Wingham, Kent: Foliage

d. Cartmel, Lancs.: Elephant and castle

PLATE 30

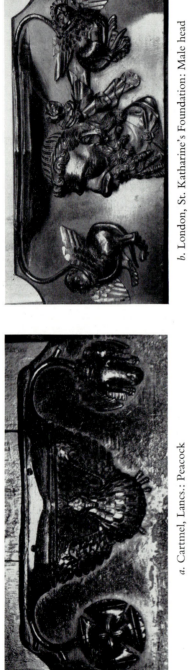

a. Cartmel, Lancs.: Peacock

b. London, St. Katharine's Foundation: Male head

c. London, St. Katharine's Foundation: Angel with bagpipes

d. London, St. Katharine's Foundation: Lion and dragon

PLATE 31

b. London, Victoria and Albert Museum: Female head

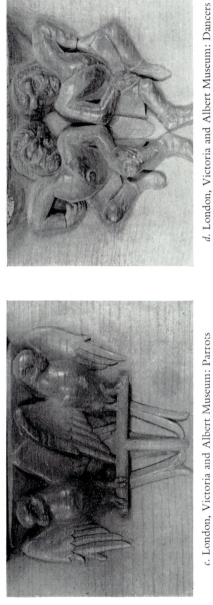

d. London, Victoria and Albert Museum: Dancers

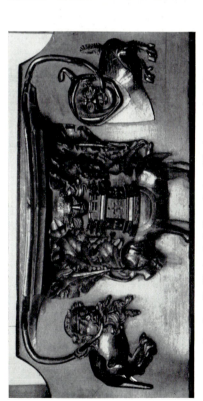

a. London, St. Katharine's Foundation: Elephant and castle

c. London, Victoria and Albert Museum: Parrots

PLATE 32

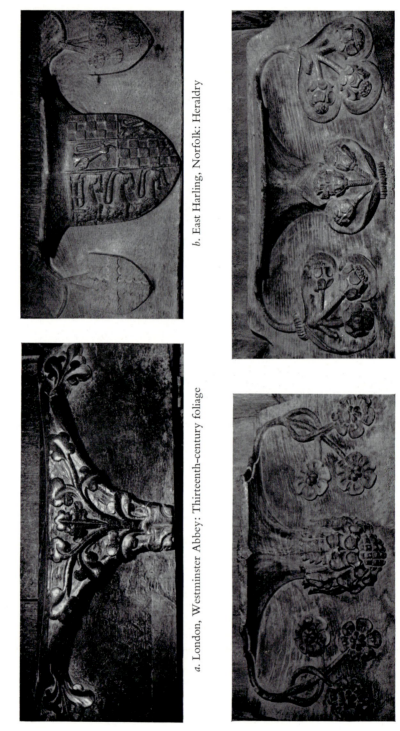

b. East Harling, Norfolk: Heraldry

d. Salle, Norfolk: Water lilies

a. London, Westminster Abbey: Thirteenth-century foliage

c. Salle, Norfolk: Roses

PLATE 33

b. Great Doddington, Northants.: Vine

a. Salle, Norfolk: Floral supporters

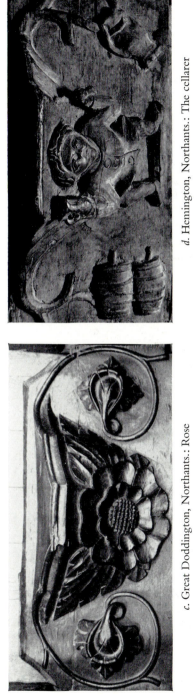

d. Hemington, Northants.: The cellarer

c. Great Doddington, Northants.: Rose

PLATE 34

b. Holdenby, Northants.: Cherub

d. Hexham, Northumberland: Foliate mask

a. Hemington, Northants.: The tumbler

c. Hexham, Northumberland: Grotesque

PLATE 35

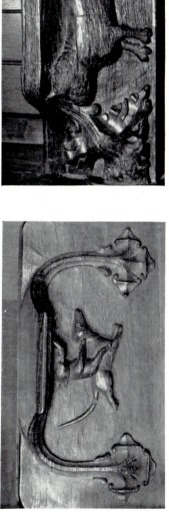

a. Nottingham, Sneinton: Fox riding hound

b. Bampton, Oxon.: Unicorn

c. Bury St. Edmund's, Suffolk: Fox preaching

PLATE 36

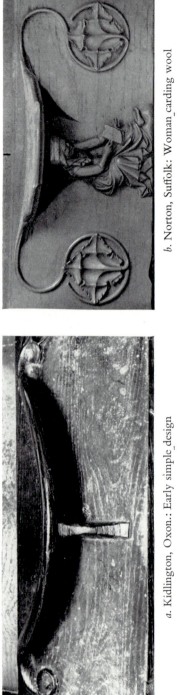

b. Norton, Suffolk: Woman carding wool

d. Occold, Suffolk: The Assumption

a. Kidlington, Oxon.: Early simple design

c. Norton, Suffolk: Martyrdom of St. Andrew

PLATE 37

b. Beddington, Surrey: Woman in caul

d. Lingfield, Surrey: Bishop's head

a. Beddington, Surrey: Bishop's head

c. Lingfield, Surrey: Woman's head

PLATE 38

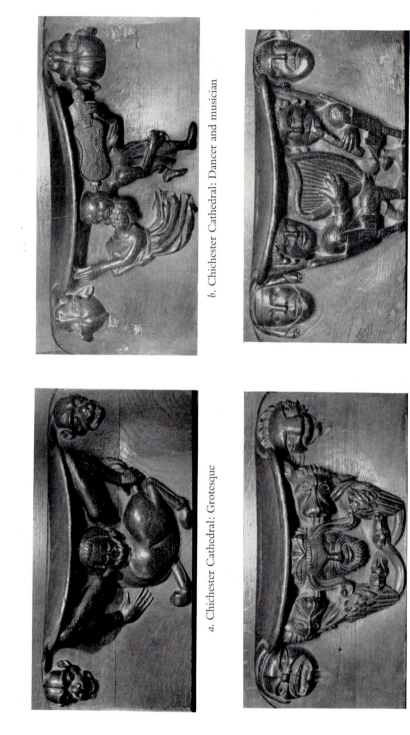

b. Chichester Cathedral: Dancer and musician

d. Chichester Cathedral: Musicians

a. Chichester Cathedral: Grotesque

c. Chichester Cathedral: Grotesque

PLATE 39

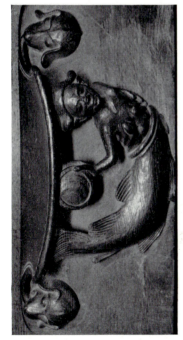

a. Chichester Cathedral: Mermaid and mirror

b. Chichester, St. Mary's Hospital: Grotesque

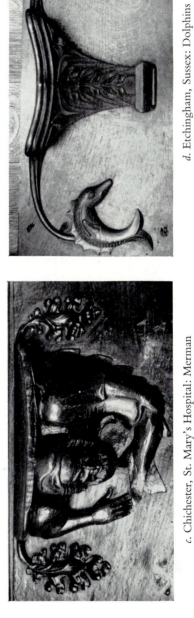

c. Chichester, St. Mary's Hospital: Merman

d. Etchingham, Sussex: Dolphins

PLATE 40

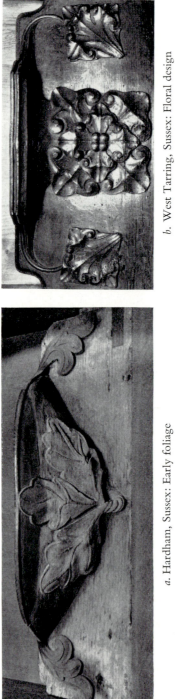

a. Hardham, Sussex: Early foliage

b. West Tarring, Sussex: Floral design

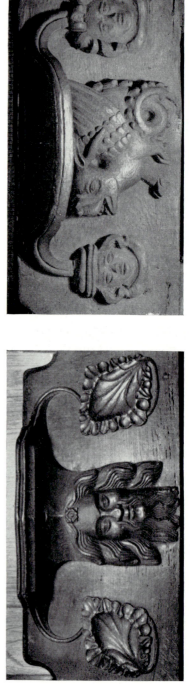

c. West Tarring, Sussex: Man's head

d. Astley, Warwicks.: Wyvern

PLATE 41

b. Mere, Wilts.: Foliage covering a fox

d. Ripple, Worcs.: Sowing (March)

a. Highworth, Wilts.: Mermaid and mirror

c. Mere, Wilts.: Angel with lute

PLATE 42

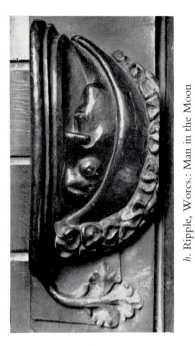

b. Ripple, Worcs.: Man in the Moon

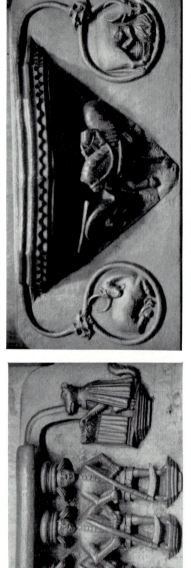

d. Beverley Minster, Yorks.: Cart before the horse

a. Ripple, Worcs.: Pig-killing (November)

c. Worcester Cathedral: Mowing (June)

PLATE 43

b. Hemingborough, Yorks.: Foliage

d. Old Malton, Yorks.: Hare

a. Beverley Minster, Yorks.: Virago in barrow

c. Loversal, Yorks.: Foliate mask

PLATE 44

c. Old Malton, Yorks.: Kneeling camel

b. Old Malton, Yorks.: Owl

a. Old Malton, Yorks.: Griffin

d. Ripon, Yorks.: Combat (relic of early set)

PLATE 45

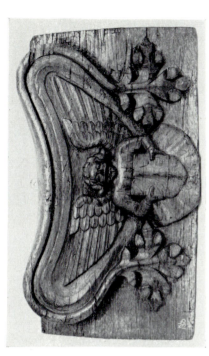

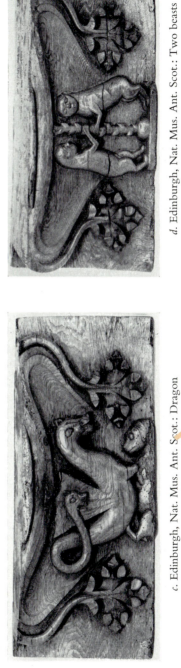

a. North Berwick, E. Lothian: Adoration of Magi

b. Edinburgh, Nat. Museum of Antiquaries of Scotland: Angel with shield

c. Edinburgh, Nat. Mus. Ant. Scot.: Dragon

d. Edinburgh, Nat. Mus. Ant. Scot.: Two beasts

PLATE 46

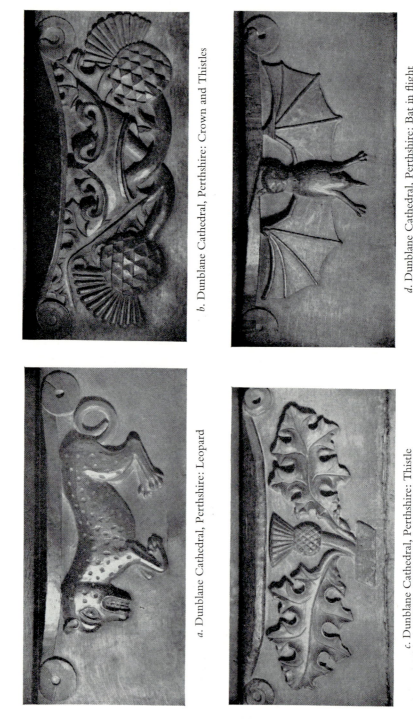

b. Dunblane Cathedral, Perthshire: Crown and Thistles

d. Dunblane Cathedral, Perthshire: Bat in flight

a. Dunblane Cathedral, Perthshire: Leopard

c. Dunblane Cathedral, Perthshire: Thistle

PLATE 47

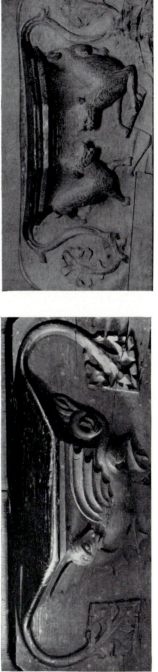

b. Limerick Cathedral, Eire: Angel

a. Limerick Cathedral, Eire: Swan

d. St. David's Cathedral, Pembrokeshire: Dogs quarrelling over a bone

c. Abergavenny, Mon.: Dragon

PLATE 48

b. St. David's Cathedral, Pembrokeshire: Lion and dragon

d. St. David's Cathedral, Pembrokeshire: Sleeping man

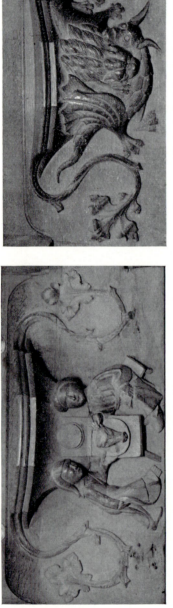

a. St. David's Cathedral, Pembrokeshire: Domestic meal

c. St. David's Cathedral, Pembrokeshire: Cowled fox